THE DIFFICULT GIRL

A MEMOIR

Helen Morse

Sparrow Press
Newbury, Massachusetts

The Difficult Girl is a nonfiction work. The events are from the author's memory. For privacy reasons, some of the names and identifying details have been changed.

Published by Sparrow Press, Newbury, Massachusetts

The author is a visual artist and can be contacted through her website at helenmorse.com.

Library of Congress Control Number: 2022902100

Morse, Helen, 1954–
The Difficult Girl, A Memoir / Helen Morse

ISBN: 978 0 578 36699 9

Cover photo by Helen Morse
Back cover photo from Morse family archive
Book design by Nancy Daugherty

Published and printed in the United States of America

Reviews of The Difficult Girl

"This beautifully written memoir by Helen Morse gives a fascinating glimpse into a world of wealth, and emotional deprivation. Morse has such a knack for vivid detail that I could picture every person, every place and feel totally immersed in her physical and emotional environments. I felt affection for the two loving people who filled in so much warmth and connection where Morse's parents were lacking. In school in New England, away from the pain and chaos, Helen took her first steps toward making a good life for herself. Her sister Debbie's tortured life and Helen's efforts to prevent a devastating loss is at the heart of the story. Although it is a painfully honest portrait of a family, The Difficult Girl is not a downer. It is a testament not only to the power of love, but the necessity of forgiveness in overcoming the challenge of a childhood filled with privilege but impoverished in what matters most. I couldn't put it down."

> — Kathy McCoy, Ph.D, author of a number of books including We Don't Talk Any More and The Crocodiles Will Arrive Later, as well as the blog, "Complicated Love" for PsychologyToday.com

"Artist Helen Morse's gripping and revealing memoir, The Difficult Girl, is an astonishing story of the improbable survival of a sensitive child exposed to generational horrors, success, privilege, and abuse, all behind the gilded walls of a story F. Scott Fitzgerald's characters Gatsby and Daisy might relate to. Her characters are incandescent from dreadful to admirable, complicated, brilliant, and painfully ill. The book is laudable in its honest, unflinching look beyond the obvious privilege. Soaring above the concealed and painful family history, the author gives hope. The extravagantly told story could be beautifully adapted to the big screen."

— Patty Ewald, former Executive Director of The Actors Studio

"Reading the description of Morse's life was like reading a Chekhov novel, but the amplitude of family wealth didn't lessen the burden. We are all 'the difficult child,' I fear. And thus the appeal of the memoir. I am so happy she got this book written!"

— Tess Gallagher, award winning poet and essayist

"The author faces her troubled past, holding each anguish and regret up to the light with extraordinary bravery. I find myself wondering how she could have survived it all... It is a memoir of remarkably vivid detail and unflinching honesty."

— Andrew Chaikin, author of A Man on the Moon

"It reads like a gothic novel, but it's all true. In this compelling and unforgettable memoir, Helen Morse has created a portrait of a life lived in a world of great wealth and greater pain. The Difficult Girl describes fraught relationships between family members where love, guilt, and jealousy are often intertwined. Despite affection and support, utter heartbreak and mental illness take their place at the table. The author describes Palm Beach and its environs as a virtual Who's Who of privilege, with everyone from Rose Kennedy to the Duke and Duchess of Windsor, as well as elaborate parties at Mar-a-Lago. All this serves as backdrop to Helen's painful search for stability and happiness."

— Nancy Brigham, author of A Fragile Enterprise:
Today's Schools and Tomorrow's Students

I dedicate this book to you, Nelson.

With love and appreciation to
my son Nelson,
my life partner, Robert,
and his daughter Chelsea,
whose enthusiastic support gave me the courage to write
and keep writing.

Thanks also, to my sister Carolyn,
who selflessly gave me her blessing to tell the truth —
all of it.

And finally, with special thanks to my wonderful editor,
Andrea Cleghorn,
whose hard work and good counsel were essential
to the successful completion of this book.

Chapter 1

Mamaroneck

It was supposed to be a fairy tale. It certainly looked like one at
the start. My parents, Joe and Claudia, seemed like the perfect
1950s couple. And when I was born, one year and a day after
their joyous union, things seemed to be moving along nicely in
that direction.

We were in the town of Mamaroneck in Westchester
County, New York, where rolling lawns sprawled in every direction across the 25-acre parcel we called home. From Orienta
Avenue, the long gravel driveway led past our Greek Revival
house to a circle on the other side, where two reclining Canova
lions flanked the front steps. The old building rose above a
backdrop of oaks, beeches, and chestnut trees with an immediate grassy view, all the way to the continuous stone wall which
marked the perimeter. Inside the wall, huge azaleas ran its
length and in springtime circled the property in a riot of color.
The sheer size of the grounds with its mature foliage made it feel
more like a park than a private residence.

In one direction, from the bronze sundial at front and
center, a path meandered under an arbor of climbing roses and
through a formal garden. A lone pillar of marble stood there, a
gift to my father from the ambassador of Tunisia. It was carved
in a spiral shape, inset with small triangular fragments of colored
stone and mirrored glass in a geometric pattern that sparkled in

the sunlight. At the other end was a huge stone birdbath with carved cherubs emerging from its center.

I remember my sense of enchantment in that spot, with its rose bushes, bearded iris, and lilies of the valley in a festival of pastels — pink, yellow, violet, and white. The tiny lilies were my favorites, with their frilly white bells and intoxicating scent, a surprise, given how small they were. Farther on were the clay tennis courts where my father played, just to one side of the orchard planted with apples and pears. Beyond the orchard stood a musty old chicken coop, still littered with the feathers of chickens who lived there long ago. In the distance, there was even a small cornfield.

At the other side of the property, the stone wall broke for the entrance to an enormous dark green barn and my grandmothers' small house across the way. Grandma Morse and Grandma Speciale (pronounced "Special") lived there together, as neither one had a husband anymore. I was taken to see them often along the long and winding pathway that connected one end of the property with the other.

Grandma Morse was a petite woman with surprisingly dark hair for a woman of her age. She was quiet, with a mild manner, and generally kept to herself. When I followed Grandma Speciale into the house, Grandma Morse was either sitting on the porch or reading in the living room. She was always cordial, but most of the time I saw her only briefly as I went somewhere else with my other grandmother.

Grandma Speciale kept a vegetable garden situated at one side of their house, neatly fenced in with chicken wire. The long rows of black earth striped with leafy green produced all sorts of vegetables she would harvest for her dinner table. She understood how things grew and spent hours every day tending her little plot of earth. I will never forget the first carrot I ever saw her pull from the soil. After washing it off under the spigot in the barn, she smiled and handed it to me.

"Go on. *Mangia*," she said, coaxing me to take a bite.

Before then, I had never tasted something directly from the place it had grown. I remember my hesitation to sample this recently dirty thing while my grandmother waited expectantly for my utter surprise when I finally did. This, *this* was a carrot? It was sweet and tenderly crisp, so different from the flat and nearly flavorless orange discs that had been sitting on my dinner plate the night before.

It was only a little ironic that the meaning of the name "Speciale" corresponded exactly with my feelings for her. Whenever we went inside, Grandma Speciale would take up the candy jar and offer me my choice from the collection of pretty sugared gumdrops. The violet ones were my favorites, with the intense and exotic anise flavor made more wonderful by the sugar crystals that scratched the roof of my mouth and melted down to the smooth chewy thing itself.

I always looked forward to those treats, but inside her house, there was something even more interesting. There, Grandma kept a sparrow which she had raised from infancy. At meals, the tiny thing would flit from chair to chair. Then, settling on the tablecloth, it would hop from plate to plate, sampling our mashed potatoes, as happy and tame as any bird might be. With my grandmother's encouragement, it would tentatively step onto my hand, its tiny warm toes wrapping themselves trustingly around my like-sized finger. Perched as it was, I could feel the tiny talons pressing into my skin, but without pain or malice, while the bird tilted its head back and forth, eyeing me with a curiosity equal to my own. Both of us were small creatures in a world of giants.

"Gentle, gentle," Grandma would say, making sure I understood that this was a fragile being that deserved my protection.

These visits always ended too soon. At some point, Grandma would decide that it had been long enough and, taking the bird onto her finger, she would carry it back upstairs. There in its cage it would have some peace and rest.

I loved being at Grandma's. It was a place where things were simple, and nothing was so fancy that a small child would be scolded for an accidental spill. The house felt homey and comfortable, and the only rule was to be polite and obedient, which was easy for a child like me.

Back at the main house, things were different. There, the opulent furniture and silk rugs required more caution. I learned very early not to climb on any of the fine furniture in the living room, and I never lingered there without supervision. In the billiards room, my father's old oak pool table was covered in a fine fringed leather blanket. Cutwork leather pockets hung below its edge, adding to the mystique. I remember my father allowing me to hold one of the heavy billiard balls in my hands briefly, but as tempting as they were, these were not for children. They had their place on the polished wall shelves next to the inlaid pool cues in their rack. The pool room and the things it contained were my parents' toys, and I needed to keep a respectful distance.

There were so many intriguing things within reach, but I was warned that these were antiques and might be damaged or stained by small hands. I have a strong memory of a beautiful stone bird that I found nearly irresistible. It was about the size of a small robin carved from translucent quartz with real ruby eyes. Its metal legs were attached to a matching round stand. I recall distinctly how dearly I wanted to pick it up, just to hold it for a moment in my little hands, but I was only allowed to look. That is what good little girls did, and I wanted to be one of those.

In the Mamaroneck house, my bedroom was on the second floor. I remember my white crib, which stood against a wall of dusty rose-colored wallpaper, a trompe l'oeil of upholstery with the image of tiny buttons placed at regular intervals across its "cushioned" surface. The mobile that floated above my crib held a flock of small flat plastic birds, with features printed in bright colors, their wings outstretched as if in flight.

I also remember my sense of accomplishment for climbing out of that crib one evening and holding on to the spindles of the banister one at a time, as I toddled down the big stairs to the sounds of company below. When I neared the bottom, all eyes turned toward me in surprise as I asked for some ginger ale and a piece of toast. My parents seemed charmed and indulged me that night. I recall well the delicious flavor of the warm rye bread, along with the adoring looks I received from everyone there as I ate daintily at a small pink marble table on one side of the room.

The only place in the house solely dedicated to children was the playroom and the adjoining bath on the third floor where Mrs. Gregory, my nurse, would bathe me in the old, deep claw-foot tub. In that room, the walls had yellow wallpaper decorated with cartoonish couples walking poodles alongside ladies carry-ing parasols and little Eiffel towers. The ceilings were canted with the roofline and the illustrations closed in around me, making it feel like I was wrapped inside a giant children's book. The Palla-dian window under the eaves gave a faraway view of the goings-on below from a height that prompted Mrs. Gregory to warn me away from standing too close to it. This was in an older part of the house, and the window's strength could not be trusted. The bare bulb fixtures were outdated, too, and sparsely placed, which made the room a relatively dark place to be at bath time. The sun was going down then, but that was OK. I had Mrs. Gregory with me, and the gathering shadows only served to mark the warm and sleepy approach of bedtime.

During the day, the playroom was bright and appointed with all the necessities. It had a child-sized square table with matching chairs and piles of children's books containing fairy tales and nursery rhymes, many of which my parents delighted in hearing me recite. On the table was a record player housed inside a small cream-colored suitcase with a central red stripe, a red handle, and metal corner caps. It was a prized possession, and I spent many hours playing records on it, one after another. My favorite was a rose colored disk of a young woman singing "A Tisket-a-Tasket." On the flip side, she sang a rendition of "Me and My Teddy Bear." I remember, too, the stack of simple wooden jigsaw puzzles of Old King Cole, Little Bo Peep, and other nursery themes. At one end of the room was a large and unfussy armchair for Mrs. Gregory, where she could sit and watch over me while I played. Soon, another girl was born, a sister, who would have to try and keep up with me.

It wasn't long before she and I were frolicking together under the watchful eyes of Mrs. Gregory, while my mother happily went out shopping or to the salon to have her hair and nails done. My father worked in Manhattan, often bringing work home with him to go over in his office on the second floor. He worked long hours, but he enjoyed his profession. Sometimes, when he was in the city, my mother would go too, strolling Park Avenue, or visiting the museums while he was busy. Afterward, she would meet him for dinner. It was easy to see they were in love. When Dad wasn't going into the office, the two of them traveled in Europe or cruised up and down the east coast on their boat.

Our days and nights were spent with Mrs. Gregory. We walked the grounds, playing in the chicken coop and gathering chestnuts. On some days, we splashed in the inflatable pool. On others, we stopped over at Grandma's. All the paths meandering among the flowering plants and trees were dappled with the sunlight of unlimited time and happy wandering. The nooks and crannies along the way offered up endless places for exploration and discovery. When it was time for a visit with our parents, we were ready, and hurried in, vying as little entertainers for their adoring glances, eventually ushered away again for bath time and bed, or simply taken away so the grownups could relax.

We relaxed with Mrs. Gregory — but sometimes, we also had a visitor.

Louise was 12 years my senior, a talkative and pixieish girl with a classically beautiful face and shiny dark hair in a stylish pageboy cut. She had a quick sense of humor, and she loved to tease everyone, often laughing at her own cleverness. Some of my earliest memories are of Louise and the neighbor boy, Sam, when they read me stories together. Louise seemed to find me endlessly entertaining, always curious to know what I was doing or thinking. I adored her.

There is an old audiotape of her interviewing me. For Louise, everything was a show, and the new tape recorder was just her latest opportunity to create one. I was two or three, and still speaking in baby-talk when she asked me what I did that day. I told her that I had been to the beach.

"And did you play with the children there?" she asked coyly.

"Uh-huh," I replied. "An de boys were *frowing* sand in my eyes!" I added indignantly.

"Oh no! That's terrible!" Louise said, as she attempted to stifle a giggle.

"An I din' cry," I assured her in a sing-songy tone.

Charmed by my declaration of bravery, she laughed, and I seemed to get the joke enough to make a retort. I cried, "Wuuurmhead!" I cried, calling out to her as I ran around the room.

Louise let out a yelp of mock surprise. "What did you say?" she asked in her sweetest tone, chuckling.

"Wormhead. You're a *wuuuurmheeeeeaaaad!*"

"*That's* not niiice," she told me, clearly amused. Now her laughter was louder, and I ran away, a tiny free bird, repeating "wormhead" back at her, my voice receding as she giggled.

Everyone enjoyed Louise. Back then, I was too young to understand her relationship to me and it was never mentioned. The fact is, I didn't question it myself for many years to come. This energetic and affectionate girl would simply appear once or twice a year, seemingly out of thin air. I never gave much thought to where she came from or how it was she got there. I just knew she was fun.

In New York, the days embraced us like a soft blanket. There was so much goodness life had to offer. Mamaroneck was all we knew of the world and all we needed to know, but we wouldn't be there forever. I was five years old when the doctors told my father that he needed to spend his winters in a warmer climate for the sake of his health. I don't remember the actual move, but it happened a year later, not long after a third child was born into our family.

Chapter 2
Joe

After a good night, my father would rise just before noon. If it had been a bad one, he would appear for breakfast closer to one o'clock. He had difficulty sleeping, invariably staying up all night reading or working until he would take a Miltown, a popular tranquilizer at the time, around six or seven a.m. Maybe it was his rheumatoid arthritis, or perhaps his chronic acid reflux or some combination of the two that kept him up. Certainly, he ate antacids like candy to treat the constant heartburn. By the time I knew him, his late nights were a long-standing habit.

Every day before he came to breakfast, he would shower and shave, coming to the table impeccably dressed, his hair still wet but neatly combed. Even before I rounded the corner into the breakfast room, the fresh scent of his favorite Royall Lyme cologne was my first hint that he was present, even before I could see him. When he was commuting, he wore a starched shirt with French cuffs, gold cufflinks and a silk tie, retrieving his suit jacket from his closet just before leaving. Otherwise, he came to the table wearing a long-sleeved shirt, slacks, belt, and his ubiquitous wingtip shoes. He didn't own a pair of loafers.

On weekends, if he had a tennis match, he dressed just as smartly, with his Jack Purcell sneakers, white crew socks, shorts, and a polo shirt that looked as clean and unwrinkled as his more formal attire. This was his norm. I never once saw him in a T-shirt of any kind, nor anything else that was not clean and neatly pressed.

He was a courtly man. With every change of day, his greetings were predictably formal. Before noon, it was "good morning," after that, "good afternoon" was the greeting. At the dinner table, he would invariably say, "Good evening." I never once heard him acknowledge anyone with a simple "hi." No one else in our household spoke in such a formal way, not even our mother. We used "hi," to greet each other, and even him, but he never altered his habit. His manner was an expression of what he felt was proper. As an editor, words and their usage were his stock-in-trade, and even this small difference in communication set him apart from the rest of us.

Although he was twenty years my mother's senior and past middle age, he was still a handsome man. At about 5-feet-7-inches he wasn't tall, but he had a wiry and athletic physique with a full head of thick and gently wavy graying hair. In his youth, it had been a sandy blond. A neatly trimmed mustache spanned his long upper lip, and his large and piercing gray-green eyes twinkled under great heavy arching eyebrows. When he smiled, his broad grin was framed by Clark Gable dimples on either side. We seldom saw this grin, but when we did, it was glorious.

He would seat himself for breakfast at his customary place, which was set and waiting for him at the head of the table. From the kitchen, the maid would appear with his breakfast, often consisting of some sort of fish. His choices were lox and bagel, a whole smoked whitefish, and anchovies or salmon roe on buttered toast. Occasionally, he shared a slice with me. The buttered toast with anchovies was a salty treat I adored almost as much as I did the gesture. Twice a week, his doctors allowed him to have his two eggs and bacon.

Born in 1902, he had rheumatic fever as a child before antibiotics were discovered. As a result, his heart had been damaged. Knowing this, the doctors had ordered him to limit his consumption of eggs and red meat. They also suggested he remove butter from his diet altogether, and margarine was the only breakfast spread we had in the house.

As he sat and ate, we could see the arthritis that plagued him made it difficult to handle a knife and fork. He wasn't much of a complainer, but I remember him mentioning his discomfort once, and I had seen the subtle grimace and the tentative way in which he used his hands to navigate his morning meals. Afterward, he would quietly linger at the table, drinking his coffee and poring over the New York Times before retiring to his desk to work for the afternoon. It's hard to imagine how he carried on with a pen or pencil in his painful hands as he wrote for hours. He was editor-in-chief of Funk & Wagnalls encyclopedia. Each new edition was a set of 29 volumes and it came out every two years. He was always adding, modifying, and editing entries, either finishing one edition or beginning the next.

My father was what they called a self-made man, coming from modest circumstances and succeeding on his own merits. Born Joseph Laffan Morse, he was the first child of Louis Morse and Gertrude Laboschin of Brooklyn, New York. His two sisters were Helen, the middle child, and Rosabelle, the youngest. Of Jewish descent, Gertrude had emigrated directly from Germany as a young woman, while Louis had been born in America. His family was Jewish too, but they were British, and had moved to America from England. Louis served in the U.S. Army for years before he became a civil engineer, while Gertrude worked as a bookkeeper to supplement the family income.

Money was tight, and my father described how one year, he and his sister Helen had each received a single roller skate for Hanukkah. Of course, they could never skate together. Instead, they would each have to borrow the other's skate to make a go of it. The story rambled on and was told with great hilarity — generally at Grandma Morse's expense. My father's lack of regard for her was readily apparent to us.

As a boy, my father contributed to the household by selling newspapers on the street corners of Brooklyn. Once, he had been out in the rain for so long that all his papers were ruined. With no one wanting to purchase them, he persisted until his uncle happened by and bought all of the bundles from him out of sympathy. Such kindness from a male family member was memorable to my father, as his relationship with his own father was strained. Louis had been a troubled man with a serious drinking problem and was regularly abusive to my father. Once, when he was a boy, Louis had beaten him so badly that he broke most of the large bones in his left foot. His mother, Gertrude, had bandaged it but neglected to take him to a doctor to have it set. His foot healed so poorly that my father needed custom-made shoes to fit around the resulting clubfoot for the rest of his life.

My dad's difficulties with Louis were chronic, and no doubt they contributed to the tough exterior he'd adopted. The reasons for his father's violent nature aren't entirely clear. Aside from problems with alcohol, his time in the army may have been a contributing factor. I can't know for sure. It was never mentioned.

Louis committed suicide in the study of the family apartment. My father was only 17 and still living at home when it happened. He had put a revolver to his head and pulled the trigger. Years later, he described to Louise how Grandma Morse told him, "Now you are the man of the house," and made him go into the study to clean up the mess. It must have been a horrific and lasting trauma to him. Daddy never talked to us about his father. It would be many years after he was gone that I heard the story for the first time.

My father had been married before. He and his first wife, Vera, had three daughters — Phoebe, Diana, and Louise. When I was born, the older two were already past childhood and out on their own. The youngest, Louise, still lived with her mother, and came to visit us on school vacations. As happy and easy as Louise was, we came to understand that her mother was quite different.

I never met her, but according to family lore, shortly after my parents' marriage, Vera arrived unannounced at the house in Mamaroneck, the same one she and my father had once shared as a married couple. With my parents out at the time,

Vera pushed past the maid and ran to the kitchen to grab a large knife. Rushing around the house, she methodically slashed the paintings and went into my father's closet to shred his best clothes. The distraught maid kept her distance, pleading for her to stop. Calls were made, and a doctor arrived to sedate the enraged ex-wife and take her to the hospital. She and my father had been married for many years. It must have been too much to bear, knowing that a new and much younger wife was living with him in a house she considered her own.

Vera and my father had met in their 20s, while he was working at Grossinger's in the Catskills of New York, a famous summer resort for wealthy Jews at the time. He was employed there as the social director, and the job was a bonus for Grandma Morse because family members were given a substantial discount. Without it, she would never have had the opportunity to chart the course of her son's life. It was at Grossinger's where Grandma Morse met Vera's mother, and the two women hit it off, enjoying the resort while watching their offspring from afar.

It was not long before the two mothers hatched a plan. My father was a handsome and ambitious young man with good prospects, and Vera, by all accounts, was a beautiful and bright young woman. The mothers reasoned that their children were a good match and agreed that an old-fashioned arranged marriage was in order. Unfortunately, Vera had different ideas on the subject. She was less than charmed by my father and begged not to marry him. Her pleas were ignored, and somehow the ceremony went forward anyway, resulting in the three daughters, and considerable misery for everyone. It is unclear how or why it was that my father went along with such a bad idea. It seems impossible that he wasn't aware of Vera's feelings on the subject.

By his account, the union was a series of horrendous events that repeated themselves for the length of their marriage. Years later, he described to me how he would come home from work to discover Vera in bed with another man. I can only imagine the fracas as the men left the premises and my father made emotional and angry demands for a divorce. At that point, Vera would lock herself in the bathroom and cut at her wrists. It happened the same way every time. In a panic, my father would bang on the door. When she wouldn't let him in, he would have to summon the fire department to break the door down, and a waiting ambulance would transport her to the hospital. Apparently, she was never faithful. He was probably away at work more often than he was home, and may have driven her to it — but he could never bring himself to leave her with the threat of suicide so clearly in the offing.

It had been an awful waste. After the divorce, there was so much acrimony that I never got to know his two elder daughters, my own half-sisters. They were much older than Louise and had already moved out of the house when the breakup happened. It's easy to understand why I never got to know them. Their loyalties rested more with their mother. It didn't help that mine wasn't much older than they were.

Dad related the whole story to me much later on, when I was a teen. When he did it, a single tear had rolled down his cheek at the moment in which he pronounced the words, "25 years," the length of his marriage to Vera. The father I knew never cried, but the feelings were deep on this subject, and the force of them was undeniable.

I know these difficulties must have damaged his relationship with Grandma Morse. The problem was, things got no better with his plans to marry my mother. He had met her in a burlesque club in Manhattan where she was the headliner. Grandma Morse had strong feelings about that too. When she was a young girl, Louise overheard the private conversation between them, but it wasn't until many years later that she finally told me the story.

"Joe," Grandma Morse had said, pleading, "She's an *Italian*. She's not Jewish — and she's a *prostitute*!"

"But Mama, Italian women make the best wives," he answered calmly.

Louise didn't know what the word prostitute meant then, but she made a point to memorize the word as the mysterious key to Grandma's objection.

For all we younger siblings knew, our father was doing his duty as a good son. He supported his mother and gave her a place to live. She was welcome in our home whenever she cared to visit, which turned out to be mainly on the holidays. She didn't come over very often. Their relationship, at best, seemed cordial. I can only imagine his private thoughts at dinner when she came to our house for Christmas or Easter, sitting across from him and my mother, the person she had objected to so strongly. Generally, she was quiet and added little to the conversation. There was no visible disapproval, but there was no genuine warmth, either. Grandma Morse seemed strangely bland to us as kids, but we knew nothing of these stories at the time. All we knew was that Grandma's opinion seemed to be of little consequence to him. By the time he met my mother, it is likely Grandma Morse had little credibility left, but I will never know more than this.

As a young man, my father had been an extraordinarily bright student, and sailed through his high school requirements in only two years. Afterward, he applied to Harvard, but was not admitted. He suspected the rejection was because of his Jewish background. It is unclear whether or not this was the case, but it is how he felt, and he never got over it. Disappointed, he went instead to New York University and earned his bachelor's degree there. Immediately after, he enrolled in the law school at NYU, and by 1925, he had become a criminal law attorney. The new career didn't last. By his own account, his final case was for a man who, in his words, was "so damned guilty" he couldn't find a way to defend him. That day, he gave the profession up for good.

A much different but more likely account of this story was that he wore out his welcome. He was simply too reactive. Although he'd only lost that one case, his success was dampened by the less than enthusiastic reception he'd received while practicing. It is agreed that he was a bane to every judge that knew him. They had seen his emotional courtroom outbursts in which he regularly pounded the wooden desk with his fists, yelling in defense of his clients. He undoubtedly took every case to heart and either didn't or couldn't maintain the decorum generally expected of attorneys in the courtroom. As the story goes, judges would cringe when he strode in, dreading the pyrotechnics they knew were to follow. It is difficult to know which explanation is truer, but eventually, he moved on to try something different.

During this time, he wrote and directed a couple of off-Broadway plays and even had a song published. He also worked for ABC as a radio interviewer and spent some time as a writer for National Review magazine. I still have his passionate resignation letter to William F. Buckley Jr. The publication took a stance against a Polish citizen in opposition to my father's personal beliefs, so he left the magazine. After that, he took the position as editor-in-chief of Funk & Wagnalls, where he worked for the rest of his life.

When he was a child, only the wealthy could afford to buy a set of encyclopedias. Indeed, his own family could not afford a set. During the 1960s, with a nod to his own childhood experience in Brooklyn, he made a move to make sure that Funk & Wagnalls encyclopedias were available for purchase by people from all economic backgrounds. In his marketing plan, he decided to abandon industry norms and make the sets available for sale in grocery stores, one volume at a time. The change would ensure that any interested parent might have the chance to provide their children with a set of encyclopedias with little financial hardship to them.

It was a point of great pride that he'd found a way to get

the reference books available to a broader audience. The campaign had been so well-received that Rowan and Martin's television show "Laugh-In" coined the phrase, "Put *that* in your Funk & Wagnalls!" He couldn't have been more pleased.

As a child, I knew very few of these stories in their complete form. They were complicated, and I was too young to hear some of them. The fact is, I took both of my parents at face value, but my father was not the only one with an interesting history. My mother had her own colorful tale of struggles lost and won.

Chapter 3
Claudia

Every morning, my mother rose around 9 or 10, emerging from the bedroom suite wearing full makeup, jewelry, and an elegant dress and heels for her cup of Lipton tea and L&M cigarettes.

"Just the usual, Roseanne," she would say, barely looking up as she sat at the table perusing a magazine or the local paper to check her horoscope. After she finished her cup, she would call friends and family to catch up on the latest news, returning to the table for another when my father came for breakfast.

My mother's undisputed role was lady of the house, a prize hard-won, after years of difficulties both familial and personal. As a child born into an immigrant Sicilian family in 1922, she had seen it all before she arrived here.

My grandmother, Domenica Bono, age 15, and her older sister Theresa were shipped off from their home in Sicily to arranged marriages to brothers who had emigrated to America earlier on. The men were virtual strangers. Love was not an option, and even the simple facts of married life were a mystery to the girls. My grandmother told a story about having just arrived the year before, and now 16 and pregnant, she made the acquaintance of an Italian woman she often saw on the rooftop of her building as they hung out the laundry. She was young and inexperienced and saw this older woman as a potential source of good information.

One day, about eight months into her pregnancy, she finally worked up the nerve to ask about something that had been perplexing her. At just the right moment, during a little bit of small talk, she said shyly, "May I ask you something? Please tell me: how does the baby come out of my stomach when it is time to be born?"

Much to my grandmother's horror, the woman replied, "Honey, the way it went in, it also comes out." This was the first in a series of many reasons my grandmother had for a lifelong dislike for men and the trouble they brought.

Still, Domenica and her husband Charles went on to have four girls. Aida was the first, followed by Josie, then Theresa (named after her Aunt Theresa), and finally Claudia, my mother. There had also been a boy, Angelo, but he died from a brain aneurysm at 18 months of age.

My grandfather Charles was a rough and abusive man. When my mother was only four years old, he caught her with her elbows on the dinner table. In a rage, he broke the meat platter over her young head.

Charles worked, among other things, as an extra in the opera in New York City. My mother described how he stood in costume during crowd scenes holding a spear in the background while Caruso sang in the footlights. He had managed to get the job somehow through Caruso himself, as immigrant Italians often gave breaks to their own in whatever ways they could. There was even one time the great opera singer came to dinner in their tenement apartment, an occasion which was undoubtedly the highlight of my grandmother's life. Charles' opera job was not a lucrative one. As a consequence, or maybe through some basic fault in his character — according to the family — he was a con artist struggling to make more money however he could. The life of an immigrant with no education or special skills wasn't an easy one. Charles and his brother had arrived from Sicily only a few years earlier as young men with little more than the clothing on their backs and the idea that they would find success in America.

Having a mate was key to this plan. A man needed someone to cook, clean, and do the laundry for him as he made his way. My grandmother was only a simple cog in his larger scheme, and Charles constantly cheated on her. She had always suspected it but said nothing. Perhaps she hoped it wasn't so. Perhaps she'd hoped he would stop on his own. Perhaps, with children at the table, she felt trapped and unwilling to admit her shameful situation to her parents. In any case, it continued until one day, Charles came home with a blonde on his arm to ask his wife if this new woman could come and live with them.

"Son a ma beetch! Live with *us*? In *my house*? Sonna ma BEETCH! I show you whadda you can do!" she screamed in a fury, striking them both and driving them off with the floppy end of a garden hose, the nearest weapon she had on hand. My grandmother never looked back, feeling no regret for losing such a useless and troublesome man.

Quickly enough, she found work herself in a Mafia-owned shirt factory where she sewed buttons, cuffs, and collars, enlisting the girls to help when she brought extra work home each night. My grandmother worked on the premises, watching as girls disappeared and rumors of white slavery abounded. Fearing for her own safety, Domenica made sure she wore her dowdiest clothing to work and left her hair uncombed. Pretending to be deaf and mute, she swept up at the end of the day around a table of mobsters as they held their meetings. During one such meeting, she heard one of them ask, "What about her?" She kept sweeping. Another man replied, "Oh, her? Don't worry about that one," then pointing to his own head, he explained, "She's stupid, deaf, and dumb."

Times were tough, and my grandmother did what she had to do to survive on her own, including making root beer in the basement of their newly rented home in Nyack, New York. She sold the bottles on the street for a few cents apiece. By all accounts, it was terrible stuff and the bottles had a habit of exploding all over the basement, depending on the weather conditions and other mysterious factors they never quite understood.

Back then, dinner often consisted of a single potato each, or a little soup, while at Christmas, an orange in each girl's stocking was an exotic and expensive treat. There was an outhouse in the backyard as there was no indoor plumbing. The pages from Sears Roebuck catalogs served as toilet paper. On cold nights, the girls placed sheets of newspaper between the blankets to warm themselves. It was a hard life then, but Claudia, being the baby, was indulged when the older girls and my grandmother scraped together enough extra money to buy her dancing lessons for a time.

Claudia never finished high school, but that little bit of dance training became her ticket out. Still in her teens, she found employment at a mob-owned burlesque club in Manhattan, where she worked alongside her sisters. Aida and Josie worked as "dime-a-dance" girls, and Theresa was a cigarette girl. Claudia managed to become one of the headline dancers, going by the stage name "Body Beautiful." She had dark brown eyes and a cherubic face which was pretty enough in a girlish way. She wore her medium-length dark hair in the classic 1940s style with a pompadour above and the sides pinned into an upsweep. She was 5-feet-5inches, with long slender legs and a physique to match her stage name. There was a rumor among family members who knew her at the time that said she was more than just a dancer. They said she was a "high-class call girl" as well, although I have been unable to find any certain proof of it.

The club was owned by one of the most famous Mafia dons in New York. It was there she met and fell in love with the mobster's handsome nephew. My mother recalled how impressed she and Aida were when they'd had a double date with him and another young friend of his. They watched by the window in delight as a shiny black limousine pulled up to the curb and the boys emerged from the car dressed in expensive European suits. When they agreed to go, some "terms" had been set for the date, which was the custom at the time. To avoid anything that might look improper, the girls would sit in the back seat of the car, while the boys would sit up front. Accordingly, when the rear door was opened for them, they slid inside happily.

To Claudia and Aida, these young men looked like something out of a Hollywood magazine. Once on the road, they told the girls they had to stop somewhere along the way. The girls thought nothing of it, and so they proceeded to an unfamiliar place and left the girls alone in the car for a few minutes. While the young men were gone, Aida and Claudia, excited by such opulence, started pressing buttons to see what they all did. When a panel in the floor opened up to reveal an arsenal of guns, they were frantic to close it again before the men returned. They weren't sure which button had opened it to begin with, and began to press all of the buttons wildly in an attempt to close the panel, finding the right one just before their dates returned. By then, the sisters were so shaken that they asked to go home straight away, saying they didn't feel well.

Despite the shocking beginning, Claudia's fascination with this good-looking, wealthy new suitor grew. They began to see more of each other, and at some point, they moved in together. After that, the initial glow of courtship faded fast. My mother was told to stay at home in a dingy little flat while she watched him strap on his pistol every morning and leave in the limo for "work" looking glamorous and full of himself. She was lonely. He kept long hours and beat her when he was at home. It was no more than a year before my mother kissed him goodbye one morning, packed all she had in one suitcase and quietly left town without a word.

My mother went to live with Theresa, who had just moved with her new husband to a military base in Virginia, but soon she moved on to Baltimore and the thriving burlesque scene in that city. She stayed away from New York for two years. Eventually, she contacted the don himself and told him she wanted to return home, where most of her family still lived. She told him of her trials with his nephew and asked for protection. He knew his nephew for the brute he was and assured her his nephew would behave.

"Come on back," he said, "he won't bother you any more."

By her account, it was only a few weeks after she had returned to New York that she ran into him on the street. She was terrified by what he might do, but instead of getting angry, he stepped out of her way and left her alone. Had he replaced her with another girl? Had his uncle put the fear into him? She wasn't sure. But not long after their brief encounter, he was found floating face down in the East River.

By the time my mother had arrived as the respected wife of the editor of Funk & Wagnalls, she had seen more than her fair share of life. She knew what it was to struggle, paddling endlessly just to stay afloat with nowhere to land and rest. She had spent years backstage, as musicians smoked their killer weed and shot heroin, stepping into the footlights to tease and entice, revealing her expanse of skin, one article at a time. She knew what it was to feel admired and she knew what it was to feel abased. She understood these things with the calloused and illusionless perspective of one who had fought hard and won.

My mother enjoyed the admiration of strangers when she'd had it, but now that she was here, no one could drag her back into the cold and murky water whence she'd come. No doubt, a sense of irony followed her thoughts there, alone at the breakfast table, as she quietly lifted the steaming cup of tea with lemon to her lips.

Chapter 4
The Move to Florida

When we landed in Palm Beach, the natural surroundings
seemed so pretty to Debbie and me, filled with exotic plants and
creatures we had never seen before, but Carolyn was still too
young to notice. Our home was lovely too, and our universe
small, confined to the house and the immediate area. We
couldn't have been aware of the shift which was about to take
place. For the time being, the world was ours to enjoy.

The house had once belonged to Robert "Believe it or Not"
Ripley and sat at the top of Hi-Mount Road, the only real hill on
the island of Palm Beach. As far as I know, there had been only
one owner since Ripley's death and for unknown reasons, that
family didn't make any changes to the property. When we moved
in, it retained the jungle-like garden that Ripley had put there
himself, now overgrown with exotic plants of all descriptions
along with strange statues from the far East. Ripley's famous
boat, a Chinese junk, was still moored at the dock. Once there,
my father hired a crew to clean up the grounds and push back
the jungle. The statues were removed and the Chinese boat disappeared too, replaced with a shinier one belonging to my father.

Within the newly open space in the yard, my father
planted tangerine, lemon, pink grapefruit and other fruit trees
to complement the mature orange trees which were already
there. By the time he was done, he had transformed the grounds

into something quite beautiful, even though it was sad to see the wild and quirky flavor of the Ripley garden go. With all the poisonous plants and animals in Florida, the tangled yard would have been a hazard for small children. Now there would be lots of space for us to safely run and play.

If we were not on the lake trail or in the yard, we spent many hours and days up on the patio and in the pool. The coral rock patio stretched broadly from the colonnaded windows of the Florida room to the far side where shallow steps ran along its length down to the pool, which sat on a high perch. There, above the rest of the sloping garden, it had a triple chromed railing on three sides which was covered in a tangle of bougainvillea. The giant oleander growing at its base provided privacy from below. Down at the water side of the yard, a thick line of hibiscus ran along a simple fence that spanned the length of the property. Beyond the fence lay the lake trail, a wide paved promenade which stretched in both directions on the island's north side along the inland waterway. At the far side of the trail was our dock, one in a series of them, each one across from its corresponding house. Most of these were parked with motorboats for short excursions along with various larger yachts. Across the Intercoastal Waterway, one could see the mainland of Florida. It was another world over there; the real world, of which we were not a part.

Palm Beach itself had a couple of drugstores, and only one small grocery situated in one of the few commercial areas. The store made deliveries to its residents by way of phone orders. Very few residents in Palm Beach did their own shopping or transported their groceries home themselves. The small number of commercial areas in Palm Beach were devoted to exclusive boutiques, a couple of museums, the Paramount (a regal old movie theater) and The Four Arts Society building that played old movies and many of the Disney classics for the resident children. There was also a post office, a tiny stand-alone building at the top of Royal Palm Way that served the residents' needs. Palm Beachers took great pride in their little world apart and seemed reluctant to leave the island for any reason but to return to their estates up north for the summers.

The island has a sense of containment which was complete. When we would leave Palm Beach by way of one of the two bridges connected to the mainland, it was as if we were leaving one world and entering into an entirely different one. Where Palm Beach was sedate, and an oasis from ordinary life, West Palm was an actual city, bustling with people and activity. The stores in West Palm carried most of the necessities of life. It had the hospital and medical buildings, department stores, and a marina and boating supply, along with the funeral homes and large grocery stores where Palm Beachers could go when they had reason. It was the proximity of those businesses which made it possible for Palm Beach life to exist on its own, keeping the more mundane and unpleasant commercial things at arm's length.

When my parents sold the home in Mamaroneck, Mrs. Gregory came with us to the Ripley house. Our two grandmothers came too, taking up residence on a separate property down the street, only a short walk away. Aside from all of us, the main house included a rogues' gallery of satellite personalities that orbited our little universe. There was a cook, a maid, a laundress, a head gardener and his crew, a handyman and a boat captain, who brought a wife if he had one. This small crowd of people all came and went through a side gate and courtyard, entering through the laundry room door. Their positions were permanent, but the turnover was high enough that it seemed every year or two we were being introduced to somebody new. Our staff moved on to better jobs if they could find them, but we always had a cook and a maid who lived with us.

I remember being aware there seemed to be an invisible barrier between them and me. It is true that I had a strong bond with Mrs. Gregory, but it was different with the other two. Even though they also lived with us, they mainly stayed in the kitchen, the maid emerging from there to clean or to serve us meals. At those times, she was too busy for idle conversation. I remember trying to be friendly anyway, but most of the time, that barrier remained. I was much younger, and what would they have in common with a girl like me anyway? It was nearly impossible to find out. My mother made it clear that we shouldn't bother them. We were to be polite and stay out of their way.

The important people in their lives, their children, relatives, and friends lived elsewhere, and rarely, if ever, did I catch even a glimpse of them. On days off, the cook and maid would return to their other lives. Naturally, if there was a serious illness in their family, my parents heard about that, as days off were granted. Otherwise, we were not privy to their everyday joys and disappointments, likes and dislikes and so, the strange and one-sided nature of our intimate connection prevailed.

The staff knew when there had been an unfair fight between my sister Debbie and me. They watched while my father
left one of us at the table to finish our milk. They watched my
mother regularly leave the house and return hours later with bags
stuffed with things they knew she probably didn't need. They
knew when we were sick, and prepared and delivered the soup
and crackers for our recovery. All this was done on a razor's edge
between friendship and something quite different. As I grew
older, I often found myself wondering how we stacked up in
their minds. Were we strange to them? Did they actually like us,
or were the smiles we saw a simple requirement of their
positions? I never knew for sure. After dinner was served and the
dishes put away, they retreated to their rooms for the evening or
home to the other people in their lives.

In the beginning, when we first moved into the house, we
all lived on the second floor. Mrs. Gregory had her own bed
and bath, but she shared her room with Carolyn while she was
still an infant. Debbie and I had a room together and our parents occupied Ripley's old bedroom. The cook and maid had
their own separate quarters as well. Their space had two bed-
rooms and a shared bath. To get there, they would take the
stairs from the laundry room at the back of the kitchen. The
back door to their area was on a small landing halfway up our
main spiral staircase, and we were strictly forbidden to open it.

The only time I ever saw those quarters was the rare occasion when they were empty because both the cook and the maid
had moved on at the same time. Debbie and I were curious and
always wanted to explore it, but I was only in there twice. Mom

told us those people were entitled to their privacy; back upstairs, Mrs. Gregory had none. We kids were in and out of her room as often as she was present in ours, with no separation between us.

The only private time Mrs. Gregory had was after we were all bathed and in bed, and even then, she was on duty all through the night. After each of my frequent nightmares, without fail, she would take me into her own twin bed to calm me. Other times, if I was sick, she allowed me to sleep in her room in the other twin across from her own.

Over the years, there were periods I slept in Mrs. Gregory's room for months at a time. I was always welcome, her soft heart unable to deny any child who needed her. Half asleep, she would throw back her covers so I could clamber in. Her soothing words and warm welcome were a great comfort to me. When I was with her, whatever the trouble was at the time would magically drift away. I remember well those nights in her room, and how the distant sounds of freight trains snaking along the mainland traveled across the moonlit waterway, adding to our reveries with their haunting call.

Mrs. Gregory gave to me what my parents could not. I think this was not a lack of interest on their part, so much as an inability to understand or address the basic needs of any child, no less their own. They themselves had grown up abused and neglected and had survived the Great Depression with a corresponding psychic thickness of skin which left them unsympathetic to children and childish troubles.

I was the one my parents called the "sensitive child," and for them, this was code for something defective. My neediness and tendency to cry when challenged perplexed them at very least, and angered them more often than not. It was true that I was unable to take things in stride. From the very beginning, it would be Mrs. Gregory who provided the anchor I would need for the stormy seas ahead. My parents could not have anticipated them.

From their perspective, what more did I need anyway? I had a roof over my head, food on the table and clothes on my back, not to mention the fact that I was growing up in the type of house that most could only dream of. They reminded me that I should be grateful that I had them for my parents. When they were kids, they would have given anything to have what I had.

And I was grateful. I was a good little girl, with all of my might. I was.

Chapter 5
Three Sisters

The terrible difficulties for my parents with their first partners were in the rearview mirror now, and for both, this was their big second chance at happiness. They married in a civil ceremony in New York City with only their mothers attending. To anyone who didn't know better, on its face, it was an idyllic story: The handsome, successful editor falls in love with the beautiful and adoring young dancer. Each of them had already tasted a kind of epic misery in previous marriages, which heightened their sense of mutual relief and joy. They were like-minded in their gratitude to have found each other.

I was my mother's first child and, more importantly, the first child of the new union. I arrived a year after their nuptials. Within weeks, Mrs. Gregory was hired, freeing my mother to devote all of her time to my father. Two and a half years later, my sister Debbie was born, and Carolyn arrived three and a half years after that. Mrs. Gregory served as a solid buffer between the three of us girls and our parents, but that was all she was able to do. We developed our own separate coping skills and we each had our roles to play.

From the beginning, I was an earnest child, the "good" girl. I worked hard to anticipate and fulfill the desires of the grownups around me. I would sing, dance, and recite on command and generally do what I was told. I craved the approval of those whose time and affection were nearly impossible to come by. Neither of my parents was soft-spoken or gentle by nature, and I coped with their often harsh personalities by being compliant in a desire to please them. It wasn't a plan I had created in order to be manipulative. I couldn't have imagined that was even possible. Instead, it was an instinctive strategy for survival that I adopted early. It came naturally to me, as I wanted harmony above all else for as long as I can remember. On the rare occasions when I got into a scrape, it was usually with Debbie. At those times, I took a submissive and apologetic posture in order to protect myself from sterner punishments. Sometimes I took full responsibility for a problem even when it hadn't been my fault. This was all I knew. Their expectations of me were high in the extreme.

It was clear to me at a young age that I was expected to be their crowning achievement. I'm sure my parents felt great satisfaction in giving me the opportunities and instruction they themselves never had in childhood. As their star attraction, they were dedicated to molding me into a well-rounded young lady. To that end, I was given lessons of all kinds and I did all I could to avoid disappointing them. They sent me for instruction in ballet, piano, art, ice skating, roller skating, gymnastics, and horseback riding.

We even had a swimming instructor, Mr. Holmes, who came to the house once a week and put me through rigorous routines. I learned to do a proper breaststroke and butterfly, and he taught me the standard way to breathe from the side as I swam freestyle, doing endless laps in the pool. On the diving board, I learned and performed various dives, including the swan and back dive. Mr. Holmes was a kind man, but the routines were rigorous. The lessons began when I was only three or four, and I dreaded the sessions despite the skills I learned.

On the other hand, I did like my art classes, which only asked of me what I already enjoyed doing. The same was true for horseback riding, which I loved. The stable was situated in the wild and dappled swamps on the western side of West Palm Beach off Military Trail. It was a thrill to move atop such beautiful creatures through the tangled and unkempt wilderness of Florida, with minimal supervision, a rarity in my childhood. With riding, the expectations of my parents were non-existent. No one was watching, and no one ever called the stables to ask how I was performing. It was here I could be bolder, riding alongside my sister Debbie in games of cowboys and Indians, galloping about with the wind in my hair away from the anxieties of being observed and evaluated. My parents didn't care about what kind of rider I was.

My piano lessons were quite a different story. The instructor came to our house, and oftentimes my mother sat behind us listening as the older woman rapped my knuckles with a ruler each time I made a mistake. The pressure was high, the ruler hurt, and I had no real ability. No matter how often I practiced, I didn't make much progress. Eventually, my parents allowed me to quit. But dancing was different. Ballet was my wheelhouse. I

loved my lessons, and my parents were told I had talent. I practiced constantly and attended two-hour classes three times a
week. In ballet, I worked hard and became proficient early on.

As a pre-teen, I was sent to something called Palm Beach
Cotillion to learn the basic ballroom dances and the general
rules of comportment that all Palm Beach young ladies of the
day were expected to know. I was also given daily math tutoring
every summer to improve my stubbornly disappointing math
grades. My parents would question my instructors after class
about my obedience and level of effort. When I fell short, they
would let me know and expected me to renew my efforts to improve by the next report.

Almost from the moment I arrived, I understood my job,
and I did all I could to satisfy my parents' expectations.

By my mother's account, when Debbie was born, she was col-
icky and bald. She was nothing like me, her first, who was easy
and born with a full head of dark brown hair like her own.
Mom would often forget to add how beautiful Debbie's blond
ringlets were when they finally did come in. Instead, she focused
on the fact that she had started out with nearly invisible peach
fuzz. She must have known that this is often the case with
babies, especially fair ones, but it was a disappointment to her
all the same. As innocuous and insignificant as these details may

seem, they were the very first of an unfortunate series of issues that set us up for what Debbie would eventually come to see as a life of constant comparison and competition.

By the time Debbie was walking and talking, it was obvious to everyone that she was a tomboy. This word was code for something unfortunate, as our parents had no interest in any girl who would not conform to girlish standards of the time. Still, Debbie was an adorable child, with blond ringlets, skinny legs, and knobby knees, always festooned with Band-Aids from efforts gone slightly wrong. She had big dimples on either side of her mouth when she smiled, like our father, and her hazel eyes were tinged with an unusual and striking honey gold color. She loved roughhousing and anything physical. She never took to my preference for more sedate and feminine activities like playing with dolls. She was happiest on the swing set in the backyard, pumping her legs to achieve lofty heights, or hanging from the strong vines of our Banyan tree, pretending to be Tarzan.

From an early age, Debbie didn't enjoy being hugged or kissed. She kept an emotional distance from everyone, even Mrs. Gregory. Years later, after she had retired, our beloved nurse spoke of it. Mrs. Gregory described how she had struggled to gain emotional purchase with Debbie even when she was small, but Debbie seemed to recoil from physical affection. She was also painfully shy with strangers, and she hung back, often hiding behind Mrs. Gregory's hem, reluctant to interact. This seemed to irritate my parents, who pushed her even harder at times, scolding and commenting as they went, heedless of her feelings on the subject.

"See how Helen says hello? See how nicely she curtsies! You need to do it more like her."

This applied to nearly any activity in the offing. In my parents' opinion, I excelled at nearly everything, and Debbie fell short in equal measure.

"No, that's not it! Come here, Helen. Show your sister how."

"See what she's doing? She knows how to do it."

Debbie was always aware of the comparisons. Even in the family photo album, while the earliest baby picture of me looked sleepy and mild; the one of Debbie looked startled and spooky. Her eyes were open too wide and staring downward, away from the camera. It was as if she could see something very scary just out of view. Meanwhile, her bald head looked oversized, ultimately accentuating the look of alarm on her tiny features. Debbie had a horror of this earliest photograph.

"See that! I have the cranium of an alien! And what is it I'm looking at?!! Ha! It's creepy! Maybe there really was something there, and it's just not in the photograph! And look at my ears! I look like an evil elf!"

Her suggestions were so absurd that inevitably, at this point we would find ourselves laughing together.

"No, silly, it's not that bad," I'd say, shaking my head. "You were just a baby. It's the photographer who did a bad job. Come on; you were a beautiful baby!"

"No, I wasn't! I wasn't! And the proof is right here!"

Throughout our lives, Debbie pointed to those two pictures as proof that there was something essentially wrong with her from the very beginning, and she enlisted me to consider it over and over again.

"Look here! Look at how sweet you look!" she'd say, leaning in to show me the page in our family album.

"This, this is a lovable child!" she'd say, pointing at my photograph. "Now let's look at me," she'd say as she quickly flipped the pages to her spot.

"Ha! You see?" she'd begin to giggle. "I don't know what this is, but it isn't lovable. This is an ugly baby!"

To her, the photograph was irrefutable evidence. I was always sorry when she would return to this point. I didn't blame her for her feelings about it. The photo was unflattering, but it was only one snapshot among so many better ones. She had been a beautiful child. I did my best to reassure her that this was just one bad picture, not an indication of anything else. I would argue that it was an unfortunate moment, a bubble of gas, or a bad angle, but still, she would insist that here was the proof, plain and simple. She knew there was something wrong with her. Debbie never relented on this point, and I suspect it was because she was trying, in her way, to express something more troublesome. The sad truth was, she had a reason for her feelings. My mother allowed it. Some might even say she made it happen. Mom would laugh in front of Debbie at the bald-headed picture and compare it to mine as some sort of shortfall on Debbie's part. Added to that, she would go on to point out that it was Debbie who had pressed against her kidneys during pregnancy and caused her problems.

"You know if you hadn't sat on them the *whole* time, I wouldn't have had so many kidney stones all these years, but you *had* to do it," she would say sarcastically.

"And then I lost most of my hearing during labor too! You really did a number on me!"

This was true. Mom had lost almost 50 percent of her hearing in giving birth to Debbie. The doctors never quite understood how it happened, but the tiny stapes bones in both inner ears had gotten very slightly dislodged during the event. All we could say was,

"It's awful, but you know she didn't do it on purpose!"

"No, of course I don't blame her," she'd answer, but we knew she did.

It became a self-fulfilling prophecy. I was the darling child, and Debbie the difficult one. My mother liked to talk about how Debbie had been born with a chip on her shoulder, but from my point of view it had been foisted upon her. Debbie felt her last place status acutely. She was always being compared to me, and the comparisons never went well. She also didn't enjoy the perks that went to Carolyn as the baby. It was a classic middle child problem, to be sure — but it was made even worse by our parent's attitudes.

Debbie was the defiant one, the self-proclaimed brave one, who loudly blazed her trails wherever she went. Carolyn, who came along three years later, was different. She had a more subtle

superpower. It was she who was able to sidle up uninvited and climb into our father's lap, snuggling in with no problem.

"Oh-ho!" he said laughing, surprised at her temerity. Carolyn was leaning into him as if it were the most natural thing in the world. He was clearly pleased, but at the same time, he didn't seem quite sure of how to hold her now that she was there.

Debbie and I observed all this with amazement as if she had clambered into a tiger's lap with no ill effects. While Carolyn was busy snuggling in, we skittered off to the playroom for a conspiratorial meeting.

"Is she crazy? Can you believe it? She just climbed into his lap!" Debbie said in hushed excitement.

"I know! I know! And he *let* her!" I whispered back.

"Would you do that? You wanna try to do it?" she asked, egging me on.

"Nuh-uh. Noooo!...", I said, shaking my head.

Was Carolyn just plain stupid? We weren't even sure. We only knew she seemed so happy for no particular reason and she always seemed relaxed, which we were not. Her eternal cheeriness baffled all of us, including our parents.

Carolyn's approach to life seemed simple. She made no waves, so she didn't get singled out. Everyone enjoyed her as the baby. She was an adorable little thing with light, curly hair and an optimistic and friendly demeanor that charmed everyone. She managed to evade the microscope that was trained on her two older sisters and consequently received less punishment, too.

All Carolyn had to do was be sweet. And she was, she was the sunny child, who didn't require much, if anything, from anyone. She was content to play alone, but she was also happy for company. Compared to Debbie and me, Carolyn was remarkably low-maintenance. She was always amenable. As soon as she was able to stand and follow Debbie, she became her constant companion. Wherever Debbie was, Carolyn was not far behind. She was not only Debbie's playmate, but at times, she was also her whipping post. But even when Debbie made Carolyn cry, she quickly got over the hurt, rejoining her sister without holding a grudge. Debbie recognized in her a willingness to forgive and forget no matter what the behavior. Carolyn never seemed to take things hard. Most of the time, she would laugh, shrug her shoulders and go away for a while, always returning later to pick up where they left off.

As the eldest, I had more trouble with Debbie's bossiness, and I resisted letting her order me around. Even so, she succeeded in getting her way more often than not. When I gave in, my reasoning was that she was younger and maybe she didn't know any better. At least, this is how I thought of it at the time. Carolyn, on the other hand, simply went with the flow, being so much younger than Debbie. Carolyn was just happy to be along for the ride.

"Give me that dog," Debbie would say to her.

Carolyn would hand over the toy she'd been playing with.

"OK. Now go get me the blocks over there."

Carolyn would get up and fetch them. Once all the toys were at her feet, Debbie would say,

"Now what we are going to do is make a house for all these animals. Mine is the queen. You can have this one instead. It's the loyal servant."

Carolyn would go along with it.

"OK. Now, don't touch the blocks or any of these toys. They're all mine now. You can just watch what I'm doing."

Carolyn would patiently do as she was told. Eventually, she might forget the rules and reach for a toy.

"No! No! Didn't I tell you not to touch them? ...Don't touch them or else!" Debbie would say, threatening.

Carolyn would withdraw her hand again and sit watching obediently while Debbie played.

When Debbie finished, Carolyn didn't necessarily get a turn. Debbie was the boss, and Carolyn followed orders.

"Go put these things back on the toy shelf. OK. Now we are going to go into the yard."

And again, Carolyn would follow.

As a coping strategy, this worked marvelously well, but there was a price to pay. Ultimately, it was Carolyn who was forgotten in the vicissitudes of our daily life. She fell through the cracks straight through into her teen years, left to her own devices more often than not. No one worried about her. Our father's health was already a looming issue for years before she was born, and there was much more to worry about in our household than the easy child.

According to my mother, she had been an "accident," an unplanned pregnancy. Mom went on to describe how it had been for her.

"She was coming so fast, they didn't even have the time to put me out. They wheeled me into the room and bam! There she was! No anesthesia. God, it was awful! You know, I never saw you when you were born. I didn't see Debbie either. I was out cold — so much better," she said, and then screwing her face into a grimace of disgust, she added, "When she came out, she was covered in all this slime and blood and goo... I've never seen anything like it. The sight of her turned my stomach. It's hard for me to forget."

I know she didn't.

Carolyn had slid into this world without any preparation. My mother seemed to see the speed of her delivery as some proof of her easy nature, but her self avowed disgust at the first sight of her always bothered me. During our childhoods, did my mother also pay less attention to her for that reason? Did Carolyn expect less because she was accustomed to it? I wish I could say it was not a factor.

From the beginning, Carolyn was the mystery no one noticed was there. She seemed to need almost nothing at all. She was so tractable that she became, in some ways, nearly a footnote in the daily goings-on. But as they say, watch out for the quiet ones. Carolyn's ease served as a cloak for a strong and independent-minded personality. While she was busy saying yes, she was also forming her unique outlook based on very private opinions, desires, and difficulties. Maybe she was waiting for the day when no one had any power over her anymore. We were unaware of these thoughts. We never could have guessed what they were, and she never gave us any indication. When she got old enough, we all came to understand that Carolyn would do what she decided to do, regardless of anyone else's opinion. She would make her own plans and follow through with them, much to everyone's shock and dismay. My mother saw no reason to expect what was coming. She didn't detect any difference of opinion or difficulty between them. Neither did we. How wrong we all were.

As it was, Carolyn's compliance was taken for granted, while Debbie's and mine were seen as choices. No one paid any mind to Carolyn's good deeds or her mistakes because they didn't expect much of her to begin with. After all, she was the baby. Her consistently cheerful disposition made it impossible to see what she might actually be feeling. I confess I worried less about her. Meanwhile, Debbie was so difficult that she set herself apart from the two of us as the "problem" child. My worry for Debbie began early and never abated. She was so sensitive and hard to please, even as a young child. My lot was that of most first children. My parents had trained the microscope on me long before Debbie ever appeared. I was destined to be the perennial exemplar and the one who felt responsible not only for my parents' happiness, but for my sisters' wellbeing too. As I matured and the dawning of my own circumstances came to me, so did my awareness of Debbie's. To my regret, I didn't know for many years that Carolyn had also suffered.

Our roles were cast early, as was our value as members of the family. I was the pretty and talented girly girl, Debbie was the talentless and defiant tomboy, and Carolyn the amusing and adorable baby. Similarly, the amount of effort we each required was evident to everyone. I cried most easily, Debbie cried the loudest, and Carolyn almost never cried at all. It may sound strange but these things explain, even in part, everything that was to come. Had circumstances or events been different, it might have been possible to see things in another light, but facts were what they were.

There was one last piece of this puzzle yet to come. It would be impossible to ignore, and I would be the one to bear its weight.

Chapter 6
The Confession and The Ballerina

When I was 10 years old, my mother made a confession to me. I was alone with her one day in her dressing room. I can picture the floor-length powder blue velvet curtains with heavy dusty rose fringe framing the large window. It was a stylish room for the day, with a blue mohair ladies' armchair and matching ottoman. On top of the French Provincial vanity were two small enameled lamps that had matching white silk shades with small porcelain birds standing beneath them. My glamorous mother was sitting on the tufted velvet stool at her vanity as she spoke.

"You know, Helen, you are my favorite child."

I searched her eyes for the joke. It took a split second for the full meaning of what she'd said to sink in. I was horrified. Tears began to fill my eyes and I cried,

"No, Mommy, don't say that! You love all your children the same!"

She replied, "But it's true. You're my favorite. That's just the way it is."

In that electric moment, I knew she was speaking the unvarnished truth. It's not that I was surprised, exactly. I had been granted plenty of small favors by then and was aware it could be true, but it was different hearing it from my mother's lips. At that moment, an indescribable sense of doom engulfed me. Suddenly, the breadth and scope of the injustice was official, and I felt totally complicit.

With that terrible statement put into words, my heart broke for my little sisters; at the same time, it broke for me. I was the one who had enjoyed too much, taken too much. It was all my fault! Admittedly, there was some small comfort to be told I was her favorite, but whatever comfort it provided was spoiled by the larger sense that whatever pleasure I got would be like taking something from them.

In response to my tears and concern for my sisters' welfare, my mother shook her head and sighed, looking somewhat deflated by my reaction. She made some small effort to comfort me, but there was nothing she could do. I left at some point with her words still ringing in my ears. I felt like a beggar who'd been invited to a glorious feast, only to find afterward that the food had been poisoned. I wished she'd never told me.

I was hungry for any goodwill from my parents, but as the eldest, I felt protective toward my younger sisters. I had no resources to do anything more than carry on and try at the same time, to shield them as best I could. The weight of that moment was a heavy burden for me. What little affection I did get from either of my parents was a rare and precious commodity. I never breathed a word of that terrible confession to anyone, not even to Mrs. Gregory. Debbie and Carolyn would never know what our mother revealed to me that day, but it made little difference — I would have to bear that knowledge for the rest of my life.

Ballet was the skill that had made me the family entertainer. It probably didn't hurt that both my parents preferred to think of my mother as a dancer in her younger years. Starting lessons at age four, I took on this role with great seriousness during the command performances when we had company.

I spun and leapt across the floor to recordings of Chopin or Tchaikovsky, creating dances as the music moved me. I focused on every "pirouette" and "pas de chat," making sure my turnout was perfect, my head was held high, and my arms and hands and fingers moved as gracefully and precisely as my feet. At the end of every dance, I would make a grand and balletic curtsy to the enthusiastic applause of my parents and the various visitors in the room. The accolades brought me a flush of pleasure that was powerfully seductive. These dances were the only times I felt a sense of unfettered appreciation from my parents. Seeing their pleasure was everything to me. It was an irresistible inducement. After I had danced to their satisfaction, I was excused. Inevitably, I would leave the room feeling victorious, appreciated, and, yes, loved. It was our regular routine. I provided them with the parental satisfaction of showing off one of their offspring. In return, I received the attention I craved so much.

I had always enjoyed dancing for them, but strangely, one day, all that changed. I was around 11 or 12, and I remember it well. I'm sure my natural preteen self-consciousness was emerging at that point, although I cannot say I was aware of it until it arrived in full flower that day.

My parents had company again, and the group was having drinks before dinner. My mother announced to me that they were all waiting. The Levys, my father's lawyer and his wife were there, along with Frank Miller from work and his wife, Ruby. I knew who all these people were, but they were not there to visit with me. To my mind, they were familiar strangers, like so many of my parents' friends, and I was sure they didn't care if I danced or not.

On this particular evening, they had arrived an hour early, dressed in their best. There was time before dinner, and they were enjoying drinks and chatting when I got the summons. Unexpectedly, I felt a rush of self-consciousness. I don't know why it happened then, but suddenly I became aware of what the command performances meant to me. It was a new and unpleasant feeling, and I voiced my reluctance. My mother ferried me into the Florida room anyway, probably thinking that when I saw the expectant faces, I would change my mind. Up until then, I had always enjoyed the attention and approval my parents gave me. I got so little attention any other way, and besides, until now, the refusal of any parental request was an impossibility.

Now, though, I found I couldn't do it. An unfamiliar sensation overtook my desire to please them and a clear idea of myself and their expectations flooded into my consciousness all at once. The picture it drew was so terrible; I was unable to ignore it. Everything changed as I saw myself as a pet monkey, *their* pet monkey. They expected me to perform for their affection, like a paltry treat given to a dog for executing a trick. I wasn't freely granted their affection. I had to earn it.

Until that moment, their approval had always felt heavenly, and I couldn't resist its call. Now, I felt used and foolish for ever having derived such pleasure from it. Once the idea of the sad and anxious little monkey made its way into my mind, it wouldn't go away. In a split second, my desperate need for their praise seemed depressing and pathetic and I said the unthinkable.

I said, " No."

"What's the matter with you?" my mother said, raising her voice.

"I don't know," I said meekly.

"Dance for us! Do it!" she demanded, her irritation visibly escalating.

"Please. I just don't feel like it."

Then she changed her strategy, her expression showing the strain of trying to disguise her rising anger.

"Come on, Helen, just *one* dance." She said it plaintively, almost begging.

Now shame-faced and lowering my eyes, I repeated quietly, "I don't want to."

Outraged, my mother declared, "Who do you think you are? You will do what you are told right now, or go to your room!"

"What's gotten into her?" she said to the others as I turned to go.

My father watched it happen without a word. I was already weeping as I turned the corner.

"She's got a lot of nerve!" I heard my mother exclaim, just loud enough that the sound traveled to me.

No one followed as I went to my room. I didn't deserve any concern, and I knew why. I had committed a cardinal sin. I had disobeyed. I took my punishment, grateful and relieved when nothing more came of it.

I never danced for company again.

Despite this change, I continued to enjoy what attention I got, but Debbie always got something else. Our parents wanted sociable and easy children, and Debbie was neither. I enjoyed meeting new people, while Debbie did not. I loved trying new foods and flavors, while Debbie's little face screwed itself into a scowl at any plate that didn't contain a hamburger or some "bisgetti' (spaghetti). Debbie had to draw with me, but she had no natural ability. I was in love with ballet and practiced everything I learned to perfection. Debbie had been forced to go to ballet class too, but her less than graceful attempts to mimic me elicited stifled smiles from the grownups. She didn't like dresses the way I did, but they kept putting her in them. Girls should be girls, and Debbie had no heart for it. All she wanted was a pair of shorts and sneakers and time to run and play.

The overarching theme was, "Why can't you be more like your sister?" The concept of seeing us as individuals, worthy of appreciation for our unique merits and talents, was not an option. My parents never saw Debbie on her own terms, and there were no accolades for her particular strengths and talents. Her inclinations and abilities lay in places they never cared to look, awarding them little to no importance. As Debbie matured, she coped by presenting a cool and self-reliant attitude that bordered on outright defiance. I saw it, even then, as an act of self-preservation and homegrown self-respect. She wasn't a pushover. She never put on a dress without a fight, and eventually, she won that war. Indeed, once we were adults, I only saw her in a dress twice — once at her wedding and the other at mine.

And while Debbie was given almost all the same private lessons I received, she had no interest in any of them except for horseback riding. I remember her saying often enough that animals were nicer than people, and horses were a special passion. Unfortunately, the activity held no thrall for our parents. They saw nothing in it, so she was forced to do almost everything with me in tandem, with predictable results. She was the foil to my good performance. I imagine our parents had no idea of the sad and terrible thing they were creating at the time.

By our teen years, Debbie and I had become like the popular TV comedy pair, the Smothers Brothers, where Tommy would inevitably tell Dickie, "Mom always liked you best." The difference was that there was no laugh track following Debbie's declarations of parental favor and no hidden well of affection for me, her sister, to soften the blow.

For her part, Carolyn saw the truth in it too, but she didn't seem to care either way. By sheer sunny demeanor, Carolyn had no detectable skin in that game. She accepted things as they were. Carolyn may have managed to secure a pass, but I was all in, and it was impossible for me not to feel the sting of every slight — and the sense of guilt I felt for my two sisters — especially Debbie.

The fact was, I was helpless to do much about it but to muddle my way forward as best I could. I had my own troubles with our demanding parents. In the end, the resentment Debbie felt toward me became so deeply rooted that it became a lifelong force field between us that never went away. We both recognized it and even discussed it openly in the years that followed, but she simply could not shake her negative feelings for me. The thing was, I also knew one more thing that she did not. My mother had seen to that; my sense of guilt for it was massive. It was Debbie's tragedy, and it was ours as her siblings.

Chapter 7
Parental Proxy

What was it like to have a governess? It meant we were seldom alone with our parents. Given the people they were, this was an absolute godsend. In Mrs. Gregory, we had a buffer and, more often than not, a safe place to retreat, but there was a darker side too. It also meant that our parents were virtual strangers to my sisters and me, especially because she had nearly sole custody. Our parents were unknown to us. They seemed exceedingly mysterious — and that mystery leant them a kind of unassailable power and glamour that kept them unaccountable to anyone but themselves.

As the story goes, when I was a toddler, I found it difficult to pronounce the words Mrs.Gregory. All I could manage then was "Eggie," then "Geggie," until finally her name became Greg to everyone in the house.

We were lucky. Having known many of the other nannies in Palm Beach at the time, I understood that Greg gave us affection and protected us in ways that other governesses did not with their children. I can remember the sensation of utter gratitude that she was ours. Greg was so unlike Shirley's french nanny, Mademoiselle, for instance, who found her twin pug dogs more interesting than her human charges. She was not unusual. So many governesses put on airs with each other and were more concerned with their own comforts and interests than those of the children they cared for. Perhaps a few were great gifts to their families, but I can only speak for our own, and Greg was our miracle. More specifically, she was my miracle.

It wasn't until my pre-teen years that I began to realize that it was unusual that my own mother didn't care for me herself in ways most children in the world took for their mothers for granted. I knew. I saw it on TV. Those moms did things my mom didn't. She never changed my diapers or fed me a bottle. She never dressed me or worked the knots out of my hair. She never bathed me or woke me in the morning for school. It was someone else who fetched a cool washcloth and baby aspirin to bring my fevers down or held my forehead as I threw up. She never even did things at my own birthday parties. It was always Greg who scurried about while my mother presided as a queen over her small country. Mom watched from on high, dressed to the teeth, never touching a dish or wiping a single messy hand. It was Greg who did these things, and it was she who attended to all of the logistics too. Greg had been there since I could remember. She did it all, and it was Greg who essentially was my mother in all ways but one.

The proof was there from the beginning. There's a home movie, a Super 8 taken by my father in Mamaroneck, in which my mother is trying to jolly me up for the camera. I am maybe about two years old, and my mother, who had little skill at tenderness, is seen tickling me hard and shaking me repeatedly to elicit a smile. Tickle, shake tickle, shake, tickle, shake. I am in her lap, facing the camera too. She checks to see if she's made me smile, but she hasn't. Her smile for the camera very quickly becomes a frown as I fuss unhappily and reach out for Greg, who is only partly out of the frame. The brief moment on film sums it up. Clearly, I felt uncomfortable with my mother, even before I could speak. Ordinarily, this statement might seem a bit unfair. It is certainly true that kids don't always cooperate for the camera, but my mother rarely touched my sisters or me. My mother had no idea how to make me smile with pleasure. All of the duties of motherhood — down to the last kiss goodnight — all were left to Greg.

I'm not trying to lay blame on my mother. Years later, she told me herself that she had lobbied with my father to care for us herself, but my father had refused. He said he wanted her to be there exclusively for him. If this is true, I can't know what his reasoning was. Maybe my mother did want to care for us. Maybe she actually thought she was up to the task. On the other hand, it is also possible that my father had the good judgment to prevent her. He might have known intuitively that she lacked the temperament needed for motherhood. This was certainly true. I used to say my mother didn't have one maternal molecule in her body. Raised essentially by her older sister in a hard-luck household during the Depression, how could she have come away unscathed? Her own mother didn't have the time for her. Perhaps there are some who survived such a situation and went on to be loving mothers, but my mother didn't. Indeed, neither of my parents was responsive to the particular needs of children, and it was the very decision to hire Greg that spared my siblings and me from worse. She was a wonderful mother, surpassing anything I might have hoped for.

Greg was kind and constant, empathetic and sensible. She understood children and she seemed to sincerely care about us. When we were naughty, she scolded us. She even delivered a swat on our backsides on rare occasions, but truly, it was her disappointment that stung for us more than our rear ends. She protected us too, neglecting to reveal some of our worst acts of misbehavior to our parents, whose punishments would have been far worse. As I see it, this was no form of treason — we knew she loved and respected our parents. She spoke highly of them consistently and often. Her silence on the subject of our misbehavior was a quiet omission which was in effect, minor protection. And we children were grateful for it.

When we were clever, she was proud of us. When we were funny, she laughed with gusto and appreciation. When we were sad, she would do anything to cheer us, even going so far as to make herself look bad in order to dry our tears. I remember well how she would slip her lower denture forward so the teeth protruded, widening her eyes, and grimacing like some sort of white-haired gremlin with a serious underbite. It sent us into sniffly giggles every time.

As I grew older, I felt increasingly protective of Greg, especially when my parents had guests and we had to make an appearance. It was expected that she would always accompany us. Anticipating the arrival, she would scurry about, dressing each of us and brushing and tying the ribbons in our hair. It was then she would rush to put on a fresh uniform herself. Greg would replace her everyday beads and earrings with something nicer, comb her hair carefully, and put on a little rouge and lipstick. I began to notice that my parents' friends virtually ignored her and seemed to view her as just an employee unworthy of much conversation. She would stand somewhere in the background and listen, or if seated, she would hang back in the periphery, minding us and keeping what she must have considered a respectful distance. No one approached to comment on how nice she looked or asked how she was doing. They treated her with the same unthinking nonchalance as they might have treated anyone who was merely on the job and not part of the group.

As a teen, at an age when young girls are so sensitive to rejection, my own feelings stung on her behalf, but nothing was ever said between us. What could I say that wouldn't point out the very thing I hoped she wouldn't notice? I comforted myself with the thought that I already knew how very special she was — how dear, and loving in ways I knew many of them would fall short. She was smart, and funny and had so much to add to just about any conversation, but they were uninterested.

My mother's position was more subtle. Her attitude toward Greg seemed to spring from a tolerance born of necessity and a burning desire to feel superior. For my mother, nothing fed that need like having someone around to follow instructions. This was her right as lady of the house. Of course, she was always cordial to her. After all, Greg was an integral part of the household, and it was she who made it possible for Mom to focus exclusively on my father. It hadn't been long before it was Greg who managed the entire household and all the other employees, too, carrying out my parents' wishes with their full endorsement.

To be overtly unkind to Greg in any way would have caused an unwanted cascade of events. It became obvious later on, that my mother had had little affection for her. By then, I realized that she suffered deep-seated jealousy for our affections. The jealousy never did, however, spur her to be kinder or more engaged with us. It was as if she felt she deserved our appreciation and allegiance without having to do anything for it. Too bad, really, because we children had plenty of love to spare, especially for our parents, whenever they had a moment to share with any of us. We longed for a show of love from them, as all children do.

My father's feelings for Greg were entirely different from those of my mother. They got on like old friends and seemed to genuinely enjoy each other's company, often lingering at the table, chatting and comparing life stories. This was natural, as they were both from another era, born closer to the turn of the last century than anyone else in the house, and Greg was his senior by 15 years. Their sense of humor was similar, and there was real simpatico between them. Had she been younger and more beautiful, there is no doubt my mother would not have tolerated her for long. As it was, she became irreplaceable. And so the years passed uninterrupted, with Greg as an integral part of our household.

I suspect that it is common among the few of us who grew up with proxies to have a sharp awareness of having missed the direct care of our own mothers and fathers.

This circumstance is the crux of the "love question," which lingered with me for many years into adulthood. Did our parents love us? Did Greg? There is a risk here that some will see this as a sort of "poor me" complaint. It isn't. My parents did all they could in this department. They simply did not have the same abilities in this regard that others may have had. Their backgrounds had left them emotionally broken. They were not withholding love so much as incapable of sharing it with us. Back then, Greg always told me my parents loved me, and I believed her because I was young, and I needed to believe it. She said she loved me too, and that was all I really needed to know. As long as she was there for me, I was OK, but as I grew older, the question of love grew more complex.

When I began to have friends from more normal circumstances, I began to see for myself what was different about me and how my family worked. Over time, I also became painfully aware of my place with Greg. It was then that a tiny kernel of doubt began to grow in my heart, leaving me unsure of my place in the universe. After all, Greg was being paid to be with me, and so her love for me was something I couldn't necessarily be sure of. If my own parents couldn't be bothered, who was to say that she should either? I was attached and wholly dependent on the love of someone who might or might not be there for me, if not for a paycheck. The idea had a profound effect on me. It affected my sisters too. I am sure many of my emotional problems began at the dawning of this thought when I was around 10. I was unaware of the nature of that shift at the time, but the benefit of hindsight tells me so. I do remember thinking that Greg must have been sincere when she told me she loved me. She had never given me any reason to doubt it — and I desperately needed it to be true. Given the circumstances, I also knew the only time I could really be sure was after she had retired and was no longer being paid to be there.

I told myself I had no right to complain. I had Greg with me, even if I wondered about it now and then, I couldn't question it too closely. She was the center of my world, and without her, my whole universe would collapse. I was utterly vulnerable. My lifeline was being paid. I had to put it out of my mind. I couldn't afford to entertain such dangerous thoughts without paying an unspeakable price, the certainty that I was alone.

Chapter 8
Our Greg

Our Greg was born Katarina Thuge (pronounced Too-guh) on April 10, 1887, in Copenhagen, Denmark. She lived in the city's center with her father and her brother Carl in a large rowhouse. Katarina lost her mother when she was very young. But for that tragic loss, she described her youngest years with great affection. Her father was a well-to-do merchant who doted on his children, especially Katarina. She described him as a very good man, kind and sentimental, who was reluctant to deny his only daughter anything, especially after his beloved wife had died. Katarina adored her father, but she confessed to me that she had not always made single fatherhood easy for him. Given the circumstances, she was not entirely above taking advantage of her widowed father's kind and generous spirit.

When Katarina was very young, she decided she wanted a pony more than anything and she told her father so. In response, her father told her gently and patiently that as much as he would like to give her one, this was not a possibility. They lived in the city, and there would be no place to keep such an animal.

When he delivered this bad news, she was standing near a windowsill in the main part of the house. It was summer, and in those days, homes in Copenhagen lacked window screens. Instead, the sills were set with bowls of black sugary poison to attract and kill the flies which might come in. In a fury, Katarina spun around and declared, "Well, if you will not give me a pony, then I will go and be with mother!" The young widower watched in horror as she quickly lifted a bowl of poison from a nearby sill. Before he could stop her, she put it to her lips with a defiant flourish and pretended to drink. She was perhaps seven or eight years old at the time. In her childish mind, she wanted to punish him, and punish him, she did.

Panicked and distraught, he carried her to bed and rushed out of the house to get the family doctor. Minutes later, the two of them returned, and her father anxiously awaited the prognosis. Had she actually consumed any of the contents, the outlook could have been tragic. The bowls contained a potent poison and her father despaired as the doctor hurriedly began to examine his little girl. The doctor rushed, checking her eyes, her tongue, and her vital signs. As the examination progressed, it soon became clear that the doctor was developing a clear idea of what sort of plan was in order. His eyes locked upon Katarina's, then slowly, with a subtle and complicit smile, he asked her if she liked oranges. Wanly, she nodded yes, still feigning the terrible illness her father feared.

In Copenhagen at that time, oranges were an expensive delicacy reserved for special occasions. The doctor turned to her father and somberly announced that the only antidote for this poison was to feed her oranges — lots and lots of them — as many as she could eat for the next week or so. With that, the doctor left, and Katarina's poor father rushed away again to buy as many oranges as he could find. Meanwhile, she sat in bed, happy and relieved that the doctor had not uncovered her ruse.

What's more, she would soon be enjoying oranges, wonderful oranges! It wasn't long before her father returned with a bushel of them, and there, at her bedside, her poor father fed Katerina orange after orange. Soon enough, the thought began to dawn on her that the doctor had guessed what she had done and managed to punish her too. Her distraught father sat at Katarina's bedside, demanding she eat more of the lovely fruit, now repulsive, with the utter conviction of a parent who wills his child to live by forcing the only known remedy.

It was her most memorable story from this time, and she told it as an example of the very height of childish bad behavior. Her nimble cleverness and worldly understanding, however flawed, had sprung from having already lost one parent at a young age. By her own description, she was a scamp and a scalawag. This little tale never failed to make her laugh to the point of tears, tears of laughter at her own unspeakably bold and shocking naughtiness, and no doubt, tears of regret for her kindly and long-gone father.

Katarina's idyllic life came to an abrupt end not long after that when her father also died. Now orphaned, she was sent alone to live with an aunt in America. Still very young, Katarina found herself in a new country with an aunt she had never met, who bitterly resented this new burden. Many years later, Greg related to me her sense of loss and the serial unkindness of an aunt who demonstrated at every turn that she neither wanted nor liked her new charge. Instead of becoming part of a loving household, she had suddenly found herself indebted to a woman whose only pleasure seemed to come with ridicule and small cruelties.

Once, when Katarina was a teen, she had taken a small amount of money she had earned herself and had purchased an inexpensive straw hat. At the time, it was the prettiest little hat she had ever seen and she adored it especially for the bright red ribbon at the crown, which was tied in a neat bow at the back and trailed past the brim. She had always wanted one like it and she brought it home excited to have something so lovely in her possession. When she walked in the door, her aunt demanded, "What is THAT?! Give it to me!"

Snatching it from Katerina's head, she threw it to the floor and stamped on it repeatedly until it bore no resemblance to the lovely thing floating on Katarina's crown only moments before. Finally satisfied that the hat was unwearable, she turned back to Katarina and told her with a sneer that red was a ridiculous color for a girl with such red hair. Katarina never forgot how her spirit was crushed that day along with her hat. She vowed to herself that she would get away from there as soon as she was of age and could fend for herself. Eventually, she did just that.

In the years that followed, she married and had two girls, Eleanor and Marjorie, and Katarina, now Katherine, moved on with her life. When her marriage didn't last, a tragic story unto itself, she went back to school to become a nurse. Now the sole support of her little family, Katherine and her daughters managed to do well. They remained a small but close-knit family, equal to the adversity that had come their way.

By the time my father met her for the first time, her name was Mrs. Katherine Gregory. She was already past 60 years old and had been in the business for some time. Usually, she would live in and attend to infants for up to 12 months or until permanent help could be obtained. She had no wish to become too attached to any one family. Because she was a nurse by training, many families of means were happy to pay for her help and expertise during their child's first year. Her former employers had given her sterling references, and the job interview with my father went well. No doubt, he and my mother were eager for her to come, having already tried a different nurse briefly, with less than happy results. And so, when she became available, my father rushed to hire her.

I was only three weeks old when Greg arrived. She was surely a relief to both of my parents, who were neither accustomed nor interested in the rigors of infant or child care of any kind. Like many wealthy couples at the time, they never intended to have children without a significant amount of help. Time passed, and even though Greg had made it clear from the beginning that her contract would be for a few months only, she broke her own rule and stayed on. She must have found our family a good fit. Eventually, they asked her to consider a permanent position with us despite her strict policy. And stay, she did.

By then, Greg was well past middle age. She was sturdy, with short white hair and a pale and freckled complexion — a remnant of the true redhead she'd once been. Every morning, Greg put on her nursing uniform — a white dress with matching stockings and white lace-up shoes with sensible heels. But for the missing nurse's cap, this was standard dress for all women of her profession in the 1950s. To finish her ensemble, she would add a single-strand bead necklace and coordinating clip-on earrings along with a tasteful smudge of rouge, and some red lipstick. Still standing at the bathroom mirror, Greg would brush her wavy hair away from her face and neatly pin the sides back with a pair of simple hair combs. Afterward, she would apply a little Jean Nate cologne to her fingertips and touch them to her neck behind each ear just before she left her room for the day. Even now, when I am in a store that carries that scent, I can open the bottle and be transported back to my time with her.

From as early as I can remember, Greg was my best friend, my protector, and my closest confidant. She was plain spoken with a mild temperament, and she had a nonjudgmental character that put everyone at ease. In addition, she had a jovial and slightly mischievous sense of humor. Greg loved to laugh and could find something funny in any given situation where others in the household might have failed. This was a great gift, especially in our house, and her presence lightened the general atmosphere immeasurably. I have no doubt it was a quality that my father adored in her.

Many years after she retired, she told me of an early disagreement she'd had with my father in Mamaroneck, before Carolyn was born. My parents were in the habit of enjoying their dinners privately in the formal dining room, while Debbie, Greg, and I ate dinner at the kitchen table, out of earshot and out of mind. One day, Greg decided to take this up with my father and pulled him aside to say that, in her opinion, it was proper for the children to share dinner with their parents. She said she thought it had gone on the other way long enough and felt it was important to say so.

Apparently, my father raised his eyebrows in response and asked her sweetly, "Pray tell me, Mrs. Gregory, whose children are these?" She replied with a smile to match his, "Why, yours, *I presume.*"

Nothing more was said. My father got the point, and from that moment forward, we ate dinner with our parents, with Greg at the table, to supervise.

It was no accident that my father afforded Greg such respect. Certainly, they both shared a sense of humor and were like-minded as peers, but she was also indispensable. Greg was up with the sun, taking care of us girls, without a day off except for one week in the summer, when she would go off to stay with her daughters in Queens. When I think of it now, it seems like nothing short of slave labor. I never got a chance to ask her about it. I can only assume she found the arrangement acceptable; heaven knows why.

Early on, when I was just old enough to understand that she would be going away for a whole week, I remember falling apart. I was inconsolable. The idea of being home alone with my parents was a powerfully scary thought for me. When I was little, they seemed foreign, and the idea of being alone with them without Greg was unbearable. While Greg was mild and laissez-faire, they were not. Where she looked the other way with small infractions and mistakes, my parents did not, and their punishments were always swifter and harsher than hers ever were. My mother, who would have to fill Greg's shoes while she was away, had little patience for small children, and in this respect, my father was no better.

I wept so bitterly that Greg was leaving that she took pity on me. Rather than allow me to suffer in separation, she took me along with her for the week. I vaguely remember my mother's displeasure for the emotional display, but when Greg offered, she quickly agreed. Doubtless, it would make her week somewhat easier too, with one less child to mind.

It quickly became a tradition, and every year Greg went home with at least one of us tagging along. I went with her most often, but sometimes Debbie or Carolyn got to come too. Greg's daughters and grandchildren were always warm and welcoming to us girls and we jockeyed for position, vying for a visit.

When I think of it now, I am amazed and grateful for Greg's real spirit of generosity. We girls adored going there. Greg must have understood why we did. In all the years she lived in our house, Greg never uttered a word to us against Mom or Dad, no matter how her private opinions may have conflicted with theirs on occasion. I felt her love for me first-hand, but it was many years before I understood how much she came to love my father and my mother, too.

Chapter 9
Grandma's House

Even though Grandma Speciale had been in this country since she was 15, she still spoke with a strong Italian accent. She was solidly built, about five feet tall, with a crown of short silver hair that turned almost black as it reached the nape of her neck. Her sense of style was unfussy and she brushed her natural waves away from her face in a neat arrangement. She favored plain and comfortable house dresses with tiny floral prints and sensible shoes.

She was no-nonsense, too, when it came to her grandchildren. She let us know that any misbehavior would not be tolerated. She liked to use a warning as a deterrent, describing a swat to our behinds if we didn't behave.

"You don' wanna make me mad? OK? I'm gonna have to give you the this! Ba-boom! Like that," she'd say, showing me her cupped hand and turning it to and fro at the wrist. "You be good for Gramma! OK?"

It was a distinctly un-scary warning, and I admit I can't remember her ever spanking me. Perhaps her saying so was enough to keep me in line, but I wasn't afraid of her either.

Grandma was up at the house often, carrying the usual rumpled wad of Kleenex in a hip pocket of her shapeless dress. She produced it every few minutes to blow her nose or wipe her eyes because of the allergies she must have had. Grandma Speciale was not one to put on airs. It's unlikely she would have known how. When we were outside, she also spat. She'd hawk one up and eject it onto the sidewalk without comment, and I took no real notice of it at the time. It took years before it dawned on me that spitting was not something most people do regularly, least of all little old ladies. But she was my grandma and, after all, she had come from the old country. Maybe they did things differently there.

Once in a while, I was allowed to go to her house for an overnight. It wasn't far. She and Grandma Morse were just down the street. Living together wasn't something they might have planned for themselves, but I'm sure when the decision was made, my parents saw it as a simple matter of efficiency. The two women couldn't have been more different. One was Catholic, the other was not. One was fairly gregarious. The other wasn't. As far as we children could see, they didn't seem to like or dislike each other, but according to everyone else, they fought often.

Grandma Speciale did all the cleaning and cooking, while Grandma Morse existed on her own plane, doing whatever she liked, which seemed to be precious little, at least from my young perspective. Her activities centered around watching "As The World Turns" and other TV shows and reading a little, without much interaction with anyone else. I have no memory of either grandmother having friends outside of the family. To us, they were simply a satellite to our home on the hill.

Their house was a neat little red and white brick ranch, its front yard edged by a low slung brick and wrought iron wall covered at the posts with climbing yellow Mandevilla. I remember the classic '50s style house fondly. Just inside the front door was a bluestone landing with two steps down into the open plan living/dining room. At the far side of the room was an alcove and past that, a doorway to the kitchen. The interior was decorated with an amalgam of Danish modern furniture and Italian decorative items. On the right side nearest the landing, there were two cushioned armchairs flanking a marble coffee table in front of the gas fireplace and its companion, a TV set. There was an abstract metal wall sculpture hanging there on the broad and modern looking stone wall.

On the left, across the front of the room nearest the landing, an undulating sectional couch was covered in protective plastic and stretched from the steps past its own coffee table and all the way to the back. The dusty moss green carpeting throughout had a curvy abstract pattern in relief. A large blond wood dining table was placed near the kitchen door beside the sliders that overlooked the patio and garden. Tucked into the alcove at the far end of the living room was a mirrored bar, an odd 1950s feature that they never used; they weren't drinkers. A number of Capodimonte clown figurines and Murano glass fish and birds were scattered about, along with Murano ashtrays for the company who rarely visited. They were always spotlessly clean. Neither grandmother smoked.

Excited to be going to Grandma's house, I would pack my favorite little red suitcase for a visit. I loved it for its neat red elastic bands on the inside of the lid, which held a matching comb, brush, and hand mirror. I would pack the little bag with Greg's help and carry it down the street myself for an overnight.

The arrival routine was always the same. Grandma Speciale would greet me at the door with a big smile and a hug, and Grandma Morse would be sitting on the plastic-covered couch in her usual spot with her hands in her lap like an aged princess with nowhere to go. I would cross the room to where she sat, and she would offer me her cheek in greeting. While I leaned in to give her a kiss, she would murmur in her wobbly voice, "Hello, dear." This would be pretty much all of the interaction I had with her for the rest of the day. While I was saying hello to Grandma Morse, Grandma Speciale would take my little suitcase and lay it on the spare twin bed in her room.

It only occurred to me years later that perhaps Grandma Morse was less loving with me because I was the product of her son's mixed marriage, a big no-no in Jewish families of her generation. Maybe I was a reminder of this disappointment. There might have been other reasons too, with respect to her feelings about our mother and her former career choices. It seems likely that any one of these reasons could explain her ever-cool reception. All I know is she treated all of us girls the same. We thought it was her personality.

Years later, I learned from one of the cousins on her side that Grandma Morse had been a very lively and affectionate grandmother. The cousin's description of her was so different from my own experience that it was hard to imagine we were talking about the same person. In any case, Grandma Morse wasn't much interested in any of us, but it didn't matter. There was someone else in the house who clearly enjoyed me and looked forward to my company.

On almost every visit, Grandma Speciale and I would make a trip to the ocean at the end of her street. The island was so narrow in our neighborhood that her house on Ridgeview Drive was virtually at the center of a three-block stretch between the Intercoastal Waterway and the ocean side. Together, we moseyed over to walk the beach, perusing the tide line for shells to bring home. We examined various specimens and put them in our pockets, celebrating when we found ones that were more unusual or in perfect condition. It was there with her that I developed a love for shells. I often brought a little illustrated guidebook with me that could tell us their names and what their former inhabitants looked like.

Sometimes, if it had been a productive search, we would make sculptures from the shells when we got home. Grandma always had a good tube of epoxy on hand for just that purpose. She'd spread out some newspapers on the dining table, and we'd get to work. We would make owls, turtles, and all sorts of animals out of them, painting in their eyes and other details with the enamel paints she kept in tiny jars behind the bar. When our masterpieces were finished, they were proudly placed on the shelf over the bar and stayed there for all the years to come. On almost every visit, we would add to the collection.

Some days, she played Italian songs on the stereo. Grandma liked to dance the polka with me while she sang along with the music. I didn't understand the language, but the music was lively, and she was an excellent dance partner. With this kind of a ruckus in the living room, Grandma Morse would quietly leave to watch her soaps or read in her bedroom. Otherwise, I quietly drew pictures with the crayons Grandma Special kept for me, and she would comment in her matter-of-fact way.

"That's nice," was all she would say, sometimes without even smiling. For her, this was approval enough, and I understood it that way.

If we weren't off to the beach, we could go out the back door to the patio. Grandma Speciale had a vegetable garden there, which was unheard of in Palm Beach. No one had one. Ornamentals were the thing in glamour land, but my grandmother grew what she liked in the sandy Florida soil, and she succeeded. I would help to water her tomatoes, cucumbers, and parsley and we would pick and eat the oranges from her tree.

I remember how Grandma would tell me about her childhood in Sicily, about the groves of olive trees her father owned and the life she'd led there. Her parents would hold feasts on Sundays and all the extended family would gather together at large tables outdoors to visit and enjoy the farm's bounty. She spoke wistfully about how families were closer there, no matter what, not like the ones in this country.

She told me of her father, whom she'd adored, and how kind and indulgent he was. At this point, she would always wipe a tear from her eye. I could see how much she missed him and the life she'd left behind so long ago. She also told me about her mother and how different she was from her father. By her description, her mother had been strangely cold and sometimes unkind, and I got the idea that she didn't care much for her.

In the evening, Grandma Speciale would make dinner. She made a wonderful chicken soup from scratch and would let me help when it was time to add in the little Pastina stars. I was never allowed in the kitchen at home, so doing things in Grandma's kitchen was an exciting and exotic activity for me. Dinners at her house were different from the ones we had at home, but they were always delicious. On special occasions, I would be given a tiny glass of wine at the table when they were having some. The wine was always Mogen David, which was what Grandma Morse drank on Jewish holidays. My Italian grandmother apparently saw no reason to waste money buying any other wine, as they drank so infrequently. I can remember sitting at their table at Passover as my Jewish Grandma Morse would raise her glass of sweet red wine to say her Hebrew prayers. In answer, Grandma Speciale would lift her glass too, and comment matter of factly, "Shoo (sure), I'll drink to that. Amen."

After dinner, Grandma Speciale would clean up, and we would have jello with homemade whipped cream in front of the TV with Grandma Morse. It was our little routine. We would watch "Mitch Miller," "Bonanza," and "Perry Mason," which were the favorites of the house. When the shows were over, Grandma Morse would retire, and I would go with Grandma Speciale to her room. There, she would tuck me into the extra twin bed, climb into her own, and switch on her Zenith transistor radio for music while we both went to sleep. It was a treat to listen to that little radio, its dial a nightlight in the darkened room while the palm trees outside brushed the window and threw striped shadows across our beds.

From her little sparrow in Mamaroneck to gardening and shell collecting, Grandma Speciale was my guide to all the wonders of the natural world. Her connection to them was just part of who she was, but she was not a woman of conventional science. Darwin's charm was lost on her.

"I'm not related to no monkey!" she would say.

She found it astonishing that anyone would have the nerve to suggest it. After all, she was a Catholic. For her, humankind began with Adam and Eve. This talk of monkeys was pure nonsense. St. Edward's was her church, and she went there for mass whenever she could. To this end, she made a habit of standing on County Road with her thumb out to catch a ride. Many times, Rose Kennedy, *the* Rose Kennedy, picked her up. She was going there, too. Mom was horrified. Not only was it mortifying to think that her 80-year-old mother had been seen hitchhiking, but what did the Kennedys think?

"Mama, Mama! Stop it! People will talk! If you want to go, I'll give you a ride." Mom would say.

Grandma was unmoved. What was the big deal? Mrs. Kennedy recognized Grandma as one of her fellow parishioners, and she was on her way there anyway. Grandma never stopped doing it, and neither did Rose. Going to church was important to Grandma, much more important than it was to her daughter. Even so, she never spoke of her religious beliefs with me. Those were private. It is likely she didn't discuss them because they were so squarely divergent from those of her Jewish son-in-law and benefactor, my father. All I knew was that "Ave Maria" was a Catholic song and it made her weep every time she heard it.

Back in Sicily, Grandma's formal education, cultural and otherwise, had been confined to Sunday mass and school up to about the seventh grade. She'd had no education beyond this. Birds were a passion for her, but she didn't learn about them from books. She had no knowledge of their habits or biology beyond the farm where she grew up. As a consequence, she had her own sense of bird science and going to see Grandma was always an adventure.

Chapter 10
Feathers and Fins

Grandma loved being around birds — most of them, anyway. It was often enough, during my young years, that Grandma would sidle up to show me her latest charge. She would have found an abandoned bird's egg and nestled it between her ample breasts in hopes of raising a hatchling.

"You wanna see? I gotta new baby! "she'd say, smiling and producing the tiny orb from the loose flesh of her cleavage.

Gleefully, we would admire the tiny egg, a lovely powder blue sometimes, other times speckled or creamy white. They were so tiny and delicate, resting as they did, snug and warm and full of promise. Once, when I raised doubt as to whether or not this was likely to produce a hatchling, she countered with a logic I couldn't refute.

"Shoo, but I keep them warm. Maybe they get a chance."

She was right. She was doing what she could, and I agreed that it was better than doing nothing.

I have no memory of how they stayed intact while she slept. Perhaps she placed the eggs under a lamp at night and then put them back in the mornings. Certainly, their safety was dicey. One time, when we were dancing the polka to one of her records, we collided accidentally. Immediately, we both stopped and looked at each other, knowing what had occurred even before we checked her bodice. There, the poor smashed egg lay in

shards- a gooey mess. She accepted the outcome with resignation, shrugging her shoulders as if to say, "What else can I do?"
and wiped it all up. Afterward, we resumed dancing, knowing it
wouldn't be long before the next "baby" would come her way.

She rescued wild fledglings as well. If one had fallen from
its nest, and she was unable to locate the nest to put it back,
Grandma would adopt the baby as her own. She would make a
concoction of raw egg mixed with ground beef, to which she
added finely chopped lettuce leaves. I remember her explaining
that this was a balanced diet. She kept the little ones in a shoe-
box with shredded newspaper for bedding, which she carefully
changed several times a day. A small desk lamp pointed toward
the box provided warmth for her little visitor. Then, making one
tiny meatball at a time, she would spear her secret recipe on a
toothpick, and convey it to the anxious baby's open and willing
mouth. As she did this, it would shake its wings with excitement, raising its tiny wobbly head as far as it would go, and cry-
ing out for what was coming. The moment the toothpick was
within range, the little bird would snatch the food, gobbling it
down greedily. Although none I saw survived on this diet, I
know that at least one must have, as evidenced by the tame sparrow she'd had back in Mamaroneck.

Going to see Grandma was like Forrest Gump's box of
chocolates. We never knew what we would get. Generally, it was
something good. Well, almost always.

One year, Debbie and I asked our mother if we could buy
Grandma a little chick at the state fair for Easter. I'm sure we
knew that our mother wouldn't like to have one at our house,

and Grandma seemed the perfect excuse to acquire one. Accordingly, we brought the little creature to her in a box we'd decorated for Easter. It was a grand gift, and Grandma was delighted. The situation was wonderful for all of us. It was a two-for-one bargain. Grandma got a healthy baby bird to care for, and we got to go and see it whenever we could. We named him Petey.

Every week, we went to visit the chick, and he was flourishing. Grandma had managed to feed him with something quite appropriate for chickens because Petey got bigger and bigger. She seemed to enjoy the chicken well enough, but we loved rushing down to Ridgeview Drive to see him, as he was friendly and so different from the pets we had at home. Eventually, Petey grew to full size. Where once the cage seemed cavernous, now he could barely manage to turn around in it.

One day, I went down the street to see Grandma. She welcomed me in as she always did and I raced to the back patio where she kept the bird. She hadn't warned me. The cage was empty.

"Grandma," I called. "Where's Petey?"

"We ate him," she said simply, busy with something else at the moment and clearly not understanding the import of her news.

I began to cry, horrified and heartbroken at the same time. This was her pet. Maybe he was a chicken, but he was her pet!

"Grandma! How could you do that?!!!"

"Whaddaya think I'm gonna do? It's a chicken. I eat a chicken!"

She shrugged her shoulders as she always did. To her, it was obvious. Chickens were for eating. That's what she knew, and that's what she had done. In the land of catered affairs, where no one even prepared their own sandwiches, my grandmother had taken Petey out of his cage on the patio and wrung his neck. After all, she grew up on a farm. She probably plucked and dressed him there too. I can only imagine now what kind of strange alarm it might have caused her closest neighbor if they'd looked out a back window just in time. But I was young then, and the thought never crossed my mind. I was inconsolable on Petey's behalf. Though Grandma was mildly sympathetic when she saw my distress, she insisted that a chicken was food, and this was life, and not to worry myself about it anymore. Ultimately, I had to put it out of my mind. She and I had so much more to do together.

On sunny days, my grandmother often walked up the street to our house just to use the dock. Fishing was one of her favorite pastimes. She would arrive carrying her rod and tackle box, along with a large plastic bucket. After saying her hellos, she would proceed out the back door and down to the waterway, where she would spend the afternoon. I loved to go there with her to see what it was she was doing. Eventually, she bought me a small rod and let me try it too, dropping the line over the side for me and helping me along the way. It is amazing how many fish I caught with that tiny thing.

When I was about eight, she came to the house one day with a grownup rod for me and said,

"You're a big girl now. It's time."

She had decided she would teach me to cast. I was beside myself with excitement. I had already been fishing with her for several years. When I was younger, she had always set the bait for me and supervised as I dropped the hook and sinker straight down over the side of the dock. She often stood with me, making sure I didn't get too close to the edge. Grandma had already taught me so much. She showed me how to maintain my child-sized fishing reel in a way that would keep the line from getting tangled, and how to avoid catching my hook on things before letting the line down into the water.

On windless days, it was easy to see the many varieties of fish meandering about in the brownish-green water by the pilings. There were large sheepsheads with their wide black and white stripes, congregating, usually four or five at a time. They were the ones we would spot most often, lurking in the shade of the dock. The Intercoastal Waterway, which connected to the ocean, was teeming with fish of all descriptions, from the odd looking sea robins, with their large and pretty folding-fan wings, to the soft and smooth catfish. We also caught stingrays, flounders and skates, brown eels, silver croakers, red snappers, and golden pompanos. My favorites were the porgies with their gorgeous yellow and white horizontal stripes and black spotted cheeks. Grandma never failed to call my attention to the fish lingering just below, telling me to drop my line in when she spotted some likely contenders.

These Florida fish loved the shrimp we used for bait. They found it irresistible. It was a while before I connected the nasty smelly things in that thin plastic bag with the lovely dishes we all ate at the dinner table. They looked and smelled so different. These weren't pink. They were slimy brownish-gray creatures with little oval eyes on stalks, their heads looking like tiny medieval helmets with jagged spear noses looking like fearsome little knights. When it was time to bait the hook, she would very casually tear off the head, threading the hook into the shrimp from the apex of the tail toward the open headless end, careful to leave the barbed point nicely hidden inside the soft flesh.

With my line down, together we peered over the edge to watch the goings-on. It was just clear enough to be able to see the creatures below as they tentatively approached, retreated, and advanced again toward the piece of tasty shrimp dangling before them. They would strike at it tentatively at first, taking a small quick nibble, and swimming away a few feet, only to return for another bite. Suddenly, they would seize the shrimp with a violent force and attempt to carry it off. Where we stood, we could watch as the ends of our rods would dip slightly, again, and again with every nibble, the activities below being telegraphed upward through the line. The fish took their time tasting our little offering. I learned to be patient until the rod took a much bigger dip and I knew the fish had actually taken the bait.

Grandma taught me to make sure the hook was set by making a quick yank of the rod away from the fish before I tried to reel it in. Even the smallest fish was a challenge. They would fight against the tether with surprising strength, moving frantically this way and that, trying to escape. Sometimes, they would swim around one of the pilings and manage to cut the line. Other times, if they were lucky, they spit out the bait, hook and all, or made off with the shrimp, leaving only the bare hook behind. The line would go suddenly slack, and we knew it was time to reel the line in and rebait the hook. The whole activity was full of excitement and mystery every time we threw our lines in. When we would have one on the hook, each of us would call to the other, "I've got one!" Then, winding our reels as quickly as we could, we watched to see what surprise awaited us at the end of the line. Sometimes it was a real fight, and we worked hard for the moment we could see what it was, landing our prize on the dock boards, still fighting and flopping at our feet. It was like Christmas every time.

Holding the struggling fish with a rag from her tackle box, she would remove the hook. I learned the proper way to avoid piercing my fingers with the dorsal spines as the fish struggled to get free. She also had a pair of needle-nose pliers to get the hook out if she needed them. Then, depending on the catch, she would either throw it back into the water or place it in her bucket filled with fresh saltwater to take home. Sometimes she gave the fish to the help, who were happy to have it. For the hours we were there, I loved observing the fish in the bucket as they circled gracefully, like small dancers from another planet, very much alive. From that vantage point, I was able to watch their wide and unblinking eyes glancing up at me from below as their mouths and gills moved open and closed in concert, fins and tails undulating.

I had seen my grandmother cast hundreds of times, but today, I was going to learn to do it myself. Except for sheepsheads, the bigger fish were farther out where she liked to cast. At eight years of age, I was going to learn to fish with the big girls. I was excited. The new rod had a spinning reel on it, and a nylon filament line like the one she used. First, she supervised the preparation of the line, allowing me to do it all myself. Carefully, I attached the sinker and the hook. She then proceeded to walk me through the whole casting process, showing me the method for throwing the rod tip overhead in an arc, while releasing the line around 2 o'clock, when the the bait and sinker would fly away toward the desired spot.

With nothing more to say, she instructed me to stand at the far end of the dock, facing away from her to do it myself for the first time. Carefully, I baited my hook and took my position. This was my moment! I took a deep breath and swung the rod upward and over, but my rod came to an abrupt stop just above my head. "What happened?!" I thought, disappointed and embarrassed by my own clumsiness. I had gotten snagged on something and turned to take a look. There, at the other end of the dock, my grandmother stood with my line leading upward to a trickle of blood that was just beginning to form at her nostrils. I had snagged my own grandmother straight through the septum of her nose.

"Grandma! Oh, Grandma!" I cried.

I didn't know what to do, I didn't know what to say. I was unable to move from the spot across from her while the sense of utter horror washed over me. My first thought was that I had killed her. How could this have happened? Should I run for help? I was scared and had no idea of what to do next.

My grandmother waved her hand reassuringly. "It's OK, honey, it's OK," she said softly.

I watched, horrified, as she slowly rummaged through her tackle box while the blood had made a full-blown Hitler mustache on her upper lip and was now dripping down onto her chin. It fell in droplets onto the weathered boards at her feet like confetti. Very methodically, and with no fanfare, she pulled out her wire cutters, snipped the metal loop from the line end of the hook, and pulled the cut end through. Quickly, she applied pressure to the spot with her handkerchief to stop the bleeding.

By now I was weeping. I was terrified and unsure of what might happen next. She reassured me calmly while maintaining pressure on her nose. It took a while, but eventually the bleeding stopped. Gently, she wiped the blood from her face at the spigot and went directly back to fishing. She told me to do the same, insisting that I resume casting as if nothing at all had happened.

She never mentioned the incident to me again, not that day or any other. To her, it was just something to deal with at the moment. She was there to fish, and to my everlasting amazement, after the whole world had seemed to fall apart, that's just what we did. Of course, after that day, I never cast again without looking behind me first — just in case.

Chapter 11
Tropical Wonderland

In the early years, life in Palm Beach was like something out of the books I read as a child. Eloise and Madeline were stories that caught my imagination, as I felt an interesting similarity between those characters and myself. I related to the glamorous but regimented life that Madeline was leading in Paris. Her parents weren't taking care of her either. She seemed fearless, but overall, she was a good girl like me. On the other hand, Eloise was naughty, naughty, naughty, in the extreme. She lived with her governess in a suite at the Plaza Hotel in New York, and I adored her creatively bad behavior and casual attitude, one that surely was impossible to imagine for myself. As it was in those fanciful books, nothing was ordinary in Palm Beach, and things that seem so unreal to me now seemed quite commonplace then.

Many governesses from all over Palm Beach took their charges to the lake trail for their afternoon walks. The trail served primarily as a promenade and bike path for the residents; no cars were allowed. The trail could only be accessed from certain unmarked entrances, and many who visited the island never saw it unless they were staying at the old Biltmore Hotel where the trail began. For the most part, it was the residents who knew where the other entrances were.

The five-mile walkway was guarded by a lone policeman named Johnny, who rode his motorcycle along the length of it once or twice daily. Johnny would always say hello, slowing down from an already leisurely pace, to stop and greet residents. He would chat with the nannies and impress the children, who crowded in to look at his shiny motorcycle and peek at his holstered gun. Aside from Johnny, the trail was not a place to socialize in particular. Most residents strolling or riding their bicycles had no interest in speaking to anyone beyond their social circle. Eye contact was scarce. For the most part, it was simply a place to see and be seen, as was the custom in Palm Beach. On any given afternoon when the weather was good, Greg would gather us together and we'd leave for the lake trail. Greg would push the carriage with one of us in it, and those who could walk traipsed alongside, ready for whatever came next. For us kids, the lake trail was something special. It was our zoo.

There were anoles, the small and lightning-fast lizards that inhabit the foliage everywhere in Florida, and we liked to catch them. Not only were they fast, but they changed color, blending in with whatever they were standing on, green for the leaves, brown for bark, or pavement. They were difficult to spot unless they were moving. The technique we developed was to watch for one sunning itself at some distance from the bushes so that we had enough lead time to jump and grab it by the tail before it streaked back into the greenery. The babies were the easiest to catch. Their little legs couldn't always carry them fast enough to escape us.

We didn't dare try to catch one once it had reached the bushes because there could be other less pleasant things hidden beneath the colorful leaves and flowers. The grownups warned us about poisonous snakes and spiders that could bite little fingers; in general, we stayed away from the bushes, no matter how tempting. The lizards, however, were safe to catch and fair game on the pathway. Sometimes, if we grabbed one too far down its tail where it was much thinner, that piece of tail would detach itself, and the slender bit would squirm for some time in our hands. Generally, that didn't happen. Usually, the little creatures were caught unhurt. I comforted myself on the rare occasions a tail came off that it would grow back. And they would. We delighted in this activity because catching a lightning-fast lizard was no small feat. Once we had one, it would generally eye us suspiciously, tilting its head and casting its tiny eyes upon us as if to size us up. Occasionally one would bite us as we petted and fussed over it, but the bite was toothless and weak and was only unpleasant for us in the knowledge that the little beast was not as delighted with their capture as we were. Eventually, we would let it go and watch it skitter back to the safety of the bushes.

There were limpets and sea snails, crabs, and schools of fish to inspect along the sea wall. Low tide was an opportunity to clamber down and get a closer look, picking up the hermit crabs and holding them in our hands until they would slowly emerge, waving their little claws at us in warning. They were adorable in their threatening postures, but we knew to respect them. We had all picked one up and gotten pinched at one time or another, and we knew that once they latched on, they were reluctant to let go. The tiny pinch could be painful, so we were careful and held them by their shell only, our small fingers well out of reach.

There were so many wonderful stopping places along the
way. Greg liked to bring us to one particularly wild and empty
space along the trail going north from our house. It was one of
the few yet untamed parcels of land on the island. It was a
rough and sandy lot and stood undeveloped and unoccupied
with lush orange trees and a huge coconut palm at the center,
which grew sideways from a point about two feet upward from
its roots. The tree traveled just above the ground for some distance before it jogged upward again with the tips of its enormous fronds still within reach. The horizontal portion of the
tree could accommodate 10 to 15 children at a time as we piled
on to straddle it. We jumped together, making the leaves sway
up and down like a giant pompom with every bounce.

Within sight of the palm tree stood a couple of shaded
trailside benches, a perfect place for the nannies to sit and mon-
itor their charges. They would congregate there, enjoying the
chance to socialize with each other. At some point during the
visit, they would pick oranges from the abandoned trees, peeling
and eating them on the spot and doling out segments to the
eager children, who ran back and forth for additional bits in between adventures. From that vantage point, the nannies had a
full view of the goings-on, while the children could run wild and
play safely under their watchful eyes.

It was a kind of a breather for all concerned, and the oranges were superb. They were not pretty like the ones in the
grocery stores today but were smaller, a mottled yellow and green
when ripe, with flat brownish scars on the smooth skins. Inside,
the fruit had a pale yellow flesh, very different from the bright

orange color seen in most grocery stores. Their lack of aesthetic beauty was deceptive, as they were delectably sweet and flavorful and rendered so much juice that it dribbled down our chins to our shirts. They were a perfect, though sticky snack in the heat of a sunny Florida afternoon.

Some days, we walked the broad flat seawall at the water's edge. It was a tropical Eden there among the numerous egrets and herons wading the shallows, searching the warm water for dinner. Farther out, the pelicans perched on dock pilings and seagulls meandered above here and there along with flocks of turkey vultures gathering on high. Most often, they circled above a portion of the trail which bordered the Palm Beach Country Club golf course.

Grandma Speciale never liked the vultures. For her, they were a bad omen. She always commented that they were circling above, waiting for her to die. As a result, I never enjoyed seeing the vultures like I did the rest of the wildlife. They did seem sinister when they congregated above, no doubt considering some dead thing they were able to see or smell far below them. I knew what they did when they found roadkill, but I could not imagine them picking at my grandma that same way. I knew somehow that it would never happen, but it was enough that they put her in such a state of mind. It shaped my dislike for them, and even now, whenever I see them gather, I think of Grandma, and what she used to say.

Florida was filled with dangers large and small, even in the inviting grassy areas alongside the trail. Once, I ventured across the grass strip between the path and the sea wall, mesmerized by something I had spotted in the water beyond. I stood still on the grass, distracted for only a minute or so when suddenly, the skin below my knees began to burn and sting with an unbearable intensity. I looked down at my legs to find they were covered in tiny fire ants, thousands of them that had climbed all the way to my knees, with no warning for me until the cataclysmic moment when they all began to bite at the same time. There were so many tiny orange ants on my legs that my skin was no longer visible. I swatted and scraped them off as fast as I could, all the while doing a dance which might have been comical, but for my screams for Greg to rescue me. From that day forward, I never set foot on the grassy areas there but passed quickly across it to the sea wall beyond, mindful of the horrible outcome if I chose to stand still.

The trail was for us a classroom full of all living things and the lessons of life itself. As we ate the oranges, the crabs ate the carcasses of fish that floated in. Bigger fish ate the smaller fish, the anoles and toads ate the bugs. Waterbirds ate the bigger fish, and the vultures ate the animals that had died on land. Once in a while, a huge fish would wash up on shore, bitten in half by what we understood to be a shark. The half that found its way to the sand could be three or four feet long, and the crescent shape of a single bite was unmistakable. As much as Mr. Disney had filled our heads with talking animals who possessed a conscience and a sense of moral justice, we walked the trail to experience the other wonders, more brutal perhaps, but equally interesting to a child's eye. No doubt some of what we saw there served our nightmares too, but while we were there, the sun was warm, the breezes gentle, and back then, everything was surprising and new to us.

Some days, we would walk south to one of the few other wild and uncultivated spots we found on the trail. It was there someone kept a kindly Galapagos tortoise named Whitey. He was a gentle and tame creature with a wise old face and large brown slow blinking eyes. Whitey was a great favorite among the children and grownups alike. The owner allowed visiting children to ride him on occasion, and for that purpose he had an ornate leather saddle trimmed in sterling silver. It was like something out of a fairy tale to be seated atop this massive and ancient beast, carrying us slowly but with his permission. Even then, I knew what a wondrous experience this was. Over the years, as many times as we passed his territory, we didn't see him often. The undeveloped plot was deep and lushly jungle-like, but we always stopped and called to him on the chance that he would appear and approach us. Sometimes he did.

Whitey was not the only large exotic animal in our neighborhood. Down the hill and a couple of blocks away lived a friendly full-grown kangaroo named Joey. Its owners kept him behind a tall chain-link fence in their yard. He was well kept, clear-eyed, and clean, with smooth fawn-colored fur across his back, changing to a flawless white across his belly. We would go there to "shake hands" with him, something he did willingly. It was an excursion we always looked forward to. Like so many interesting aspects of living in wonderland, he was our neighbor. Sometimes Joey would escape his confinement and bound down North County Road, much to the consternation of the residents and local police. The kangaroo would jump in great broad leaps down the main roadway with cars slowing down cautiously to let him pass. Inevitably, the police would get word that Joey was out again and make chase in their patrol cars. It would take some time, but eventually, they would surround him, only to watch helplessly as he would hesitate, then bound easily over the circle of cars and continue on his way.

One afternoon, my mother's good friend Polly entered the house in a panic.

"Claudia! Claudia! I swear I haven't been drinking! I wouldn't have believed it myself if someone had told me this, but I swear I haven't had a drop to drink!" She was breathless.

"As I was coming here just now, a giant kangaroo passed my car on the road! I swear I am telling the truth!"

The grownups couldn't stop laughing. We understood her absolute conviction that no one would — or could — believe her story. Our tropical wonderland was familiar to us, but we children were learning how odd it might seem to anyone else.

Chapter 12
Friends

It might have been surprising to the Palm Beach crowd that my parents had any social life to speak of, since they didn't attend many events that were the mainstay of the Palm Beach calendar. The truth is, they were seldom invited.

Unlike most Palm Beachers at the time, my father didn't care much about anyone else's religion, bloodline, or bank account. He didn't hold their success against them, but it didn't elevate them in his eyes either. His standard was a matter of the heart. Social status and ethnicity were only incidental factors for him. Instead, he socialized, for the most part, with those with whom he had some history, and his friends saw no reason he shouldn't be proud of his Jewish heritage.

Many of his friends had modest beginnings similar to his. They included artists, musicians, lawyers, educators, athletes, and intellectuals — all showing up to relax and spend time with him and my mother. My father's enjoyment of those who came to visit was genuine. Most of the time, they were his friends, but my mother never objected. Her own friends could be counted on one hand, and his friends became hers too. My mother was his support and his lieutenant at these events, as she was in all aspects of their life together. I never saw her question him or go against even his smallest request. Instead, she did all she could to accommodate him, and then some. For my mother, his happiness was primary, which was obvious to anyone paying attention.

There were regular nights in the summers when my father had his friends over to play pinochle. When they arrived, my mother scurried about, supervising the staff, even serving the men herself in a grand gesture of conviviality. Once the games were in full swing, they were left to themselves. My father and his friends would smoke their cigars and drink whiskey, neat or on the rocks, late into the night—shouting, laughing, and sharing the banter of old pals.

"Oh ho! Morty!" my father would boom.

"You lucky bastard! The damned cards are yours tonight!"

There would be a short pause and then, louder. "Who invited this guy anyway!" which would be followed by a roar of laughter from the group.

His voice carried with theirs throughout the house, echoing with an aspect of our father we rarely saw otherwise. We were a household of women, and this demonstration of playful masculinity was so different for us. It was fascinating to hear it, and on those nights, an atmosphere of wellbeing, however fragile, permeated our small planet.

Card nights were not exclusive to my father. My mother had corresponding canasta nights with her cohort as well. Most often, and nearly without exception, the women who came to play were the wives of my father's friends. It was clear to us that for her, the social stakes were high. She sought their goodwill and tried to be the consummate hostess in their eyes and his. Still, she was determined to focus on her cards once they were all seated together. To this end, she had a station for iced drinks, both alcoholic and non-alcoholic, along with a selection of sandwiches, crudités, and sweet nibbles on trays. She gussied up the tables with small-footed cups containing fresh cigarettes, filter-end up, with small individual matchboxes and ashtrays at every place. This way, her guests could serve themselves, and our maid and cook could retire at a reasonable hour.

We children were kept out of the way on both of these nights, as they were for grownups only. Greg kept us sequestered after dinner in another part of the house and ushered us to our rooms, where we could occasionally hear the goings-on, but we would not be seen. Usually, when our parents had company, it was not a family affair. The only exception was when the entire Dania jai alai team came to our house for a yearly barbecue.

My parents were frequent spectators at the jai alai fronton, and over time, they became personally acquainted with many of the athletes. Somehow, my father managed to convince Tasio, one of the players, to give him jai alai lessons on off days. My father was the only local ever to make such a request, and the subsequent lessons cemented a friendship between him and the entire group. On barbecue day, Tasio and the other players would arrive together, carrying the ingredients for an authentic paella. Some of them busied themselves at the grill, while others stripped off their street clothes in the cabana for bathing suits, jumping into the water for an impromptu game of water polo.

The event took place on the patio area facing the pool, where countless bottles of Spanish wine were poured for the guests and the staff carried trays of crab legs and assorted hors d'oeuvres from person to person. While the paella took its time cooking in huge, dome-covered metal pans on the grill, the heady aroma of chorizo, clams, shrimp, and chicken filled the air. It was a festive party, and those who brought guitars would sing Spanish ballads long into the evening.

Most of the men were young and single, but Tasio and his wife Polly came as a pair. They were our favorites. My father had forged a warm friendship with Tasio and Polly and they had become very friendly with our mother. We girls knew them both because they came to the house on their own now and then.

Tasio was the star player at the fronton and was a little older than many of the other men. He spoke little English, but Polly was an American. She was always smiling at his side, indulgently translating for him with an enthusiastic manner which was endearing. They were a warm couple and their presence added something special to any gathering they attended. It was obvious they adored each other, and their delight in receiving us girls was the same. Tasio's face would invariably light up when he spotted us. His English was poor, but words were unnecessary. He spoke to us in Spanish using grand gestures to demonstrate what he was saying, all the while peppering his speech with an occasional word in English. We all understood him quite well. Opening his arms, he would call us to him with a broad and eager grin spreading across his handsome, sun-weathered face.

"Mis chicas estan aqui! Bueno! Bueno! Ven a mi! Good! Come!" he would cry, motioning us over to him. We were delighted to comply.

Jai alai had given Tasio tremendous upper body strength, and he was fond of lifting us up and gently tossing us high into

the air, only to catch us again just before we might land. It was
something our own father never did with us and it was great
fun. We might as well have been tiny kittens for all the effort it
seemed for him. We loved the wild abandon and begged for
turn after turn, while he indulged us enthusiastically.

After we'd each had many turns, Polly would gently intervene on his behalf, and he would reluctantly admit that he was
getting a little tired. By then, we'd all had more than our fair
share, and we were content to hang by his side and talk with
Polly, who translated whatever we said to him. Best of all, they
would not allow our parents to shoo us away.

When Polly and Tasio came to visit, we would hang around
them for as long as we liked. They stood out as people who
wanted to interact with us regardless of where our parents were,
asking us questions and listening intently to our answers. We
children knew instinctively that their interest in us was sincere,
although we couldn't have known why. As it found out later,
they had both dearly wanted children of their own but hadn't
been able to conceive. They liked children. Polly and Tasio's real
warmth endeared them to us, and of course our parents loved
them, too. They became treasured family friends long after my
father finally had to quit his lessons.

As close as we were to Polly and Tasio, they couldn't have
known that what they saw when they visited was not the world we
lived in when no one else was watching. When guests arrived, we
knew as long as we behaved, we were safe from unpleasantness. If
we were lucky, we might even have a nice time. On those days, we
were dressed and held up to be admired by all, and my mother

would behave more solicitously. She would even seem proud of us and stroke our hair or give us a maternal hug as we stood near her, something that rarely happened otherwise.

One of my parents' friends might engage us in some conversation, and my mother would join in, straightening our dresses or smoothing our hair as she spoke. She liked to discuss the ins and outs of motherhood with them, and she'd shake her head in sympathy with the other women, saying things like, "Oh, I know what you mean. There's never a dull moment! Haha! ...Thank you, she *is* adorable."

Turning to me, she would ask, "What are you doing today, honey?" I remember experiencing a flash of happiness for the term of endearment. At the same time, I knew she wasn't really asking for her own sake. I would answer her, "I'm going fishing with Grandma when she comes up."

"That's nice," she'd say. Then, turning to her guests, "But they *are* a handful, you know what I mean. We worry about them, and do you think they appreciate it? Ha!"

Taking my hand and squeezing it, she would say smiling, "Have you had something to eat, honey? Go ask Roseanne for some crab claws. You too, Debbie!"

While she spoke, she never quite managed eye contact with us but would watch instead for the visitors' expressions of approval. Any direct look was often a private one and a signal of disapproval, something we dreaded. Those moments never ended well for us. A heavy shadow of stress was cast over our house, but it was invisible to those who visited. For them, it was a beautiful place of love and bounty.

Mom regularly held forth with others on her role as a mother, and as we got older, Debbie and I began to notice the inaccuracy of this presentation. The two of us would exchange secret and knowing looks. Her words, we knew, were for the benefit of her guests. Debbie's eyes would lock with mine, and nothing more needed to be said. Nurturing was not her strong suit. She was too busy tending to our father, but that was not all. It was that she was so different when we were alone. She simply showed no interest in us unless it was to scold. We might be passing through the Florida room on our way to the back yard, and if we were wearing something that she didn't like, or if our hair was out of place, she never hesitated to speak up.

"What's the matter with you? You look ridiculous! Go change those pants! What will people think when they see you dressed like that? Is that what you call combing your hair? You look like a slob!"

"And take those shoes off! Dammit, I didn't spend good money on them for you to scuff them up on the lake trail. Did Greg see you put those on? Greg! Take her up to find something else. God! I think you children enjoy aggravating me!"

Sometimes, she would lurk in the hallway outside our rooms and appear with some grievance or another. We had the feeling she almost wanted to find something. Our room was a mess. There was a towel out of place in the bathroom. The crayons weren't put away properly. There were items, *any* items on the dresser. And if she'd bothered to come all the way upstairs to speak to us, we knew it would be worse than if we were downstairs.

She always felt freer to speak when no one was nearby. We were wasting her time, causing her aggravation. In her fits of anger, she would grab us roughly, throwing us over her knee and yanking down our pants. She would spank our bare backsides for even the slightest infraction. Her hands were large and hard, and she didn't hold back. To our amazement, as much as it hurt us, the repeated loud slapping never seemed to hurt her hand at all. Other times, if there was a wet washcloth, a hairbrush, a hanger, or anything else that was handy, she applied them to our bare skin with equal enthusiasm. Once, she even used a wooden spoon. When it was over, there was no discussion, no hug, no sense of forgiveness. She would simply leave the room and not return.

When we got a little older, we began to call her "old leather hands" behind her back. It was a giddy feeling of minor defiance. We wouldn't dare say it to her face. Life was complicated enough, and there was no sense in making things worse. The next time we saw her would be at dinner. We would sit at the table, eyes averted, while she sent irritated glances at us, making sure we knew she hadn't forgotten. We squirmed in our seats, as she made allusions to our bad behavior, worried that our father might catch on and things would escalate. Greg would usually do what she could to diffuse the tension.

"This is a *wonderful* lamb chop. Where did it come from? Publix?" Greg would say.

"It'd taste better if these kids would behave," Mom would reply drily, her eyes trained on us and unwilling to shift her focus.

"It's not easy to find such fine meats here in Florida. By

the way, I saw Smiley again today," Greg would add.

"Smiley? Which Smiley was that?" my mother would respond, her mood brightening, the flicker of a smile crossing her face.

Greg called everyone Smiley when she couldn't remember an actual name. My mother found this hilarious, and Greg knew it. She found many ways of calling attention away from us when needed, and she often succeeded with Mom. Looking back, it is clear that Greg had some sense of how things were. She never said a word of it to us children, but she did what she could, stepping out of the way when necessary, doing what she could when it was possible.

As young children, we generally accepted what was, with little sense of reproach for anyone but ourselves. It was only as we matured and saw more of the world around us that we began to compare our experiences to others. Within the small list of children we could call friends in that town, we came to know a few who had it worse and some who clearly had it better.

A deeper understanding of how things were for us came slowly, and perhaps too late, in some ways. Like all children, our psyches were forming at a time when we had no self-protective armor. We learned to navigate the world as best we could, but it was often confusing. There was no denying we had two mothers — the one we knew when friends were over, and the other, when no one else was watching. In some ways, our father was more consistent, but our relationships with both of them weren't simple or easy. And for us, there were consequences.

Chapter 13
Discipline

Even though our parents were separated by a 20-year age gap, fundamentally, they were not so very different from each other. Still, it would be easy to focus on the obvious differences, which were stark. Education and intellectual pursuits were as important to my father as they were unimportant to my mother. He had many degrees that trailed his name on publications, while she hadn't even finished high school.

Culturally, he was Jewish — and she, an Italian Catholic, but they were both New Yorkers from ethnic backgrounds which, although different, had certain things in common. Epithets like Kike, Yid, Wop, or Guinea were familiar to them as they each had experienced prejudice in their youth. They both had gone through some of the harshest things life had to offer: he with his father's physical abuse and subsequent suicide, she with an equally brutal father, and the crushing poverty of an immigrant household.

In adulthood, they responded to those experiences by burying their vulnerabilities and insisting their children do the same. For them, disciplinary behavior like what they got from their own parents was considered "old-fashioned" and completely acceptable. It was still the era of "spare the rod, spoil the child." Children who did not conform or behave to their exact standards received the kind of punishment that fell out of favor in

later generations. Our parents had no reservations in this regard. It was their right. If we misbehaved in any way, they
thought nothing of raising a hand, often out of proportion to
the infraction itself. Their words were no gentler than their
physical punishments, and there were no laws, no government
agencies or psychologists that would tell them to do otherwise. I
have no doubt they considered their parenting approach a vast
improvement over those of their own parents, and perhaps it
was, but many similarities remained. As much as we craved our
parents' approval, we also feared them, and it was probably a bit
of both that kept us in line. We knew we were under constant
scrutiny, and making any misstep was a worry. We could get into
big trouble for anything — insignificant or not, it didn't matter.
The tyranny of that scrutiny combined with the memory of
what happened when they were angry last was usually enough to
sustain the tension we sisters felt in their presence.

As much as there was a good deal of strain in the household, there were reasons for it. Mom had lost much of her hearing and she had problems with her kidneys too. Between her
health problems and his, even the most easy-going family would
have been stressed. Mom always worried about Dad, while at the
same time, she struggled to hear even ordinary conversation.
She suffered through several extremely painful and unsuccessful
surgeries on her ears, along with multiple surgeries for kidney
stones. Eventually, her once-gorgeous belly was riddled with
scars. When Dad had a bad night from the pain of his arthritis,
she worried. When he had a heart attack, she was beside herself.
We kids were incidental to the drama taking place for them,

and, for the most part, we were kept out of the way. When we were around them, we were there to give them pleasure, not add to their troubles. They had known only harshness from their own parents, and in this regard, it would be fair to say that history did repeat itself. They may have been soft with each other, but they were not with their daughters. And, given our good fortune, they were also determined to raise us to be well-behaved and grateful girls who would take nothing for granted. And we didn't.

Sometimes I would see my father around noon at the breakfast table.

"Good morning, Helen," he would say, peering at me over his slender reader glasses, a quiet smile crossing his lips.

"Hi, Daddy," I would say, settling myself at my empty spot at the table next to him, careful to express my interest.

"What have you to say for yourself this afternoon? What are you doing today?"

"I've got my piano lesson in an hour, and then I will have to do my homework."

"Good girl. Make sure you get that done."

With that, the conversation was over, and he would resume reading his paper. Most of our interactions were like that: vaguely formal, requiring me to show respect by keeping it brief and to the point, presenting myself in the best light possible.

Dinnertime was generally the only real time we spent with our parents daily, and once Greg had shamed my father into it, the pressure was on. There were so many things that could go wrong. Spills and stray bits of food on the tablecloth were always a worry, and of course, we were expected to drink all of our milk and finish everything on our plates. Thankfully, our Pekingese, Pitapat, was always lurking under the table. She waited for whatever we might pass her way if we could manage it unobserved. Lucky for us, she even ate brussels sprouts.

Strict discipline had begun early. I was born left-handed, and early on, my father decided that this was an unacceptable habit to carry into adulthood. Life as a lefty was inconvenient, in his opinion. His method of convincing me to use my right hand was to correct me at the table whenever I reached for anything with the other. Without a word, he would sharply smack the offending hand with the butt of his knife whenever I tried to use it. Eventually, the strategy worked. It was only recently I noticed that when I am in the shower, I still use my left hand to wash. It seemed curious at first, until I remembered that he had never been present at my bath times, which resulted in this oddly amusing relic of my innate left-handedness.

Even finishing a glass of milk became a monumental issue. Strangely, in Florida, despite refrigeration and air conditioning, milk seemed to spoil quickly. At those times, we would say nothing, hoping no one would notice we weren't drinking it. This strategy usually didn't work, but it was worth a try. I had always hated the taste of milk anyway, even when it was at its freshest. They already knew this, and felt it important that I drink what I'd been given. They saw any reluctance to drink as disobedience and a way to skip the milk that night. It's just that when it went bad, it wasn't that easy. More often than not, my parents took note of my full glass and I was told to sit at the empty dinner table until I'd finished it. My parents never drank milk, and what's more, for some odd reason, my father was unable to detect the flavor when it had gone off. I don't know how my sisters accomplished it then, but sometimes they managed to get it down when I could not. I remember having to sit alone for hours after everyone had gone for the sake of finishing a 16-ounce glass of sour milk.

What's worse, the longer it sat, the milk only got warmer and more horrible. It was a bad day for me when my father would be the one who returned to the table to check on my progress. My timid suggestions that the milk had gone bad would only irritate him more. He would take a sip, and tasting nothing, would order me to drink it on the spot.

"It's fine! There's nothing wrong with it!" he'd say angrily. "Finish!"

Much weeping and gagging would follow each effort to drink even the smallest amount until in frustration, my father would take up the glass himself and hold it to my face until I had finished it all. If I was lucky, he might stalk off in anger instead, leaving me alone with the glass. Then it was the maid Roseanne or Greg who then came to my rescue, but occasionally, it was even my mother who would come in to taste the milk herself. They all knew Dad couldn't detect the flavor of spoiled milk, and he remained unconvinced. They would sneak in and sample it, and with a grimace, they would carry the offending liquid away without a word. Shooing me to my room, they would return the empty glass to my place at the table so that when he checked again, he would see it had been drunk.

Finally, when I turned 14, he decided I was no longer required to drink milk. Once I had permission, I never drank it again.

Both Carolyn and I managed somehow to cope with our father as best we could — she, as the baby and I, as the favored eldest. But for mysterious reasons, when Debbie was about seven or eight, she had a terrible time coping with our father's harsh persona. During that period, if Dad so much as looked sideways at Debbie during dinner, she would either lose control of her bladder or gag, and throw up into her plate. My father had a horror of bodily functions, and his reaction was unbridled revulsion and irritation. The maid would be called and rushed to remove the plate and mop up the table or the seat, while Greg took Debbie upstairs. Once all was clean again and Greg had settled Debbie upstairs with some toast and ginger ale, the rest of us would return to the table. My parents never treated Debbie's actions with anything resembling sympathy or concern for her welfare. It was her problem, not theirs.

"Disgusting," my father would say with a grimace.

"Yes," said my mother in agreement.

And that was the end of it for the time being. Everyone knew that Debbie wasn't technically sick, and the dinner would resume without any more mention of what had happened.

How is it even possible that a child could be so afraid of a parent that she would vomit into her plate? What would push a little girl to such an extreme? None of us had burns or broken bones to show for our abuse; it was sheer fear that ruled us. And rule us it did. I know full well that to some, Debbie's responses might sound like a fabrication. Understandably, it would be hard for most people to imagine this level of fear if they hadn't experienced it firsthand. But I was there. We all were.

Living in the shadow of my father's rages was simply a fact of life for us. He had a hair-trigger temper and it was legendary. Even grownups tiptoed around him, knowing to stay on his good side, as there was hell to pay on the other. He was masterful in his ability to cut anyone down to size with only a few choice words and the vitriol he brought to the fight. I can remember distinctly the anger Dad directed toward his stockbroker or anyone at the office who crossed him. His voice would boom throughout the house as he screamed into the phone, calling them on the carpet for one mistake or another and cutting them into ribbons with his invectives.

"Christ, what is going on over there? What? What do you mean? I gave you clear instructions, damn it! Oh, you did, did you? It doesn't look like that to me! Put John on the phone. I want to speak to him. The hell I will! If you can't do your damned job properly, John and I will find someone else who *likes their job better* and has *the talent to do it!*"

His standards were high. He expected as much from himself as he did from others. With his colleagues, at least, he confined himself to general social norms. With us, it was different. He didn't direct his fury at us often, but those times were memorable. Louise always said that my father only had to raise his hand to you once, and you never forgot it, and this was true.

Our mother's temper was also fiery, but it was by degrees less frightening than his. She was not a petite woman, and her large hands were painful when they made contact. Her ridicule was deeply hurtful in its own way, but our father's anger seemed to well up from something primordial and boundless like the ocean. When it swelled, it was a fearsome thing like nothing else. At those times, we knew that it would be best to run and hide, and pray to God he didn't find us before the explosion came. It didn't happen often, but my mother and the others would step out of the way when he was like that. No one could stop him. No one dared try.

He had only spanked me once before when I was about four, but I remembered it well. Otherwise, it would be his verbal expressions of anger alone that were frightening enough. I always did everything I could to avoid a spanking, but I don't know what I was thinking on that day. I likely wasn't thinking much at all. I was about 12, and I was walking across the living room dressed in a pair of jeans and a midi top, the latest fashion, which was tied in a knot just under my chest. The short top and my hip-hugger pants left my belly bare, and he didn't like it. As he passed me, he commented with a frown,

"Take that off, and cover yourself. You aren't coming to the dinner table wearing that!"

I don't know what possessed me that day, but I suppose the budding teenager inside me was emerging. I replied under my breath,

"Oh, shut up."

I had never done such a thing before. It was the first time, and it would certainly be the last. I didn't think he could hear it anyway, but to my surprise, he had. From behind me, came his voice, strong but controlled,

"What. Did. You. Say?"

I knew before I turned that I had made a terrible mistake, but it was too late. Looking back, I saw him standing stock still with his arms at his sides, his fists clenched. His entire frame was trembling as he attempted to contain himself, but his eyes were wild, and the veins on his neck and forehead bulged with the pressure building up inside. The rising fury was physically palpable even with the distance between us. It was only a split second before he bounded toward me, raising one fist and swatting me hard across the face. The blow landed on my cheekbone and knocked me off my feet. I lay on the carpet, seeing stars as he loomed above.

"Get up!" he said, breathing hard, his voice quavering.

I got up. I could barely steady myself on my feet before another blow came. Again I fell to the floor.

"Get up!" he said.

He looked dangerous. I had a vague awareness at the time that my mother had come into the room, but she stayed at a safe distance from where we were.

"Not in her face, Joe! Not in her face!" she called to him, apparently unable to intervene directly.

When I managed to stand again, I was back on the floor in an instant. I can't honestly say how many times he struck me, but I do recall wondering when he would stop, as it got harder and harder to right myself.

Eventually, I couldn't get up again and he stalked off, leaving me alone. Everyone was gone. No one came to check on me or help me get up. I don't know how long I lay there, but I remember being in pain, exhausted, too afraid to move.

At some point, he stalked back out of his bedroom and
scooped me up in his arms, carrying me to a big chair in the living room. There, holding me in his lap, he rocked me back and
forth with his face bent to my shoulder, repeating, "I'm sorry,
Helen, I'm sorry," over and over again.

It was the first and only time my father ever apologized to
me. It was also the first time I had been given a peek at my
father's softer side, ironically, at the very moment in which I
had experienced his most brutal. It was a moment that changed
my impression of him forever. Up until then, he'd never held
me, never spoken to me tenderly, much less asked for my forgiveness. In all my young life I'd had no understanding of who
it was behind the iron facade, a person with a conscience and
tenderness I'd never experienced before.

Now I had seen the whole man, and however oddly, it
served to soften my view of him. My father was human, after all.
Still, this new perspective was not enough to make me abandon
my sense of caution; how could it? To fear him was only sensible.
Now, the new and more comforting perspective took up residence in my mind alongside the fear. None of us could defy
either of our parents without disastrous results, and as a matter
of survival, we almost never did.

Chapter 14
In the Balance

It wasn't all bad. My father was brilliant and unlike anyone I have ever known. The mixture of emotions we felt for him — fear, affection, and the desire for his approval — battled with each other in our hearts, with no one attribute winning out over the other. While he commanded our absolute respect, he could also be silly, even hilarious at times, with a hearty laugh and a deep appreciation for the absurd. Despite the ambient intimidation we all felt, he had undeniably endearing qualities, thereby creating a mixture of clashing emotions. Simply put, our father managed to make a place in our hearts despite his worst qualities. When he was feeling good, we were, too.

One of the things which served as a balance to his authoritarian personality was his love of parlor tricks. He could easily write in script with either his left hand or his right. He was genuinely ambidextrous in everything he did. This skill alone would have been amusing enough, but he could do it almost as quickly when he wrote upside-down and backward simultaneously. Even though the ability was fairly useless, I have never seen it demonstrated before or since. More interesting than this was his memory. Once, he handed me a book he had just read and told me to select any page from it I liked, so I flipped through the pages and chose page 153 at random. To my utter shock and delight, he was able to tell me what was on that page, not verbatim, but in great detail. It was hard to believe, and he repeated the feat many times before I had to concede that his ability was real.

Daddy was the one who taught me to wiggle my ears together or separately. Even better, he taught me how to cross one eye at a time. He demonstrated it with great patience until I could do it myself, turning one eye inward toward my nose while the other remained looking straight ahead. These were quirky and wonderful little tricks, which I enjoyed doing for others, proud to have inherited those peculiar abilities from him. But there were also tricks I never could master. He had fantastic muscle control and could make his eyes move in rapid and tight circles, an effect that was creepy and funny both at the same time. He could also shift his whole scalp back and forth like a loose toupee. As hard as I tried, I failed, but my efforts to do it always made us laugh.

Starting when I was around eight years old, in the evenings we were allowed in, one at a time, to visit with our parents for 15 minutes before bedtime. When we entered their suite, we would find them propped up in bed in their nightclothes watching TV. If Daddy was in a good mood, we could ask to see the toys he kept in his nightstand. Smiling, he would open the drawer for us to see what lay inside, and then ceremoniously, he would bring out each toy and wind it up. He would laugh with childish delight at the little tin band he created while the little tin frogs jumped willy-nilly around his table. I can still hear the metallic sound of the gears as the frogs wound down and the peculiar *ching ching* of the monkey's cymbals. It was clear he liked the monkeys best, but they were all favorites to us.

"Ah-ah-ah — nooo touching! These are *my* toys!" he'd say, in a sing-songy tone, smiling and wagging his finger if one of us reached for one.

The more we pleaded to touch one, the more he laughed and said no, relenting only rarely and with close supervision, lest we overwind them or otherwise do them damage. They were his treasures, and we had to treat them with great respect.

My mother once explained this peculiarity privately, telling us that when he'd been a child, he'd had no such toys and that this is what made him so possessive of them. No doubt he enjoyed watching us as we tried to navigate his strict instructions, and I imagine too, it was the unbridled longing he saw on our faces that amused him so.

But this behavior was not only confined to children's playthings. He also cached cookies and candy for himself and was just as possessive of them as his toys. His two favorite candies were black licorice and French jellies, which he brought back from Schrafft's in New York. We didn't care much for the licorice, but we loved the jellies. They were oversized pastel-colored blocks covered in powdered sugar, which came nestled in pleated paper cups inside a flat box emblazoned with the Schrafft name. He kept the box, when he had one, in the top drawer of his dresser. They came in lovely fruit flavors, about two bites in size, and they were softer than any ordinary gumdrop. On special occasions, he would dole them out to us, one per customer, when we were in his room for a bedtime visit.

The cookies he held aside were the ones made by Mrs. Hewitt, our neighbor. She would make spice cookies for all of us around the holidays, which were crispy and incredibly delicious. She had to make a tin for the general household and one specifically for my father. It was inevitable that we would polish off our whole tin way before he did, and eventually, we would have to come begging for one of his. With this in mind, he always hid his cookies in a secret location in his closet. When we asked him if he would share some of his, he would question us as to where ours had gone. Then he would make us wait outside his closet door lest we see where he had hidden the tin.

"Stay right here," he would say, exaggerating his tiptoe on the way into his closet to find them and emerging with one cookie for each that asked for one.

"Eat it slowly! Make it laaaaast!" He would admonish us with a mischievous grin.

He knew how peculiar and miserly this behavior was and seemed to be tickled by it himself, along with our whining pleas as part of his little comedy. We found it funny too. We were willing participants. We surely wanted a cookie, but it was also good to have a way to make him smile. When I think about it, I imagine he might have used all of these things as a way to bring us to him, as he was not entirely comfortable with children. I wonder now if he was aware that through his toys and treats, he had found a gentler way to interact with us outside of his typical harshness and punitive behavior.

Once, during dinner, when the basket of hot dinner rolls arrived, I remember how he pulled back the cloth which covered them and selected one. He discreetly whispered to me to watch this while silently and ceremoniously, he examined it from every angle in a pantomime. When satisfied, he gave me another conspiratorial look before leaning over the side of his chair to drop the roll on the carpet below to see how it bounced. No one else was watching. This bit of comic theater to test the bread's springiness was a joke meant for me, as his manners were nearly flawless. If I had tried the same, the result would have been entirely different. I would have been sent from the table without dinner. But this was his table, and they were his rules to be followed or broken, and the sheer hilarity of such behavior was our little secret. He was misbehaving for my approval, and it made us both giggle. Once the roll had bounced well and passed inspection, he retrieved it discreetly, with a wink, and proceeded to properly butter and eat it one small piece at a time, as if nothing out of the ordinary had just happened. I recall he did this more than once in the years I knew him, but it was by no means his usual behavior.

Thus, the dichotomy between the frightening father and the one who was lovable and funny was squarely seated. It is what it was to know him. He never fully pulled away the curtain that separated us, not, at least, until he was nearly gone. His ministrations were transactional. We visited with him at appointed times. If he felt good, we could see the toys, but he alone could touch them. We had to ask for a treat, and we would get one, but only if we met his requirements.

He never did say, "I love you," but these moments with him were enough to keep us from concluding that he didn't care. We were his children, and he, the ruling adult. These small gestures were tantalizing hints now and then which telegraphed his interest in us and served in part to soothe the wounds which were broad and difficult to bind. It is common knowledge that men of his generation were less interactive with their children, and he was, in some general sense, on the far end of that spectrum. We lived for those moments of kindness and connection because they were as close to the feeling that he loved us as we could get, and they sufficed. They had to.

Aside from these times, most of what we knew of him we heard from others. We knew he had a solid moral compass for the outside world. He made significant contributions to many different charities and causes for which he seemed to feel a true passion. He regularly donated to the efforts in Israel and Boys Town in Italy. He gave away full college scholarships to a good number of the children of friends, family, and colleagues. He was also politically active and contributed to many election campaigns, standing up for his own beliefs and supporting those who championed them.

Knowing these things made us feel we were growing up in the house of a man who deep down, had a good heart, but he was hampered by the amount of time he had for us and the limits of his personality. The fear he had instilled kept us in the periphery, reluctant to step forward except when invited. Our father was practically all we knew of men, with no others in the house, not even brothers. We longed for his affection, and this fact made us sharp observers. We all loved to see him happy.

To this end, I often drew pictures for him, but I learned quite early that to present my father with artwork would only elicit a need to educate me further. He would say,

"That's very nice, but look here...."

And taking a pencil from his desk, he would draw directly on top of my lines to show me how they could be improved by direct comparison. I recall being proud of a particular rendition I had done of a horse. The moment I presented it to him, out came the pencil.

"Very good, but your horse's head is far too large for its body. If you reduced it here and here... Do you see what I mean? You need to extend the line from the head to the body this way... There! You see? That is how you do it!"

I was disappointed. I had only wanted to present my father with my best effort, my prize horse. As he drew on top of my drawing, every stroke of his pencil made me cringe. I had worked so hard, and he was busy destroying what I had done. I felt so proud of that horse. It's not that I thought he was trying to be hurtful. Instinctively, I knew he only wanted to help. He was an excellent draftsman — but I was young then, and all I wanted was for him to love the pictures as the gifts they were. These moments weren't working out the way I had hoped. Eventually, I kept my pictures to myself, preferring to enjoy them privately, where they were safe from his pencil.

Although the magic of my artistic abilities may have fallen short somehow, there was one thing that always brought a smile to his face. Cigars. They were his weakness. After a bout with throat cancer at 49, he'd given up cigarettes and replaced them with cigars for the remainder of his life. Back then, the belief was that cigars were harmless, and Cubans were his favorite. He had managed somehow to have the illegal items shipped to him regularly. When a box would arrive, his excitement was almost childlike.

Telegraphing his pleasure, he would place himself at ease in a chair with the unopened package in his lap. Putting one foot up, then dramatically crossing it with the other, he would make a show of getting comfortable before he would slowly un-wrap the package. Then, breaking the twine which tied the box and slowly tearing off the plain brown paper wrapper, he han-dled the box as if it contained something extremely rare and fragile, savoring the cigars within, long before a match was struck. He would break the seal and open the top, skimming his nose over the fragrant array, breathing deeply to take in their aroma. Then with evident satisfaction, he would smile devilishly and select one from the box. Carefully nipping off a bit of the pointed end with his teeth and spitting it out, he would light the blunt end and take his first draw, gently blowing a stream of thick and acrid smoke into the air before him. It was forbidden fruit, and his pleasure was so evident, it was nearly contagious.

"Now that's a cigar!" he would exclaim, grinning like a pirate at all of us, showing off his cleverness at having procured such booty.

At times like that, the comedy was intentional. He knew how funny it was. My father's favorite comedians were Sid Caesar, the Marx brothers, and Spike Jones. He had many Jones records, and he watched Caesar's Show of Shows whenever he could, but Groucho Marx was his very favorite. On rare occasions, he would, for our benefit, walk the floor in a crouching stride, hold-ing his cigar aloft as Groucho did, all the while wiggling his own prominent eyebrows. I remember well how he would produce a perfect toothy Groucho grin, announcing, "That's the most ridiculous thing I evah hoid!" My father and Groucho sounded strangely similar, which wasn't surprising, as Groucho was of his generation, and they grew up in the same area of New York. Whenever I see a Marx brothers movie now, I hear that flavor of my father's accent in Groucho's, and I remember his impersonation fondly.

Chapter 15
The Centerline

Who can say how it happened? Siblings aren't born with some genetic guarantee that they will become best friends, or even get along. There are the lucky ones who start out close and stay that way, sailing smoothly into adulthood. There are others who never quite find a way to gain the connection that the word family suggests.

The ones who have lifelong closeness and harmony are lucky indeed. Even as a child, I longed for it myself. While it was clear my parents adored each other, there wasn't a strong connection among the rest of us. Our relationships as sisters were tested and damaged time after time, with the lion's share of strain occurring between Debbie and myself.

She and I shared a room from when I was four or five. It wasn't long before Debbie drew an imaginary line down the center of the room that I wasn't allowed to cross. From around the age of five onward, she needed to be the boss, and this was just one of the ways she did it. It was always easier to go along with her plan than to fight with her. I was her big sister, and I was generally more tolerant.

In our room, Debbie was in command as overseer and ruler of the centerline and all the goings-on in our bedroom. The toys on the shelves along with the ones in the closet were on her side; the bathroom was on mine. Whenever I wanted a toy, I would have to wait until she needed to use the bathroom. I had nothing to do on my side but sit on my twin bed and wait, playing with whatever was already there. Eventually, she would need to use the bathroom, but she made a point of delaying as long as she could, tickled by the idea that I had to wait for what I wanted.

"Don't you need to use the bathroom yet?" I'd wheedle, clearly pained by the desire to get another toy.

"Nope," she'd say, smiling. Her eyes alight with pleasure. It was easy to see how she relished this proof of her power.

We both knew she had no interest in my baby dolls or the tea set on her side of the room. I had to wait to gain access to them, as these were *the rules*. All I could do was comply. There was humor in the situation, which we both recognized, along with a flavor of one-upmanship which, for some reason, I accepted. As it was, Debbie preferred the stuffed animals, Disney figures, and blocks. The bother was that she savored being the warden of my toys, whether she wanted to play with them or not. Occasionally I looked to Greg for intervention when I felt Debbie was taking her self-appointed powers too far, but that didn't happen often. Usually, I could find a way to bargain with her.

When we played games outside, Debbie was the commissioner, captain, and umpire. Whether it was hide and seek or Marco Polo, we could protest, but we always ended up playing by Debbie's rules. Often, they were stacked in her favor, but she shrugged off our complaints. If we wanted to play with her, we had to do it her way. As we grew, this mode of interaction never changed.

Once, when she didn't get what she wanted, I learned how

vindictive she could be. After a typical sibling scuffle where she felt I had gotten the upper hand, she went off and pinched herself until it left marks. Afterward, she ran to Mom, saying I had inflicted the damage. While I got the inevitable spanking, Debbie crouched within eyesight and giggled quietly under her hand. My mother never heard her. The marks were all the proof my mother needed anyway, and I was beside myself with regret for Debbie's cruel cleverness. I even scolded her afterward, but she brushed me off. She felt I deserved it. There was no reasoning with her. Exhausted, I gave up trying.

But these weren't her only qualities. She could also be brave and fiercely protective of all of us. From the very beginning, if she perceived a threat from any of our peers, she always stood up for what she thought was right. She seemed to think of herself as a champion for the downtrodden.

One day, Debbie and I were in front of the house when a neighbor boy came over to us. I was probably eight, and she was about six, the same age as the boy approaching. Frankie had flaming red hair and a face so full of freckles that there seemed to be no breaks in the pattern. He was closer to my height than Debbie's, and he had on a baseball jacket covered in patches and logos which gave him a kind of tough guy aura. With a swagger, Frankie stepped close to me and spoke.

"Do you know what I'm going to do with you? I'm going to tie you up, stick you in our motorboat, drive you out to the middle of the waterway and throw you in!"

His eyes were on fire to match his hair. I was terrified and on the verge of tears. Debbie who was much smaller, answered back,

"Oh, no, you won't!" and punched him squarely in the stomach, turning on her heel as the boy crumpled to the pavement. I followed along behind, her wimpy big sister, grateful and proud of her extreme fearlessness in the face of such an obvious threat.

Combat was her happy place, and Debbie was never so happy as when she was competing. She loved card games of all kinds and Mousetrap, Monopoly, and Yahtzee, which never failed to raise her spirits. She loved to stir the pot, claiming that one of us was doing something wrong, often just to see how it would all play out.

"You're *cheating!*" she'd exclaim with the self-righteousness of an avenging angel.

"No, I'm not!" I'd protest, genuinely hurt by even the hint that I would stoop so low. There was nothing to be done but to let her play out this little scenario and suffer through it. It was all part of the fun for her and after all, I was her willing opponent.

"Yes! Did you see that, Carolyn?! She's *cheeee-ting.*"

She would say it gleefully, repeating the word insistently while she placed her sneer as close to my face as she could. It was her favorite position, especially if she was losing a game. Debbie hated to lose. Carolyn and I both knew that a game with her might require such mock humiliations. But as insistent as she could be, Debbie knew we didn't cheat. We just knew when our fortunes began to rise, we had to prepare for the onslaught.

When Debbie was at her best, she was funny. She had a wicked sense of humor and a mischievousness that made us all laugh. As a pre-teen, Mad Libs was a great favorite, and she never failed to think up the best and most appropriately offensive words when asked for a noun or verb. Her laugh was loud and unreserved, fueled by her boldness and equally bad behavior. These were times I relished with her, because she could be as outrageous as she liked, and the only result was a hearty laugh between us.

Along with Debbie's fondness for competition and noisy mock battles, Debbie was also territorial in the extreme, and at those times, fairness went out the window. Forget altruism. It was Debbie who demanded outrageously extravagant gifts at Christmas from our parents, and she would get them. While Carolyn and I would hesitate to say what we wanted from Santa, Debbie was outspoken. She was boldly precise about what she would and would not accept. It was her way.

One year, when she was about 10, she asked for a Sunfish, a small sailboat, to use on the Intercoastal Waterway. Carolyn and I both shook our heads at the gutsy request, knowing that there would be no way in the world she would get it. Our parents were children of the Depression, and signs of avarice or selfishness were roundly rebuked. They had scolded both Carolyn and me for lesser requests. Asking for something expensive was considered bad behavior, but Debbie didn't seem to care. She argued bitterly with my mother about being too young, but Debbie never backed down. When Christmas finally arrived, and the boat appeared, Carolyn and I stood agape and rethinking our own Christmas strategies. We were shocked! Santa had delivered the impossible.

In the months that followed, Debbie managed to take the Sunfish out onto the lake only once or twice. Then it sat unused

at the side of the house, a symbol of her sky-is-the-limit auda-
ciousness. We repeatedly asked her if we might take it for a
quick trip, maybe just out and back again. After all, she wasn't
using it — but she was emphatic.

"No way! Why should I let either of you use it? You'll only
break something, and even if you don't, you'll get your cooties
all over it. Next Christmas, you should ask for your own boat.
This one's *mine!*"

We were raised to be generous and share what we had, but
Debbie never allowed either of us to use it. We were surprised
too, when our parents never countermanded her or scolded her
for her selfishness. It is hard to understand their reasoning on
this point, but the fact is, they didn't intercede. It may have
been the same reason we sisters let her get away with things.
They probably didn't have the energy to cross her. Debbie was
so difficult, and when she dug in, she was relentless. My father's
health wasn't good, and my mother needed to focus on him.

In any case, Carolyn and I gave up on asking, and the Sunfish sat in the side yard for several years. When the tropical sun
had done its work, the boat went to the trash heap. It was telling
that Debbie preferred to have her boat junked than share it. It
was all about her peculiar kind of selfishness, which she viewed
as correct and only fair. We had our stuff, and she had hers.

Animals were Debbie's one true passion in the world, and
this principle also applied to them. The family dog Pitapat, the
parakeet, gerbils, and fish belonged to all of us. This wasn't
enough for Debbie. By her teen years, she figured out a way to
have her own personal pet. Debbie had discovered a cat living in

our neighborhood who seemed to have no owner. She was a lanky, underfed creature with long and dirty fur in stripes of white, gray and brown. Every day for months, Debbie lured the cat in with treats and bowls of food until it finally let her pet and even brush its long coat. Debbie named her Toto, and eventually, with more food and incredible patience, Debbie was able to pick Toto up and bring her indoors.

No one else could befriend Toto. True to form, Debbie would not allow us near her, and the skittish kitty remained hers and hers alone. Most of the time, Toto lived outside, doing what she liked and going where she wished. When Debbie was home, all she needed to do was to go to the back door and call to her, and she would magically appear out of the greenery, ready to greet and spend time with her friend. By then, Toto's general appearance had improved remarkably. She allowed Debbie to groom and fuss over her in every way. Toto took to delivering mice in a neat line outside our back door for Debbie, a tribute to their closeness. At dinnertime, she would take Toto back outside, where she preferred to be.

It was around then that Debbie confessed to me that she liked animals better than humans. It was easy to understand why. Debbie pushed people away when their needs conflicted with her own. It was simpler for her to bond with animals. Toto would never talk back, hurt her feelings, or disappoint her. And as Toto's owner, Debbie could also rightly claim every minute of her attention when they were together. The cat would be the first for Debbie in a lifetime filled with creatures of all kinds. They would fill a gap for her that people never could.

Just a few years earlier, around the time she got the boat, my parents had taken Debbie aside for a chat. It was a chat she never forgot. Indeed, it was an event that changed Debbie's life for all the years to follow. She mentioned it often, well into adulthood, as the moment when our parents broke her heart. Even Carolyn acknowledged it was a seminal point in Debbie's attitude and outlook.

Carolyn described it to me from her perspective. As she told it, she and Debbie were playing, and Debbie suddenly got very excited about something and wanted to tell Mom or Dad. Debbie took Carolyn with her. As it turned out, Mom was out at the store, but our father was at home. As they approached, they could see him entertaining a group of guests in the living room. Hesitating, Carolyn said to Debbie,

"Are you sure you wanna do this? He has company, and I don't think we should."

Carolyn stepped backward, indicating that she wouldn't follow, but Debbie strode into the room anyway.

"Daddy! Daddy," she exclaimed excitedly.

"Not now, Debbie. I have company!" he said, annoyed.

"But Daddy..."

"Enough!" he growled. "Go to your room!"

"But..."

"GO!" he yelled in full-throated anger. "You have no business interrupting me!"

Debbie, deflated and head down, left the room in tears. Later that day, my father called Debbie in for a chat. Mom was there too, in a show of solidarity.

My father said, "Debbie, we want you to know that you have been demanding too much attention for some time now... You are not the only person in this house."

The message was clear.

He went on, "We want you to understand that you and your individual needs are just not that important in the grander scheme of things." Mom sat at his side in silent agreement.

"We will not indulge this kind of behavior. We have done enough of that. There are other people in this house, and you need to fall in line or suffer the consequences."

Debbie took this speech as proof of our parents' utter disregard for her. She felt the world was full of people who didn't love her or feel she was important. Had the very same message been delivered to Carolyn or me, we probably would have taken it well enough and felt chastened. We would have thought they had reasons to say so and resolved to be more mindful. For Debbie, it was a battle cry for her and only her. She took the message into her heart, where it festered and turned her against them for the many years to come. She would refer to it later on as the moment when everything changed for her.

Once wounded, Debbie could never find a way to recover, no less forgive. This was always true for her. She took even minor difficulties to heart. The idea that she could expect to come up short informed her every thought and action. The problem wasn't only the family dynamic, even if it may have contributed. Debbie seemed to lack the ability to find simple happiness. The good things that happened were somehow less good than she'd hoped. Meanwhile, she protected herself with a bravado that bordered on aggression, in an effort to camouflage an exquisitely sensitive and vulnerable underbelly. It was this overcorrection that created nearly every one of the miseries she ever suffered.

I was only two years older than my sister Debbie, and I didn't have the words back then to describe what the problem was, but I knew there was something wrong. I knew it the way you know the sky is blue. You just know.

Chapter 16
The Help

Over the years, staff members would come and go. With the turnover, each arrival was a new and different experience. Sometimes it meant only a small adjustment for us. Other times, the personalities were as outsized as our own, with results to match.

Whether there was company or not, we ate our dinners in formal style. Occasionally, however, some welcome levity broke our vaguely oppressive sense of proper etiquette. We had a cook named Jessie, whose claim to fame was that she liked to entertain during dinner. No one ever asked her to do this. It was something that sprang from her natural and exuberant personality and what looked like a true fondness for my father. She had been with him for some years before his new marriage, and who knows what she'd seen back then. Perhaps the whole tradition sprang from a moment in which she had sought to cheer him when things had been difficult.

Whatever the reason, both uninvited and unannounced, Jessie would emerge from the kitchen occasionally to serenade us with her harmonica. She would play one or two upbeat tunes, accompanying herself with a comical rhythmic stamping of her feet, which she did with much gusto. It was quite a show. She was not a gifted player, but she made up for it with sheer enthusiasm. My father saw these moments as entirely entertaining and funny, and the faces across the room lit up when she did it, all of us applauding and calling out "Bravo!" loudly at the end. In later years, after some time away, she briefly returned and resumed the tradition. I remember feeling slightly embarrassed not only for her but for us as a group. It seemed we were taking part in something that felt strangely wrong, even as it appeared she was enjoying herself. I wonder now what motivated her. Surely she must have understood what a strange and awkward scene it was: The privileged family sitting at a formal dinner table, while she, our cook, stomped and played her bluesy riffs, as she danced around us.

The whole thing left me feeling uncomfortable even though her performances came as a welcome break from what had always been a stressful time for us kids at dinner. We loved Jessie for her exuberant kookiness, and her penchant for comic relief, as we enjoyed so many of those who came and went from our household.

There were others with strong personas. We had a series of boat captains, mostly single men, who lived aboard our boat, the Feliz Ano, docked about 200 yards from the house at the lake trail. The captains always lived on board while they worked for us. At some point, my father hired a captain who arrived with his wife. They had been with us a year or two before one night, the captain and his wife got into a heated argument in their private cabin.

The captain was a rough-looking older man with a white and unkempt beard that made him look like a haggard Ernest Hemingway. His soft-spoken and reclusive wife was in her 40s with a lanky build, an extraordinarily plain face, and a crown of overly tight and colorless curls. We never really got to know her, because she stayed on the boat most of the time and kept to herself.

On the other hand, we knew the captain pretty well. He came up to the house regularly. There was always a maintenance issue to discuss with my father or to make plans with him for their next excursion. It was also the captain's job to chauffeur us to school every morning. We knew he didn't much like children. He barely spoke to us, preferring to drive in silence as we sat happily chattering to each other in the back seat of the car.

Before the incident, it seemed the captain might have a drinking problem, but maybe my parents weren't sure and chose not to notice the telltale signs. They probably felt it wasn't their business anyway, as long as he was sober when he was on the clock. Allowances were made. Finding a knowledgeable captain for the boat was not an easy task.

The night it happened, no one heard the argument, as it all took place on the boat, some distance from the house. Apparently, it was a terrible and drunken quarrel. It dragged on into the wee hours and reached its climax when suddenly, in fear for her life, the wife threw herself overboard wearing not a stitch of clothing. Unwilling to return, she proceeded to swim across the Intercoastal Waterway in the darkness. She made it to the other side, which was a feat in itself, as the mainland was at least half a mile away. The nighttime swim had been a clear act of desperation, as the ocean fed the waterway on both ends, and sometimes sharks were spotted in that area.

At some point during the night, my parents got a call from the West Palm Police Department to pick her up from the station.

The captain was fired that night. Immediately, my father set about searching for a replacement, and from that time forward, we kids were sent to school by carpool.

Conflicts between the house live-ins were generally minor, but one other fight in particular stands out in my memory, mainly because it took place during the day for all to see. The fracas was between Inez, our cook, who was a homely and cantankerous older woman, and Virginia, our maid at the time, who was as young, sweet, and as pretty as Inez was generally unpleasant.

Whatever the offense, in a sudden fury, Inez proceeded to chase young Virginia all over the house with a butcher knife. Up and down the spiral staircase they went, with Inez wielding the huge knife above her head, bellowing as she went. She chased a screaming Virginia through the living room and Florida room and back again through the dining room and kitchen. At that point, someone was able to intervene, getting Inez to surrender the knife and pack her things.

We children speculated that it must have been a fit of jealousy that sent her over the edge, but none of us kids ever knew for sure. All we knew was that Inez seemed angry all the time anyway, with never a smile for us kids. We wouldn't miss her, and we were relieved that Virginia was still with us, happy, and unhurt.

Not long after Inez left, Sonja, a Finnish woman arrived, bringing along her daughter, Jennie. While Sonja cooked for us, Jennie, who was all of five years old at the time, took a mysterious liking to our father. After dinners, she would sidle past the kitchen door and into the living room to clamber into my father's lap for a snuggle. What surprised everyone was that she did it so boldly and uninvited. She used every wile she possessed in her childish arsenal to charm him, pronouncing the word "Daaaaa-ddy," when she saw him in the most seductive baby talk we had ever heard.

The move was so daring, it was charming in its way, especially for my father — and of course he allowed it. Debbie and I looked on, amazed. After all, neither one of us had ever presumed to behave that way ourselves, but it was Carolyn who took real offense. That was Carolyn's special thing with him, and as the baby of the family, she made sure to let Jennie know she disapproved.

"He's my Daddy, not yours!" she scolded.

After all, Carolyn was Jennie's age and felt the threat of displacement keenly. In response to Carolyn's quiet objections, Jennie simply smiled back at her knowingly, all the while wordlessly telegraphing her defiance and returning each night to do the same thing all over again. Carolyn's resentment was growing so obvious to the grownups by then that my mother had to take Carolyn aside to correct her. She told her that Jennie had no father and that she was selfish to be so unwilling to share a little. After that, and for as long as they lived with us, the post-dinner activities continued, accompanied by Jennie's knowing smiles and Carolyn's grudging silence.

Back in the kitchen, Sonja had the distinction of being the very worst cook we ever had. The exception was her Finnish cardamom bread that was not only delicious but beautiful to behold. It came out of the oven a perfectly braided oval with a glossy and heavily sugared crust, subtly sweet with a tender interior. We couldn't wait to pull off the warm sections of braid and dab them with bits of margarine, taking bite after greedy bite. The exotic cardamom fragrance filled the house whenever it was baking and sent us all to the kitchen door to ask when it might be done.

Unfortunately, the bread was a one-off in a repertoire of dishes that were often nondescript and oddly difficult to describe. To us, it was clear that she was making every effort to serve things with as much creativity as she could muster, having no idea of the basic principles of cooking. This resulted in over-seasoning some things and under-seasoning others. She also seemed to have no real sense of what flavors and ingredients went together.

We quickly learned that, although she had presented herself as a cook, she had only done so in a desperate scramble to find a job to support herself and her child. She probably had no previous experience at all. We would sit at the table expectantly, knowing that whatever arrived would be a surprise, but not the good kind. I imagine Sonja managed to stay on as long as she did because of Jennie. I'm sure she had gone to my parents with a hardship story and it's likely they felt some sympathy for her plight as a single mother.

Aside from her wonderful bread, Sonja's most famous dish was the dessert she called "floating island." None of us had heard such a thing before, although years later, to my surprise, I found a listing for the dessert in an old thrift shop cookbook. The first time she set it out before us at dinner, it was introduced with great fanfare as her specialty. It was still early in her tenure, and the extreme pride with which she announced its arrival led us to believe that what we were about to experience would be extraordinary, like her bread. And in a way, it was.

The individual desserts were served in our fanciest dessert bowls, with a small matching plate underneath it. At the bottom of each delicate bowl was a sea of what looked like beaten un-cooked egg yolk and what appeared to be egg whites placed in the center, like an island. It was a bit of artwork in a bowl, but as we learned, the best part of this dessert was its name.

As we began to eat, we learned that the soup of egg yolk was as plain as it looked, and the frothy egg white island was not much tastier than its humble uncooked beginnings. Perhaps more sugar and vanilla or maybe some lemon zest would have made it more palatable, but they were sorely lacking, and it left us with the queasy feeling that we were consuming raw eggs with nothing more to disguise them.

None of us, my parents included, had the nerve to tell her that the dessert which made her so proud was terrible in equal measure. We felt obligated to eat it, and we did our best, prais-ing her for it afterward as we did everything she made.

"Thank you, Sonja, that was delicious," we all said politely, only confirming to her that the floating island had been the spectacular success she had expected it to be.

As a result of that desire to be polite, every few weeks the dreaded dessert would reappear at the table. As soon as the hor-rible yellow and white confection was delivered, we were left alone to contemplate our bowls. We would glance at each other, the impossible comic tragedy of it all visible on every face. Dutifully, we attempted to eat it all up, stifling our giggles, all the while suffering from utter disgust and the necessity of keeping the sounds of our titters and moans from carrying into the kitchen during our attempts to swallow what we'd been given.

The dessert became a family legend. For years after Sonja and Jennie were long gone, whenever any food was deemed truly bad, the memory of Sonja's floating island would be invoked. Irrepressible laughter and knowing looks would always follow any reminder of that unforgettable dish.

And then there was Roseanne, an unforgettable character who had been our maid for many years. She was an older woman when she came to us and had worked far past the time she probably should have retired. Around 7 a.m., Roseanne had the table set for our breakfast in the Florida room and Greg would bring us children to the table where she would take our requests.

"I want some Rice Krispies," Debbie might say.

Roseanne would stare back at Debbie, waiting, without response, quiet and unmoved.

"May I *please* have some Rice Krispies?" was Greg's gentle correction.

"May I please have some Rice Krispies?" Debbie would repeat, parroting Greg.

With this, Roseanne would relax the scowl that had crept across her face and adjust her shoulders in a slight gesture of satisfaction.

"Of course," she would reply dryly, dipping her head to one side in courteous acknowledgment.

"Miss Helen?" Her eyes would land on me.

"May I have some scrambled eggs, please?"

Roseanne would nod again.

"And you, Mrs. Gregory?"

"Oh, I think I'll have my coffee with one of those Danish we got in yesterday, if you don't mind.

Touching her hand to Carolyn's highchair tray, she asked, "And would you please bring a little oatmeal with a splash of cream and sugar for this one?"

"Thank you," Roseanne would say to us all. Then with a solemn and slightly more formal nod, she would head back into the kitchen.

We had to behave for Roseanne. She had no patience with rudeness from us kids or irregularities of any kind. She carried herself in a prim and dignified manner but often muttered resentments to herself under her breath as she went. She never did it when my mother or father asked for something, but with us kids, and even Greg, she felt free to let her minor displeasures be known. If we asked for an afternoon snack, even one sanctioned by Greg, she would turn, and on her way to get it, she would mutter to herself just loud enough for us to hear.

"It makes no sense for children to be snacking now, so close to dinner! I've got no time for this, a woman is busy, busy, busy."

Roseanne's duties were wide-ranging, from making the beds and straightening up after us in the mornings to cleaning the whole house — vacuuming, mopping and dusting everything. When she had any extra time, she would make sure the many silver pieces were perfectly polished and bright. Still, she never refused us when we called. She simply had her opinions, and we knew what they were most of the time, if only in some general sense.

It's funny, though. We didn't mind. We had special feelings for her that were unaffected by any mild crankiness on her part. We had something important in common. She kept a place in her heart for our dog Pitapat, who had always been her special friend.

In her final years, Pitty required extra attention. It was sweet for us to see cranky old Roseanne fussing and preparing scrambled eggs and boiled chicken for Pitapat. She adored our dog and had taken it upon herself to do this without prompting from anyone. No, she wouldn't serve Pitty ordinary dog food — it simply wouldn't do! Pitapat no longer had her vision, her hearing, or even her teeth, and by then, Roseanne was nearly as elderly herself, while she fussed over our dear dog with complete devotion.

We would overhear Roseanne uttering endearments as she served her the fancy dinners she'd prepared. No matter how formal and mildly judgmental Roseanne might have been with us, we had a true sense of affection for her. When poor Pitapat finally died at the age of 20, Roseanne was beside herself with grief and didn't manage to stay on much longer, as her one source of great pleasure was gone. We were sorry to see her leave. Our maid Roseanne had been with us longer than anyone besides Greg, and it seemed to us that this was the end of an era. Perhaps it was.

Chapter 17
Kings Point

Only a year or two after the sale of our old house in Mamaroneck, my father decided to look for a summer home in New York. At the time, he was flying north for in-person meetings at the company. When he did, he stayed at the Carlyle Hotel, which was just around the corner from his office on East 77th Street.

We girls loved the fancy hotel soaps he brought back for us. The pale yellow bars in their cellophane wrappers with gold seals were so pretty, each with a crisp imprint of the hotel crest on them. The soaps had a delicious and delicate aroma unlike our usual bath soap, but these little souvenirs weren't reason enough to keep things as they were. It wasn't long before he found the house at 50 Pond Road on Long Island, in the suburb of Kings Point.

I was eight years old when we spent our first summer there. It was the place where my own troubles began, but that wouldn't be for a while. Despite everything, it was the home I would love most. Those summers on Long Island were special for our whole family. I remember our first trip there. The new house stood on the northwestern edge of Long Island, facing the city. At night, from our backyard, the Long Island Sound stretched all the way to the Throgs Neck and Whitestone bridges. The city beyond them sat lit up and twinkling like a distant festival, the prominent outlines of the Empire State and

Chrysler buildings towering above it all.

The broad stone house stood in the center of three acres at the dead end of Pond Road. It had a large circular drive shaded by old-growth trees and a grand entrance complete with steps up to a set of four pillars, very much like the former house in Mamaroneck. My father had even managed to move the old marble Canova lions there. The former house was a wooden Victorian, but this one had been built at the turn of the century with broad granite boulder walls and a barrel tile roof in the Arts and Crafts style. At the front of the driveway across from the entrance, the peonies — thousands, it seemed — served as a colorful and fragrant message of welcome.

Passing the familiar lions, we entered through the portico directly into the living room. At the far end was an enormous central staircase with a landing halfway up that split the stairway in two, with those stairs doubling back and up to the second floor. The master bedroom, guest rooms, and servants' quarters were all on the second floor.

Our rooms were below, on the first floor, just past the living room through a vestibule to the left of the staircase. Our space was quite private and kept us out of the way so that our childish enthusiasms and tribulations would not disturb or disrupt the lives of others in the house, but we loved it in there. Our room and Greg's were connected by a central bath we all shared. We had our own exterior door leading to the porch and down some steps to the pool.

We would swim there in the chill of early May or June, and I remember fondly how Greg would fill the bathtub for us when it was time to come back in. It would be late afternoon, and racing through the brisk air, we would bound up the side steps to where Greg stood at the door. Taking our damp towels, she would help us peel off our wet bathing suits to get into the bath she had prepared for us. By then we were all giggles and shivers and I remember our "ooohs" and "ahhhs" as we clambered into the blissfully warm water.

Our bedroom was quite large. It had a playroom area with a TV, a couch, and a couple of upholstered chairs. All of our toys were there too, along with a child-sized wooden table and chairs where we could draw or play records. A pair of twin beds were some distance away on the other side of the room. A night table between the two beds was topped by a small lamp with a pair of lambs cavorting. This was where Debbie and I slept. Initially, Carolyn slept in a crib in Greg's room. We spent many happy hours inside playing games, drawing, and playing music when the weather was bad.

Since Daddy was in the publishing business, he always made sure we had plenty of things to read. A large bookcase divided the room and was filled with countless storybooks and illustrated volumes. A 20-volume set devoted to dinosaurs and prehistoric life was a particular favorite of mine. When I wasn't reading, I liked to paint the round and weathered stones I picked up from our beach, putting them on display alongside the books and other natural treasures we'd collected.

In those rooms, we had everything any child might wish for. Greg's room was more grownup, of course, but it was comfortable, too, and she always made us feel welcome. While we

played, Greg would settle into one of the armchairs in the playroom to do her needlework. She always had a project going for
friends or family. When Carolyn got older, she joined Debbie in
that room and I moved into a bedroom upstairs. But for now,
this was our suite, and we used it well.

On Thursdays, when the cook was off, we had our dinners
there. Our parents ate elsewhere while we sat on our couch with
little folding tables in front of us and the TV on for entertainment. Greg would heat up the Swanson TV dinners and would
eat beside us while we watched "Soupy Sales," and "Diver Dan,"
shows they didn't have in Florida. Sometimes Greg would make
a special grape juice and ginger ale drink with slices of lemon
which was always a big favorite.

We adored those dinners. The compact meals in their little
foil trays with compartments for each separate item seemed so
fancy to us. We thought they were divine. Our favorite one was
the Swanson fried chicken dinner, with its small serving of vegetables, mashed potatoes, and even a tiny dessert. These meals
were completely exotic to us, and eating dinner so informally
was a real treat. We were out from under all the rules of comportment and our parents' noses, a welcome departure from the
usual. It was wonderful to have dinner where we could jabber at
each other and make silly noises. Being allowed to watch television at the same time made it even better.

Kings Point was a stark contrast to our place in Florida.
The spiky palm trees, harsh sun, and oppressive tropical heat of
that place had an atmosphere quite different from the gentle
summers in New York. I remember opening the front door in

Kings Point to the perfume of pink peonies aloft in the fresh air of early summer. I liked to cup them in my small hands and bury my face in the enormous blooms, soft and cool on my skin. Their fragrance was so sweet that there was always an ant or two on the yet-unopened buds searching for sugar they smelled. The heavy canopy of old trees everywhere gave a safe and cloistered feel to the place.

Some days, we were in the pool for hours and hours. We'd be in it so long that our fingers shriveled into little pink raisins and our lips turned a slightly purplish color, jaws aching from the chattering of our teeth. Nonetheless, like all children, we didn't care. When Greg noticed the telltale signs, she would call us out of the pool to warm up in the sun before she let us jump back in to begin the whole process all over again.

We played Marco Polo, swimming to locate each other with eyes closed or Greg would toss pennies into the pool for us to find and retrieve from the bottom. There would be silly jumping competitions off the diving board and comic attempts at water ballet. Sometimes Debbie, Carolyn, and I would duck under the water and sit on the bottom, speaking to each other as loudly as possible, the sounds seemingly emanating from the bubbles billowing from our mouths. We made a game of trying to understand what the other had said. We'd exchange messages and when we couldn't hold our breath any longer, we'd burst to the surface to verify the latest nonsense we'd heard underwater. Sometimes the neighbor kids would join in too, and sometimes we would go to their houses.

A couple of friendly families nearby included us in whatever they were doing when we turned up. All that was needed was a phone call to Greg, and we could stay even longer. There were no such informal families in Florida. There, everything was by appointment, and our schedule was much tighter. In Palm Beach there were so many after-school activities, and nobody ever just dropped by. In New York, things felt more relaxed. If we weren't in the pool or at a neighbor's house, we would explore Pond Road, where ring-necked pheasant roamed the leafy underbrush, rustling and cackling at us as we went along. The landscape was mild with no poisonous plants, animals or insects to worry about. We did spot some poison ivy down Pond Road, but we learned to avoid it.

Debbie and I were allowed to roam by ourselves without supervision along the long and quiet expanse and into the wilder areas where chipmunks would peep at us and the squirrels overhead chased each other endlessly in games of tag. All along the dappled roadside, tiny yellow snapdragons grew on slender green stalks, and there were buttercups, which we held under our chins to see the brilliant yellow of their petals reflected there.

Ranging far and wide, we examined everything we could find. We searched under trees collecting horse chestnuts and pulling off their spiny green covers to pocket the glossy brown nuts. We knew they were inedible, but they were so pretty. We walked the leaf litter, upturning stones to find creatures that would scuttle away or squirm in surprise at our curious attention.

Those summers, we spent the days with no awareness of time, like water spilling from an endless pitcher. Eventually, the sun dipped low and sent us back from the wilds, flushed and hungry, across the mown grass and past the pink blooms at our door. We'd hear clattering in the kitchen as we crossed the living room to go wash up and dress for dinner, feeling grateful for the free time we'd had.

Most days, after dinner, we would go outside again for an hour or so before the sun would go down to wander the vast rambling yard as we liked. Behind the house was a large round outcropping of rock that emerged from the pristine lawn. It was there we held many after-dinner games of King of the Mountain and tag, running across the lawn undisturbed until Greg would call us in for our bath.

Sometimes at twilight, the yard would be sparkling with fireflies dancing and twinkling in the still air, beckoning for us to try and catch them. One evening, before Greg came to get us, we had raced around, catching the tiny creatures in our hands and placing them in a jar to make a fun lantern for our bedroom. I remember we filled the jar with a large number, securing a piece of foil to the opening with a rubber band and poking tiny holes in the foil so that they could breathe. I placed the jar on our bedside table before we went to sleep. Later that night, I opened my eyes to see the fireflies flashing everywhere. We had accidentally made the holes in the foil a little too big, and they had escaped. Debbie and I sat up in our beds in wonderment as our room was transformed into an insect carnival, the whole room twinkling with tiny lights. Poor Greg awoke too, hearing our happy cries, but seeing the reason, she no doubt rued the fact that she had allowed us to bring the jar inside at all. The next morning was devoted to locating every single bug before my mother could arrive to see them loose in our room.

The house and its environs were a pleasure to all of us. On the near end of the pool to one side, my father planted his perennial flower beds. He would often return home from Manhattan in a happy rush to tend his lilies, iris, and roses, never managing to change out of his suit pants beforehand. My mother would stand at the side porch calling for him to stop.

"Joe! Joe! You're going to ruin those pants!" she'd call out to him with some urgency.

"All right, all right. I'll be right in," he'd call back, continuing to water and weed, obviously finding it hard to tear himself away.

On weekends, Aunt Ida (Aida) and Uncle Joe would often arrive for the day in their latest two-tone car, always clean and freshly waxed. Uncle Joe worked as a used car salesman, and he loved his cars. Aunt Ida would bring a particularly heavenly deli ham — always the same kind — along with kaiser rolls, swiss cheese, half-dill pickles, and a delicious potato salad from a favorite deli in their Yonkers neighborhood. Congregating at the one-room pool house, Mom and Ida would busy themselves happily chatting, putting together sandwiches, doling out potato salad and pulling sodas from the small fridge to arrange a feast on the tables outside.

Cousin Joan, their daughter, would come too if Louise was around. The teenagers would find the furthermost corner of the pool to spread towels and sunbathe, with their foil reflectors strategically placed to focus the sun onto their faces. They were too young to be much interested in the grownup chit-chat and too mature to want to turn themselves into bedraggled urchins with us kids. It was the big girls' corner, and we younger ones thought they were ever-so-glamorous. Later in the day, my father would join everyone when he finished whatever business he had attended to in his office downstairs. As the sun began to sink lower in the sky, they would all retire to the Florida room, while Greg toweled us kids off and got us changed and ready for dinner.

No doubt, my father enjoyed being in New York. It seemed to lift his spirits. He probably felt more vital there in his home state and directly managing his business on a day-to-day basis. Mom loved New York, too. She relished the days she could spend in the city. She was nearer to Aunt Ida too, and they could visit each other more often. In later years, Ida also moved to Florida, but for the time being, they could only spend time together in the summertime.

On those days, when everyone gathered and we kids splashed in the pool, everyone else would be arranged in the chairs and chaises nearby, talking and laughing over lunch as if this were the happiest family in the world. It would have been hard to guess that any child could be troubled in that place.

I was just 10 years old when my difficulties began. I moved to a pretty bedroom upstairs so Carolyn could leave Greg's room and share with Debbie. I loved my new room, but problems came suddenly, with mysterious physical symptoms that appeared out of nowhere and multiplied over time. This was when I began to suffer from a terrible and profound form of insomnia.

It was there in New York, after a visit to my father's psychiatrist friend, that I was put on a regimen of phenobarbital to help me sleep at night. It was the secret my parents, Greg, and I all shared but never discussed. Still, there was an undercurrent of concern as Greg and my parents were aware that something was going on. I knew they were worried that something was wrong with me, and I was too. Still, we carried on as usual, and my love for Kings Point seemed to mitigate at least some of it.

Everything there seemed so perfect. We were leading a life of plenty in beautiful surroundings. Therein resided the massive and largely invisible paradox. Certainly, to my parents, it didn't make any sense at all. They chalked it up to having an over-sensitive child, and I was sure they must be right. Greg may have known better, but she wasn't saying. I do know that when we left again for Florida every August, I felt a pang, but when we were in Kings Point, it was glorious.

And there was one more thing that made those summers as special as they were. When we were in New York, I got to visit Greg's family, times that were precious to me.

Chapter 18
111-22 75th Road

Everyone loved Marjorie. She would greet us at her door in Forest Hills, New York, with a broad smile followed by enthusiastic hugs and kisses.

"Mother! Welcome home! And Helen! How *nice* to have you come to visit us! Do come in!"

Marjorie was Greg's daughter. She had a personal warmth that put me at ease from the start. A slender and elegant woman about 10 years older than my mother, she had long brown hair pulled tightly back and pinned into an intricate braided bun. She had been a fashion model in her youth, and her high cheekbones and beautiful arching eyebrows remained a clue to her former profession even into her later years.

Vonn, her husband, was a compact and stocky man with a neat little mustache. He was gruff compared to Marjorie, but in his terse way, he managed to make me feel welcome, too. He was a brilliant art restorer, repairing tears and holes in antique paintings and then repainting the damage with incredible skill. Vonn never lacked for work. At mealtimes, he would magically appear upstairs from his basement studio, only to disappear again when the meal was done, going back downstairs to continue his painting. He spent most days there, tending to various projects.

It was easy to see that Vonn suffered from substantial hearing loss and, as I learned later, occasional fits of depression.

Although he wore hearing aids, it was obvious that he heard with difficulty and was less socially inclined as a result. His studio in the basement was not only his workshop but no doubt a respite for him.

Once, Vonn showed me a painting he had worked on, a 19th-century farm scene in which he had to fill in large areas in the exact style and colors to match the original. The painting was delicately rendered and pristine from edge to edge. When he showed me the back of the painting, I was able to see the broad patches of canvas that had been added during the restoration process. I was amazed. From the front, it was impossible to detect where he'd painted on the original.

Marjorie and Vonn had been together since they were young. They had three children, Ethan, Cassie, and Ellie, who were also kind hosts when I came to visit. They were quite a bit older than I was but always welcoming, including me in their conversations and activities.

Greg's other daughter Eleanor lived with them too, but she was more of a mystery. She had moved in with Vonn and Marjorie sometime after her own husband died. Eleanor never spoke of her old life but for a mention of her son Robert now and then. She was always cordial, but she let her sister take the lead. Marjorie owned a small antique shop off Austin Street in Queens, and Eleanor worked there with her. Every morning, they would leave Vonn to his studio and walk arm in arm to a local diner, where they would have breakfast before opening shop for the day. When I was older, they took me with them a few times. They would sit in the same booth each morning, and the waitress knew well enough how they would order.

"Coffee and Danish if you please, dear," Marjorie would say graciously, flashing her bright smile at the woman.

The waitress knew them well and didn't stay to ask Eleanor what she wanted. The waitress knew Eleanor would have the same thing. This weekday breakfast was their little extravagance, and they enjoyed it thoroughly. After the meal, it was a short walk from there to the shop.

The shop itself was tiny but tightly packed from floor to ceiling with beautiful antiques, mostly "smalls," the things which could be lifted and taken away without help from anyone else. Marjorie's shop carried a wide array of items. There were fine examples of porcelain by Minton, Sevres, and Limoges, among others, along with all kinds of sterling silver items mixed with curios and countless objects of art. There were figurines of all sizes, whale teeth carved by 19th-century sailors with scenes of nautical life, and carved ivories from China and Japan. Along with those, there were exquisite pieces of art glass and estate jewelry. The shop walls displayed oil paintings and framed autographs and letters of famous people from earlier centuries. It was like a little museum. There was so much to look at that a person could well spend hours on any one visit and still miss something. To a child like me, the shop was utterly fascinating. Others must have agreed, as it was always busy. Some visitors were regulars who knew Marjorie and Eleanor personally. It was not only a place to buy something unique, but a spot for friends to congregate and catch up on the news. The two women were gracious and welcoming to every visitor.

Back on 75th Road, their home was a modest but charming brick row house, with three floors filled with all of the lovely things they had collected over the years, things that they could never part with for the shop. Many of the walls at home were similar to the ones in the store on Austin Street, with the special autographs, and old paintings that Vonn and Marjorie loved and would never sell. Over the fireplace in the center of the living room was a beautiful pastel drawing of their daughter Ellie. The furniture there was elegant like at our house, but less showy, giving an old-fashioned and homier feel to the house.

The narrow first floor consisted of the cozy living room at the front, with stairs leading to the second floor at the center of the house. On the other side of the staircase was the dining room, leading to a galley kitchen. From there, one could either go downstairs into the basement or outside to the back of the house. Past the back door was a tiny fenced-in garden, just large enough for the roses that edged its inner perimeter. It had a large outdoor table with chairs where Greg and her daughters loved to sit.

On the left side of the fence was a gate that opened into an enormous open area with towering trees where kids from the neighborhood could play within sight of their parents, as it was, enclosed by an entire block of row houses with back doors facing inward. It was here that I first learned how to jump rope with Marjorie's daughter Ellie. I remember how she brought me out with her and introduced me to some of the kids, coaching me on my jumping skills and generally playing the good hostess. Ellie was older, and I looked up to her as a benevolent big sister.

Meanwhile, there seemed to be an endless supply of kids playing outside at all times of the day. Double Dutch was favored by Ellie and the older neighborhood girls, using two oversized jump ropes at once. Two girls would power it in a giant four-armed helix, one great arc of rope rising to its apex just as the other smacked the ground. I watched, amazed, as Ellie would jump in and hop to evade the ropes underfoot with impressive precision. It was the first and only time I ever saw it done. Once I got older, I got to try it too, but it surely wasn't an easy feat and I never quite mastered it.

When I visited, I always stayed on the third floor with Ellie. It was the bedroom she shared with her older sister, Cassie, who moved somewhere else while I was there. In their room, the angled ceilings created a cloistered feel, and I remember how pretty it was to see the soft morning sunlight filtered through the tangled curtain of English ivy that grew past their windows. Dappled shadows and highlights thrown from the leaded glass panes blanketed the room in a gentle woodland effect. It was a romantic place to wake up, and I wished our own house had such a wonderful aspect.

Downstairs, on the second floor, I remember Marjorie and Vonn's large bedroom. Marjorie had a beautiful vanity at one end where she sat each morning to apply her makeup and fix her hair just as my mother did. Greg's smaller but equally pretty room was just down the hall. In the bathroom, there were formal photographs of Marjorie as a young woman, dressed in different outfits and looking very chic. The room had a few enormous and empty perfume bottles decorating a high shelf.

The stopper alone from the Chanel bottle must have weighed at least a couple of pounds. I was intrigued. I didn't know they made them that big. Greg explained to me the bottles came from Marjorie's modeling days.

The house had other mysteries. I don't recall if I ever saw Ethan or Eleanor's rooms. I wasn't one to snoop. Eleanor was very private, and I would never have visited Ethan's room. He was older, and very handsome. I had no brothers, and young men were mysterious creatures to me. I recall having a crush on him. It's likely his room was also on the third floor where the girls were, but I have no recollection of it. I can remember finding myself outdoors alone with Ethan once.

At the time, he was leaning casually against one of a few brick archways between the houses. His eyes were trained on me while he made a little small talk, asking me about school and other things. I could sense his fondness for me as he spoke, and I recall I had an overwhelming sense of shyness in response. At the time, I was still a very young girl, and I'd had no idea of how to put all of those feelings together. I loved the attention he was giving me, but I was tongue-tied and didn't know how to converse with him. His face with its fine features were a distraction. Of course, nothing else happened. He was so much older than I was, and no doubt he only saw me for the baby I was. I had no idea of how to behave as casually as he did. Looking back on it, I'm sure he was just being friendly. Ethan treated me with the same warmth as everyone in that house, but for me on that day, it had been a tiny bit more.

Downstairs on weekends, it seemed there was always tapping

at the screen door, with friends and neighbors calling inside to say hello. Marjorie and Greg never failed to invite them in for a cup of coffee and a chat. There was always a white box on the kitchen counter tied in red and white cotton string from the bakery and filled with Danish or some other confection ready for such occasions. Most often, it was people they knew from the neighborhood who came to their door. They seemed to have so many friends. Other times, a client might appear with some old treasure to show Marjorie for her consideration. Much of the merchandise at the shop was acquired by word of mouth. Still, no matter who showed up, they were treated with the same genial welcome and an offer of refreshment. Even Cassie, Ethan, and Ellie's friends were met with the same warm welcome.

"Come in, dear. Come in! *Won*-derful to see you! Here, have a seat. Can I get you a cup of coffee or something cold to drink?"

Whatever Marjorie and the rest were doing, it could wait.

"Now, tell me, how is everyone?"

"And your mother? How is she doing these days? Any better? Here, have a slice of crumb cake, I just picked it up this morning."

All visitors got the same warm welcome. Everyone loved these people, kids and grownups alike, which was no surprise.

I remember wishing with all my heart that they could be my real family. I knew it was impossible, but I remember thinking how nice it would be if only they could adopt me. There was never an angry word or disapproving look between them, even when things went wrong, and being there was intoxicating. I felt safe with them, and every day was like a great gift, virtual heaven on earth for me. I looked forward to those visits every year. Over time, I watched their family grow older and the kids grow up. They, in turn, watched me do the same.

After Greg finally retired and went to live there for good, I continued to visit, and they always welcomed me warmly. Greg spoke with such fondness about my family and me. How they tolerated all her stories, I will never know, but they listened and laughed along with her, interjecting with asides and compliments in my direction. They were always interested, as far as I could see, and genuinely appreciative of their mother's happy memories.

I still marvel that they made me feel as welcome as they did, particularly when, over the years, they'd had precious little time with Greg to themselves. Rightly or wrongly, I felt responsible for this loss, but they were never the source of such feelings. Those were mine alone.

Chapter 19
The Secret Room

When we moved into the house in Palm Beach, it retained some
subtle reminders of Robert Ripley's previous ownership. The
famous purveyor of all things unusual had left his distinctive
mark on the house, and for me, there was one hidden feature
that stood out. The house had a secret room.

The master bedroom suite was on the second floor off a
long hallway with two facing bathrooms, a black and white one
for my father on one side and a more feminine one with peach
and white tile for Mom. Each bathroom had a walk-in closet,
paneled in cedar beadboard and equipped with plenty of rods
and hooks to accommodate a sizable wardrobe. The oversized
bedroom was beyond at the far end of the hall.

Ripley's secret room was inside my mother's closet. It was
impossible to know it was there, as the mechanism to open its
door was a closet hook amid a row of identical hooks. The pan-
eling on the walls disguised the outline of the door. All we had
to do was turn the special mechanical hook counterclockwise by
half a turn, and with a click the secret door would pop open.
The room was a small one. Originally, it had contained a cot
and chair, but my parents had moved those out. The room had
a fixed window overlooking the pool area, overset with stucco in
a grid pattern. The grid made it difficult to see into, and it
would have been hard for an intruder to determine the exact

location of the room. This was useful, as the room also contained a small wall safe.

When we moved in, my parents decided to use the room to store their valuables. My mother kept a rack in there for her fur coats. Her best jewelry was stored in the safe along with important papers. I loved to go with Mom when she went in to retrieve things. I remember her standing, combination in hand, carefully turning the small knob in one direction and then back again several times before the door of the vault would give way. She told me that Mr. Ripley built the room because he felt he needed a place to hide. It was like a strange little clubhouse, and it was our family secret. It made sense to me that a man who made his living combing the world for the most bizarre things might have developed some strange fears of his own. I imagined I could feel just a little bit of that fear every time I stepped into it, and I never went there alone.

Once Carolyn got a few years older, my father and mother moved into a more private and elaborate addition they had built downstairs at the other end of the house. Along with his and hers bathrooms and walk-in closets for each of them, the wing had a large dressing room for my mother with the master bedroom beyond that. When I turned 10, the new master suite downstairs was finished, and as the eldest daughter, I was given the old Ripley bedroom for my own. Now we kids and Greg had the whole upstairs area to ourselves, and Carolyn, who had been sleeping with Greg, took my place in Debbie's room.

My mother, who loved decorating, had the room repainted and carpeted in rose and cream, which she felt more suitable for a young girl. She got rid of the black lacquer bedroom set they had been using and installed new cream-colored French Provincial furniture. She also bought me a queen-size bed to replace the king and put a low stone table and large tasseled floor cushions around it in the far corner. This was where she placed my small stereo. When I had friends over, we could sit there and play records. She didn't consult me about what I wanted, but I was thrilled with her choices and to have my own room with everything fresh and new. It all looked very grown-up to me compared to the room I had shared with Debbie, and I reveled in it and the sudden privacy, at least until nightfall.

In my bed at night, across the big room, I had a full view of my mother's old bathroom. The nightlight inside it illuminated the closet and the hook for the secret door. Lying back on my pillow, I can remember watching compulsively, fearful that I might see the hook turn on its own.

This was a time when vivid dreams and nightmares became common for me. They arrived in technicolor and included monsters and the supernatural. I believe they spoke of my fear of death and dying and the helplessness I had begun to be aware of in my daily life. And waking up from a nightmare in that room brought little comfort to me. I would simply find myself back in my own bed with a view of the dreaded door.

Many of the bad dreams I had were recurring ones. They played themselves out in my sleep in frightening repetition. Each time they did, I knew what was coming next. Each time, I was unable to stop it. I had my first nightmare at the age of six. It involved a genie that I discovered in my parents' room, the same room that was now mine. The genie would be standing above my motionless parents, bloody scimitar aloft. He was wearing a turban and bright silk clothing with a red sash, red silk shoes, and he had a long and pointy goatee with a waxed mustache above his feral-looking teeth. Both my parents were splayed and gutted, their shiny insides spilling past the blankets to the floor.

At the moment of discovery, the genie's eyes would lock on mine, twinkling with evil intent, and a sinister grin would creep across his face. The chase was on. I remember running as fast as I could down the spiral staircase, all the while calling for my toddler sister Debbie to hurry along with me. With her hand in mine, and the genie closing in, we made it to the round carpet in the front entryway, the front door, and safety beyond it, just barely out of reach. Suddenly, I could not move Debbie. As I turned to look behind me, I could see the genie had gotten a firm grip on Debbie's other hand. At that moment, I knew our deaths were imminent and I had to decide whether to stay and fight or let go of her hand and try to save myself.

At that precise moment, the choice was unbearable and the extremity of it would wake me up. The dream was so real, I would call out to Greg for comfort. It repeated itself many times in those younger years, always the same scenario, and now it followed me into my new bedroom, the one with the secret door. It was in that room I also began to have a new recurring dream.

I don't know why, but it was the most frightening dream of them all. In the beginning, I would be on my back, in bed, unable to sleep. The line between reality and my imagination was entirely blurred. The large room was dark, and straining to see, I slowly became aware that something was happening. Blinking my eyes, I could just make out the wisps of a mustard yellow fog that were beginning to float into the room at the top of the doorway. I was familiar with this entity, and my horror and sense of helplessness were total each time, as the slow and gathering swirls of vapor began to thicken and converge with increasing malevolence.

In the dream, I recognized the presence and knew it meant my doom. I could not move or cry out as it gathered, hovering in the air above me, thick and faceless. I could feel a sickening sensation in my bones. It was as if the black plague itself was taking form above my recumbent body, preparing to infuse itself into me. It was fear itself that visited me on those nights, unstoppable, inevitable, and beyond rational description. I lay there frozen, knowing I would soon be enveloped in the queasy bleakness that now hesitated above me. I was paralyzed with fear and couldn't cry out. I felt beyond helpless and could do nothing but lie there, a prisoner to this shapeless thing that was my own special torment. At the point in which I knew for a certainty that it was about to descend, I would awaken, never quite sure it wasn't still with me.

The nightmares were bad enough, but I can remember the nights when I was awake, and watched the hook for so long that it seemed to turn ever so slightly on its own. The first time it happened, I sat bolt upright in bed, unable to avert my eyes. I was frozen in fear, unable to scream. A distinctly metallic taste filled my mouth, and the breath went out of me as if a giant vacuum was attached directly to my lungs.

I wasn't sure I could make it out of the room. I tried several times to call out to Greg, but I couldn't produce enough breath to make a sound. The trouble was, I had to move toward the secret door to leave the room because the hallway was also the only way out. Trembling and panicked, I managed somehow to make it past the bathroom door, but the hallway was long, and I crumpled about five feet from the exit, depleted by the white-hot fear coursing through me. I don't know how long I was there, yearning to reach the closed door just in front of me. At last, a fresh surge of energy propelled me out to safety.

I never told Greg what it was that sent me so suddenly to her room on those nights. I knew it was just crazy, thinking I'd seen the hook move. I feared my own bedroom at night and I blamed myself. I was too big for such childish things, I thought, but I couldn't control the dreams nor the fear. All I could do at those times was get myself to Greg as quickly as possible.

"Can I sleep with you?" I would ask. She didn't question my sudden arrival, but seeing it was urgent, she would offer me a place beside her in her small bed. With her ubiquitous hot water bottle jammed between us, I would fall asleep warm, safe, and grateful. During those four years, I slept with Greg in her small room more often than my own.

From the beginning, I had been a sensitive and anxious child, and it is no wonder that all that anxiety spilled itself into my slumbers. I was aware that my father had his first heart attack during my first year of life, and he'd had at least four or five more by the time I was 10. He was always dying. What fears I might well have had anyway were given more detailed shape and form when my sister Louise took me at the age of six to an unauthorized triple feature horror movie. No doubt, the ideas that came to me at night had their genesis there. My mother was furious.

"Louise! What were you thinking?!" she said bitterly, trying to contain her anger.

But the damage had been done. By the time I occupied the room with the secret door, my fertile imagination had already taken off, and I had nightmares regularly, all of them in vivid and lurid color. The dreams that dogged me and the secret room were part of what became a very memorable, perplexing, and complicated time for me back then. I imagine it wasn't easy for Greg or my parents either, even as they had no idea of the specifics. Being so young, I had only a diffuse understanding that I was unhappy.

"Honestly, Helen, you're too sensitive," my mother would say, and I believed her. I thought it must be true. Whatever daily stress I felt was illustrated by the constant sense of fight or flight which pervaded my childhood in subtle and less subtle ways, leaving me meeker and milder than I might have been otherwise. As I got a little older, the combination of free-floating anxiety and my home situation got the better of me.

My state of mind had not always been readily apparent, but by the age of 10, it became undeniable to everyone, both inside and outside the immediate family. It was at this age I began to experience migraine headaches that, despite aspirin, sent me to my bed. I was in a fetal position unable to move all day until the crushing pain passed after a period of sleep.

At the same time, I began to have panic attacks. I would

experience a sudden urge to vomit, and I felt compelled to get up from wherever I was and run away — anywhere. I had developed a phobia of throwing up, and so I never ran to a bathroom. I was afraid that if I went in there, I would surely do it. I would stand up from my desk with a great sense of urgency and run out of the classroom. It could happen without warning. And it did. I never knew where I was going when I ran, I only knew that I must go. Because of this, I missed about half of sixth grade. After each episode, I would be sent home. Sudden nausea and ensuing panic seemed to come and go at random, even keeping me home before I ever went to school.

I had already had difficulties with insomnia. During the previous summer, when that symptom first appeared. I was up at all hours, lying in my bed, eyes open. Even when I was tired, I was often unable to sleep. I was unstable in other ways too. Often, I would weep unexpectedly, with no apparent cause. I remember how strange it felt. I wasn't sad, but copious tears flowed anyway, and once they began, I couldn't stop them. My father and Greg took turns trying to find ways to make me laugh.

One time, my mother had a whack at it, but she quickly lost patience. She had come into my bedroom, clearly intending to cheer me up. As I continued, unable to control my tears, angry frustration overtook her.

"Stop it. Stop it!" my mother hissed, as she grabbed me by the throat with both hands, squeezing so hard I was unable to make a sound.

There in my room, she towered over me, maintaining her

grip. I couldn't breathe. Her face was only inches from my own and the black look in her eyes showed a fury that was terrifying. I didn't dare fight back. She held me there so long that I began to black out before she finally let go of my neck. At that point, I fell to the floor, coughing and gasping for air while she stormed out of the room. She never came back. No one saw it happen, and neither she nor I spoke of it ever.

My father, who resolutely refused to recognize mental illness, began to arrange for medical testing in hopes of pinpointing my physical problem. As an aside, my father's denial of mental illness is curious, given the fact that his own father had suffered from it and we all knew his sister Rosabelle had too. In any case, he made a series of appointments with doctors who sent me for tests, and even an EEG, but none of them could come up with a diagnosis.

Finally, at the end of that summer, out of desperation, he and my mother took me to see the New York psychiatrist who was a close friend of Dad's. He questioned me while my parents sat outside in the waiting room. I recall being aware of my parents' proximity, along with the likelihood of his immediate report to them, and I remember answering his queries with what I knew they wanted to hear. I had only a rudimentary understanding of what a psychiatrist did at the time, but surely knew enough to tailor my answers to my parents' approval.

"Are you happy at home?" he asked me, once we had settled into our seats.

"Yes," I answered simply.

I'm not sure I knew how unhappy I was.

"Is there anything you can tell me about how you feel when you think you need to run away?" he asked, probing further.

"No, I don't know why it happens."

And I didn't. It was a mysterious, frightening experience. The symptoms were so real. Spontaneous weeping aside, I thought I must be physically ill.

"Are you enjoying your summer?"

"Yes."

This was only half true, I was being sent to a day camp during the week, and I hated that part.

"What are you doing with your days?"

"I am going to camp."

"Do you like it there?"

"Yes."

Of course, this was an outright lie. My fellow campers had been more mature than I was and laughed openly at what they identified as my awkward social skills. I was too polite, and their vocabulary was new to me. I hadn't been exposed to the bawdy songs and humor of more worldly children, and I lacked confidence. This left me with a decidedly uncomfortable feeling, and every day that I was sent there, I counted the hours until I could come home and play quietly in the yard.

"How do you feel about your parents?

"I love them."

This answer was entirely truthful. I did love them. Still, I recall thinking this was a loaded question, and I knew not to elaborate further. I chose to say the one thing which was truest and would make no trouble for me. Any further elaboration would be reported back to them, and I knew I couldn't.

"Is there anything they can do to help you feel better?"

"I don't know."

This was also true. I didn't know. They were who they were, and given that basic fact, in my view, there was nothing I could ask for that would be remotely possible. I might have told him otherwise, that they needed to be gentler and more loving with my sisters and me. I might also have said that I found them frightening, but this was not possible.

The interview was basic and brief, and I went and sat with my mother in the anteroom while my father went into his friend's office to discuss our conversation. No doubt, it was reported to my father that there seemed to be no detectable problem. I was of sound mind and seemed to be happy enough. My father looked gratified as we left for home, smiling to himself and at me, as there was nothing his friend had said to him that countermanded his own beliefs.

Eventually, after all the medical tests came back negative, the doctors determined that some medication was necessary, whatever the cause of my symptoms. They gave me paregoric — a camphorated tincture of opium — for my occasional nausea and more aspirin for my headaches. There was nothing they could do for the panic attacks, but I was put on a regimen of phenobarbital at night for my insomnia. The barbiturate made the call to sleep profound and irresistible. It reduced the number of nightmares, as it conveyed a deep and often dreamless sleep which was a blessed relief to me. One tablespoon of the thick red liquid at bedtime did the trick. The medicine had a pungent, aromatic quality mixed with a syrupy sweetness, and it made my tongue slightly numb when I took it. Once the flavor filled my mouth, I knew that comfortable sleep was soon to follow, and for this reason, I even came to like the taste. This liquid was my salvation.

By the time I was 12, the dose had to be doubled to have the same effect, but it didn't matter. It was working. The familiar bottle of phenobarbital was my best friend and I took it with me wherever I went, whether it was for an overnight stay at my grandmother's house or traveling anywhere else. I felt panicked if I left it behind. Now I needed it every night, if I were to sleep at all.

Joe and Claudia at their wedding.

Dad

Mom

Greg

My parents, two grandmothers, and friends in Mamaroneck, NY

The Palm Beach house

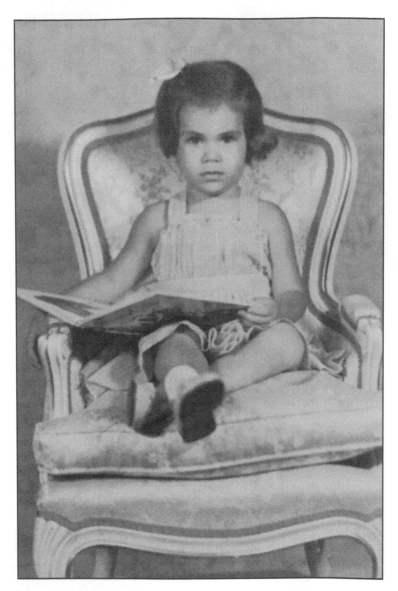

Me

Debbie

Grandma Morse

Grandma Speciale

Grandmas Speciale and Morse in front of their house

Palm Beach. Mom, Dad, and Grandma Morse

The Kings Point house

Get Well note

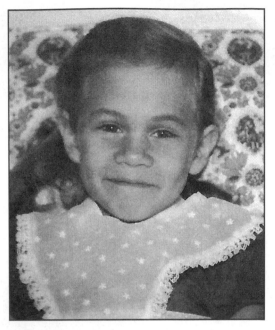

Debbie

Me and Debbie

Carolyn

We three

Debbie and Toto

Debbie, ca. 1971

Mom, ca. 1971

Greg and me

My last portrait of Debbie (in front of the dining room wallpaper)

Chapter 20
The Heart Attack

His lips were blue. I heard the paramedics as they stormed through the front door with my mother, racing toward the master bedroom at the far end of the house. His breath was shallow, but he had refused to be put on a stretcher. Instead, my father was carried, each of his arms slung over a younger man's shoulder, their hands grasping his in support. His jaw was slack. The sweaty skin on his face and neck was pale and grayish and contrasted with his happy pink gingham pajamas. Wordlessly, he glanced over at me with weary eyes as he was ushered past. His feet still in his slippers, the toe fronts dragged across the living room carpet and around the corner to the front hallway. My mother hurried behind, hastily checking her purse for her car keys while urging the men toward the waiting ambulance.

The front door closed behind them, and suddenly, all was quiet. I stood for some time in that same spot. I felt lost. He was such a powerful man that it was a shock to my young eyes to see him looking so weak and vulnerable. I hadn't been present at the other times he had been ushered away. He'd had many heart attacks, but I only heard about them later, when he was home and convalescing. In our house, they were like war stories told at the fireside, related with reverence and tinged with the astonishment that he'd survived yet another one.

There had been the famous episode in Kings Point in the

middle of the night when, reluctant to wake my mother, he'd crawled down the massive double staircase and called the ambulance himself. And now I'd seen it myself. Still fighting, he refused to leave the house lying down.

That day in Palm Beach, many hours later, my mother arrived home without him. She was beside herself with worry.

"The doctors aren't sure he will make it this time," my mother told me, the exhaustion and worry stretched painfully across her features. Her hair was a mess. She wore no lipstick and barely any makeup at all, aside from what had run from the tears she'd shed. I had never seen her like this. It was obvious she'd thrown her outfit on in haste, without regard to what went with what. She didn't look like the mother I knew. It was as if she was playing at looking as messy as possible. The effect surprised me and made me feel truly sorry for her, even as I was busy worrying about him. She asked me to take a walk with her, so we set off out the back door to the lake trail.

"They told me he has pneumonia and that he's suffering from heart failure due to another attack," she told me. She needed to tell someone. I didn't know what to say or how to comfort her. I was only 10 years old. I kept my eyes to the shell-speckled pavement under our feet as we walked.

She continued, "His lungs are filling up with fluid, and his heart is weak," and with this, she took a mighty breath and began to weep in earnest.

"Oh," I said, at a loss for words. The tears that welled up in my own eyes were in response to my mother as much as for my own feelings.

"They told me they will do everything they can to save him," she said, but her shoulders only spoke of defeat and were as droopy as her mismatched outfit as we walked the trail, unaware of the people who passed us as we went.

We walked and we walked, side by side down the cruelly sunny trail. A gray day would have seemed more appropriate. She cried openly as we went, and I wept along with her. It was a moment that was unprecedented in my young life. I suddenly experienced as never before a sense of closeness and empathy for her. The fear for my father's life was all-consuming, but I also felt the undeniably delicious sensation of being needed — really needed — by her. These feelings came to me all at once, both abject terror and utter delight, mixing inside my young chest. It was as if someone had poured two competing chemicals inside me to make some kind of bomb that might go off at any moment.

My mother and I walked in silence for a while, at which point she did something stranger still. Suddenly, and out of the blue, she offered me a cigarette, saying, "Have one of these. It'll make you feel better."

"Is she crazy?!" I thought, but I didn't dare break our moment of closeness to remind her how young I was — and that of course, I didn't smoke. Instead, I took the cigarette from her, and she proceeded to light it for me as if she'd done it a million times before.

We walked until she was tired, then we returned to the house through the back gate and up the lawn to the back door. Over the next few weeks, she went back and forth to the hospital as he slowly recovered enough to come home. The story was always the same, he would have a close call, and eventually, he would be brought home and sent straight to bed, where he had doctors' orders to stay for months on end. Friends would send their good wishes by phone or post, and my father would remain in the bedroom to recuperate, my mother hovering nearby at his beck and call.

When I was younger, I had given him my favorite doll at one of these times. It was a little cloth clown with a child's face and a fabric body and legs that flopped every which way. It had small jingle bells at the ends of its arms and legs and one at the tip of its pointy hat. The many bells made a lovely sound as it was carried. I gave it to him in a moment of pure altruism, meaning for the doll to be a comfort to him as it had been to me. He kept the doll on his side of the bed until the day he died, but that would not be today.

We weren't allowed to go see him; the hospital had a no-children policy, but now he was home. When I entered my parents' bedroom, he held his arms aloft in greeting from his place on the near side of the giant bed. I will never forget the expression on his face, a mixture of purest love and delight, something I'm not sure I had ever seen before. In answer, I ran down the few bedroom steps and across the room to him. He pulled me close and kissed me forcefully on the mouth with a kiss that was more earnest than any I had ever experienced from either parent up until then.

It was never his custom to kiss anyone on the mouth except, perhaps, our mother. I confess I cannot remember him doing even that. Maybe there had been a very occasional peck on the cheek when they were leaving each other or returning home. But this kiss was different. It felt to me that the extremity of his warm greeting matched the extremity of a brush with death. I believe he hadn't been sure himself that he would live to see me again.

For an instant, a sensation of love, now utterly requited, gripped my heart. I shall never forget it. The impervious and scary giant was vulnerable, and more than that, I now felt his love for me. I mattered to him! It was the first time in my life I felt this so deeply. I was grateful for the moment and horrified by it at the same time. Suddenly I understood I would never have experienced this glorious flash of my father's feelings if things had gone the other way. I almost lost him, and the thought sent a shiver down my spine.

The experiences of this particular event were, in every way, an anomaly for me. It gave me a hint of the insight I would gain much later on, but at the time, nothing changed. Everything returned to the old normal. As he recovered, he grew busy again and more distant, just as my mother too, seemed to have forgotten how close we had been when we walked the trail and smoked a cigarette together. It was as if nothing momentous had happened, when indeed it had, at least for me. If I entertained any illusions about my everyday life changing, I quickly learned that it was not to be. But the experience tucked itself into a small corner of my mind, and I called upon it whenever I felt the need. I could remind myself that these people did in fact have deep feelings, even when they could not seem to access them as often as I would have liked. Ever the optimist, I never once considered a more cynical view, which was, instead, the one my sister Debbie had. I gave them the benefit of the doubt. As far as I was concerned, they really did care, even if they weren't good at showing it, and that knowledge was a comfort to the child I was, ever yearning for their love and looking for it in every thought and action.

My father regained his general health, although each heart attack caused just a little more damage. I was aware that despite his forceful personality and general appearance of vigor, he was fragile right there at the center of his chest. No doubt the scares fostered my all-around talent for worry.

He was never far from being gone forever to all of us, and at times, our stone house felt more like a house of cards, liable to come crashing down at any moment.

Chapter 21
Palm Beach

The move to Palm Beach wouldn't have been my choice. It was the winter home for America's rich and famous, where my sisters and I would eventually feel like perennial outsiders. Our parents might have been able to afford a home there, but they had come from humble beginnings, quite different from many other residents. In addition, our collective family ethnicities did not match up with most of our neighbors. For these reasons, among others, it was a bad fit for us girls.

There are aspects of our Palm Beach experience that stand out in my memory as strangely horrifying to relate. If you lived there, the shameless and intentional display of wealth and seemingly pathological need for fame and status were unavoidable. By the time I was a young teen, I understood all too well that Palm Beach was a town that thrived on and fostered the worst aspects of human nature. The sheer spectacle could also be fascinating and even amusing at times. No accurate description of our lives in that place would be complete without an attempt to describe those details.

Many of the residents in Palm Beach were direct descendants, or the actual founders of some of the largest companies in the American industrial complex. Others were heirs and heiresses of the most prominent and blue-blooded among us. They were the "kings and queens" of society, descending from the

Mayflower or international royalty, both actual and political.
Many were directly related to some of the most famous and infa-
mous characters found in American history books. The Dodges,
the Rockefellers, and the Phippses had houses there, to name a
few. Douglas Fairbanks Jr. was there, too, along with Lily Pulitzer
and Estee Lauder. Even the Duke and Duchess of Windsor win-
tered there. They all had chosen Palm Beach for its privacy and
exclusive reputation. For the most part, these people were not
only aware of their places in the social register, but they themselves had written and edited its pages. Some of their children
were my first playmates.

Those boys and girls were familiar to me, but I had very little
in common with them apart from financial security relative to
the world at large. From the beginning, I felt a distinct sense of
"otherness" when I was with them. Like the Kennedy family, we
had a house on the north side, where most of the Jews and Catholics lived. Back then, the Jews had only begun to make their way
in, a goodly number of years since the Catholics had done it.
Real prestige in Palm Beach was Protestant, on the southern side,
where Bethesda-by-the-Sea, the Episcopalian church, was the old-
est and most beautiful place of worship on the island.

Before its present owner purchased it, Marjorie Merri-
weather Post built and lived at Mar-a-Lago, a place that was more
like a castle than a residence. Many legendary parties were held
there and my parents had been invited to one of them. I remember my mother's description of it the following day.

"You wouldn't have believed it, Helen! The silverware at
the table was solid gold! I'm not kidding; I checked! And there

were 100 people there — maybe more, I don't know. What if someone was inclined to stuff a fork or two into their pocket? Nobody was watching! It was unbelievable."

My mother described how the legions of guests were attended by a seemingly equal number of waitstaff.

Excess ruled everywhere in Palm Beach when the yearly season of charity balls were at The Breakers and the various private clubs. Delivered by their chauffeurs, the guests streamed forth dressed in tuxedos and spangled gowns fashioned by top designers of the day. There were costume balls too, soirces with women arriving in opulent, theatrical ensembles complete with feathers, silk velvets, and piles of real jewels. Outside, uniformed men stood and watched over parking lots filled edge-to-edge with Roll Royces, Bentleys, Jaguars, and Bugattis. No one seemed to care for understatement in Palm Beach. It was all "show it so they know it," and to a little girl like me, and for many others too, I'm sure, it all looked pretty glamorous. It certainly did to Greg and my mother.

Meanwhile, the daily procession continued as always on Worth Avenue, Palm Beach's most famous shopping area. In the early 1960s, the socialites strolled along, chauffeurs at curbside, awaiting their return. The women greeted each other, all with perfect hair and makeup, and what looked like their best jewelry all at once. One modest ring or bracelet was simply not enough. The practice of stacking multiple gold bracelets three and four inches wide up at least one wrist was popular.

These women fairly jingled with jewelry, and they were show-stoppers. They often dressed in full-length sable or real

leopard skin coats and sometimes crowned themselves with diamond tiaras to finish the look. Their fur coats must have been
oppressive in the tropical heat, but they were determined to
browse Cartier, Dior, and Chanel on Worth Avenue in their
outrageous best. They were probably relieved whenever they
were able to go inside for the air-conditioning. Still, in their
promenades along the avenue, they expected to be noticed and
perhaps even photographed by Mort Kaye for a mention in the
local paper, the Shiny Sheet.

At the time, Worth Avenue billed itself as the most expensive retail street in the United States, and going there was like attending a sort of royalty parade, but without the benefit of a
marching band. Some residents even walked the avenue with an
ocelot on leash. When I think of it now, I am amazed they managed to do this. Anyone knows how difficult it is to walk an
ordinary house cat. Still, the exotic animals were there, walking
alongside their owners.

Greg loved the social hubbub. She liked to peruse the
Shiny Sheet and speculate about what she knew of the various
families and scions pictured there, speaking in hushed tones
about the Dodges, the Munns, or the White Russians, no doubt
picking up much of her gossip from the small army of governesses she saw all the time on the lake trail. Even Greg, my source
of sanity and balance, was a fan of high society. She had inside
information, and it was her guilty pleasure.

The Shiny Sheet newspaper, like everything else in Palm
Beach, did its best to appear exclusive. Its pages were high-grade
white paper, almost shiny, which protected its readership's

spotless fingers and fine furniture from the unpleasant ink transfer of ordinary newspapers. It was also easier to handle than broadsheet papers, with a total of just six to eight sheets folded to half size. It carried a few ads, a smattering of local news, a horoscope section, and the ever-popular society gossip column.

The column served as the heartbeat of the Shiny Sheet and, in some ways, of the town itself. Celebrity visitors, houseguests, and their hosts were mentioned there without fail, along with their activities and whereabouts on the island. Of course, it featured charity balls and galas during the busy winter season. Even the birthday celebrations of Palm Beach children got coverage. Lucky invitees were listed and pictured in its pages as a strange sort of medal of approval. The official photographer, Mort Kaye, never failed to turn up at most celebrations to take pictures, just in case the paper would decide to run that event. Over the years, he had been to our house to cover various festivities. My parents had even hired him at least once for a portrait session with us girls. Days after one of our events, we would check the Shiny Sheet to see if our family had made it into print. Greg and my mother noticed these mentions with a good bit of excitement, whereas my father seemed to have no interest in them at all. When one of them would find us there, they would pass the paper, one to the other, both Mom and Greg excited as little children.

"Here we are! Look, Helen, that's you with Anderson! And look! There's a picture of Debbie with Rocky and the McGowan twins! Oh! And they've printed the guest list here below! Ha!"

It seemed to be something of a big deal, and because of that, it seemed a big deal to me. I had no real sense of what it meant for them at the time. I can only imagine now that my mother felt a thrill akin to being admitted into an exclusive club she had never thought was a possibility, given her start in life. For Greg, it earned her bragging rights in her circle of nannies. I can remember what a pleasure it was to see the pride on their faces.

We children liked to see the pictures too. But as I grew up, I began to recognize the Palm Beach adoration of wealth and exclusivity for the thing it was — the innocuous tip of an impossibly large and ugly iceberg. We girls would come to know it all too well and suffer because of it, as I imagine some others did, too.

Occasionally, the obsession with standing out from the crowd had a lighter side. The creativity of the residents could be entertaining. Often, in March and April, they would have their white toy poodles dyed in Easter egg colors: pink, yellow, blue, and violet to go along with the holiday theme. These colorful pups sported matching nail polish on their little toes and wore satin bows in their perfectly coiffed top knots. For us, they were a delight to behold. These were fluffy little Easter creatures, and we children adored spotting them whenever they were out with their owners for a stroll.

The love of whimsy was not only confined to the animals of Palm Beach. A woman whose identity we never learned used to ride her bicycles on the lake trail. She would pass by on her Zebra striped bike, wearing matching zebra pants, blouse, scarf, and shoes — and the next time we would see her, she would be riding a lime green bike with a matching green outfit. We lost count of how many matching sets she had, but it was a vast array of colors, plus stripes, plaids, florals, and of course, animal prints.

In Palm Beach, there was a need for attention that lined up perfectly with the American fascination with monarchy. The wish to be associated with royalty was commonplace. It was, in fact, so prevalent that it was rumored some made appeals to various European royal families to obtain titles for themselves, even when they could not establish a substantial familial connection. When no link was found, a generous donation could secure a title instead. Certainly, the community was atwitter any time its perennial residents, the Windsors, were seen in public. And many others visited the island regularly, including Prince Charles. As a young man, he played at the polo grounds in West Palm Beach. We never saw him, although I do recall an idle wish to go. I would never have gotten close enough for even a peek at him anyway, given the crowds of would-be barons and baronesses and general hangers-on, pressing in wherever he went.

I remember seeing the Windsors myself more than once, a smartly dressed elderly couple walking arm-in-arm along the lake trail. The first time I ever saw them, I remember Greg's excitement.

"Do you know who that was?" she asked me under her breath.

Of course, I didn't. I was young. I remember looking behind me to watch the pair strolling away while Greg told me what she knew of their story.

"That was Edward, the Duke of Windsor, the man who was the *king of England* and Wallis Simpson, the woman he gave it all up for. She's an American and a *divorcee*. He wasn't allowed to marry her, so he gave up the throne just to be with her! Such a handsome couple, and so romantic! They may be old now, but they still look so happy together, God bless them."

It is unclear how many people knew then that the Windsors had once fraternized with the Nazis. I'm sure Greg hadn't any knowledge of it at the time, but such facts would have made little difference to many other Palm Beach residents. Antisemitism was commonplace in our town — one might even say it was the town's open secret. It was common knowledge that Jews were not permitted to join either the Everglades Club or the Bath and Tennis Club, the two most sought-after memberships on the island. They were not even allowed to enter the premises as would-be guests of a member in good standing. As late as 1972, it is a matter of record that C.Z. Guest, a well-known socialite, had her membership suspended for some time for trying to bring Estee Lauder and her husband in with her. Both were Jews.

Even though we were only half Jewish, eventually we girls would experience this prejudice directly. I can remember my tension as a preteen when I ended up with a friend, the daughter of a member, inside the Bath and Tennis Club. Her parents probably didn't know of the plan, and my friend insisted we go in, as she always did with others. I was afraid to say anything, and so I went along. I can recall how nervous I was as we sat by the pool, not being sure that someone wouldn't suddenly appear to eject me from my seat. It was strange, even back then, to feel so unwelcome anywhere in my own town, but this was Palm Beach, and it was a fact of life. It got much worse for me by junior high school.

Chapter 22
Legacy

However perfect it may have seemed to others looking in, the manicured estates of my hometown served as screens to shield their occupants from further scrutiny. Elegant hedges and stone walls hid a host of ills, and the children who grew up there were not immune to them.

Palm Beach was not the same experience for me and my sisters as it was for our parents. In hindsight, I can see why school wasn't a happy experience for me. In general, the dramatically skewed value systems and abundance of money combined with a dearth of parental emotional involvement damaged these children. Many were angry and anxious to exert their own power wherever they could, most often upon the weaker and more defenseless. For my mother and father, the attraction to Palm Beach was simple. It was beautiful and it had warm weather, and that was enough. My parents may not have held the same values as the others, but even then, I had an inkling of what a lack of parental care had done to me. Still, a few fond memories remain.

My first playmate was Anderson, whose father was the cousin of a British prime minister, while his mother was famous in her own right. Anderson's parents indulged him with magnificent toys of all descriptions. At the age of four, he rode a mechanical pony-drawn pedal carriage, its body covered in animal skin with a horsehair mane and tail. The carriage was crafted of the finest materials — lacquered wood, leather, and chrome — and there was even a child-size leather crop for its young driver.

In his backyard, Anderson had a spacious toy castle with turrets and a second floor. But most eye-catching of all was his bedroom, filled with trophies his father brought back from safaris in Africa. There were multiple big cat pelts on the floor with their heads still attached, jaws open in permanent snarls of fierceness. Real elephant tusks jutted from the walls, and I remember an impossibly large Steiff stuffed giraffe that towered over the heads of the grownups.

Anderson's paternal grandmother lived across the street in a famous villa on the oceanfront, where we often went for a swim. I remember being invited there for lunch one day, and sitting on the long covered patio overlooking the pool. The sky was cloudless, and the tropical sun blazed harshly on every surface. We sat at the table, shaded by the portico overhead, and squinted out at the vista. While we waited, our hands folded properly in our laps, the butler filled our bowls expertly with a strange looking creamy concoction.

It was my first taste of oyster stew. I hesitated as I lifted my spoon, but didn't dare refuse it. To my delight and massive relief, it was unspeakably delicious. My friend and I sat beside our governesses, with Anderson's elegant and largely silent grandmother presiding. To me, it felt as if we had been given an audience with the queen herself. The luncheon proceeded with little conversation and of course, no misbehavior.

When the grandmother retired to the house, we stayed and swam, as we often did, with our governesses attending. The villa's pool was filled with salt water pumped directly from the sea beyond. Salty pool water was new for me. It burned our eyes — and if we swallowed it accidentally, as kids do — it burned our throats too. But Anderson was my young companion, and where he went, I went.

For a while, we did everything together. Anderson was a handsome boy, with blue eyes and blond hair and a courtly manner, if that is possible to say of a four year old. He was sweet natured, and treated me with a kind of deference which is rare among small children. He was always happy to share his toys and seemed to think I was his "girlfriend", sending me several notes — my first Valentines — and even a get-well card once, all drawn by hand.

As the years progressed, Anderson and I lost contact. We had only been together while our governesses looked for activities for us as very young children, but I always remembered him affectionately. On a visit home in my early 20s, I picked him up hitchhiking along South Ocean Boulevard. As soon as he got into the car, I recognized him. Although it had been years, there he was! He had longish sandy hair now, with a bit of a blond beard just coming in. The baby fat was gone, but I had no doubt who it was, an extremely handsome version of his childhood self. Filled with excitement and warm memories, I immediately identified myself. His expression was impassive. He didn't remember me or appear to have any curiosity at all. I can't say I was devastated exactly, but it was disappointing to have such fond memories of a boy who had so clearly forgotten me.

My memories of Anderson are entirely positive, but I was so

very young then. Who knows what it had been like for him with his parents? I never knew. But I did know of a good number of children whose lives were less than blissful. Some of them suffered outright.

During the same early days when I knew Anderson, a governess friend of Greg's frequently brought her charge Wallace to our house. The governess was concerned for the infant's health and brought him over for extra feeding. Wallace was sickly and she felt he was not getting enough nourishment at home. His parents were also blue bloods, but with a direct connection to one of the most notorious figures in American history.

These parents seemed to have no real attachment to their own child. As the years went on, Wallace and I became friends in our teens. By then, Wallace was tall and painfully thin, with a long shock of blond hair that flopped seductively over one eye. He became part of a small coterie of friends who came over to hang out in our pool house. I saw him often then, the long fingers of his large hands flying over the keys of our piano, a favorite place for him when he visited. Wallace was talented and self-taught; he impressed us with the melodies he composed, most of them strange and melancholy. He had a black sense of humor, too, which we understood on some level as an expression of his life experience. We enjoyed Wallace's company, as he was very bright and always seemed in good spirits. We admired his brand of courage in coping with what we perceived as evil circumstances. We were aware, too, that he needed us and a respite from his life as it was.

Wallace had told me how his cousin lived with his family.

The cousin had lost both of his parents in a tragic accident. Wallace's own father made it more than obvious that he preferred the cousin over him, because, in part, the cousin had gained a sizable inheritance. The boy was given a bedroom upstairs, while Wallace was relegated to a room away from everyone else on the lower level. He went on to describe how the whole family would gather upstairs for steak dinner, while Wallace was given hot dogs to be eaten alone, down below.

On visits to his house, I saw how he suffered at the hands of parents who mistreated him to the extent that they put a chain and padlock around the refrigerator to keep him from grabbing a snack between meals. My understanding was that everyone else had a key. In a place of plenty like Palm Beach, reports of a chain and padlock on a refrigerator might have sounded like a total fabrication, but I saw it with my own eyes.

The cruelties of his parents were unrelenting. Once, Wallace invited me to be his date for the school prom. His mother had given him permission to go. As the time approached, however, his mother told him she had decided not to pay for his tuxedo. Wallace had no means to pay for it himself, and suddenly the date was off. I remember his apologies and his corresponding black humor on the subject. He tried to laugh about it, but I knew he was stung.

That same year, Wallace had managed to scrape together just enough money to buy his mother a box of chocolates for her birthday and she returned the unopened candies to him as his one Christmas gift the following December. Once again, he made jokes about it, but I knew how much it must have hurt. At some point, he painted his basement bedroom black and showed it to me with much pride. I saw the color as a commentary on his situation.

The sad stories of the children of privilege were more numerous than I can recount here. Another young friend Marion lived in a house with her brother and their governess. The parents lived separately in a house on a neighboring lot. I remember going with her for dinner to her parents' house. I cannot recall if they ate dinner together every day or less often, but I do remember the dinner was a somber and formal affair, and her parents' demeanor struck me as chilly at best.

What made the dinner more memorable was the butler, Wesley, who had a wooden leg. He sat in a chair behind the dining room door and unstrapped his leg in between courses, laying the prosthetic to one side, always at the ready to strap it back on. I recall feeling sorry both for my friend and for poor Wesley, whose leg pained him. As difficult as things were for me at home, this seemed so much worse. Marion had parents who didn't even want to live in the same house with her. I could only imagine what it was like for Wesley; these people couldn't possibly have been any kinder to him than they were to their own children.

Of course, dysfunctional families are found at every economic level, and there was no shortage of them in Palm Beach. At the vast estate of another of my youngest playmates, the father, one of the great captains of industry, was in the habit of relaxing in the pool on a gigantic float while his butler went back and forth, bringing drinks and tea sandwiches to his floating tray. Reclining all the while, the man would slowly eat, removing the crusts from the sandwiches or taking only one bite, then tossing the rest directly into the pool, knowing full well that someone else would have to fish them out later on. At the same time, the governesses watched over the rambunctious children playing at the far end of the palatial, free-form swimming pool. We children never noticed what was going on, we were at such a distance. And we wouldn't have noticed how drunk he was at the time either, but years later, this was what Greg related to me, marveling at the dissolution of such a successful man. I cannot help but wonder what it must have been like for his young son. If behavior is any indication, I do know the boy showed the effects of such a childhood later on.

Even as a child, I knew this was not an ordinary American life. Television shows like "Leave It to Beaver" and "Father Knows Best" illustrated a different kind in great detail, and I longed for that one. It was worlds apart from the way we lived. The shows highlighted loving families where the father was largely present, and the mom would emerge from the kitchen to serve the food she made herself — breakfast, lunch, and dinner. Sure, their TV houses were smaller, but so what? Times at the dinner table were intimate ones, where the parents expressed interest in their children, asking them about whatever was going on in their lives that day. When the kids got into trouble, they turned to their parents for help and advice, and their good parents were concerned and available. We watched the children in these shows walk right into the family kitchen and get a snack for themselves, with no one to scold them. The kitchen was their domain, too. To top it off, when the kids got sick, the moms and dads took their temperature and tended them, as a matter of course. I watched these programs, and others like them, marveling at the way family members could treat each other and wished ours was like that.

When I was in the sixth grade, I made friends with Jane, a girl who lived near us in a modest ranch house on North Lake Way. I will never forget being there for the first time for lunch. Jane's mom called from the kitchen, telling us we should come put something together for ourselves. She had laid out the various sandwich fillings on the counter for us, along with the condiments and some bread. I remember the sheer joy of making my own sandwich and returning to the TV room with Jane. We didn't have to sit at the table. Not only that, but Jane seemed to be completely comfortable around her parents. There was no detectable distance between them; they joked and laughed together, often teasing each other with obvious affection. There were generous hugs on arrival and departure, but it was more than that. They actually touched each other with a brief but conspiratorial hand on a shoulder or a pat on the back here and there. The generally close and easy atmosphere at Jane's was a revelation to me.

For the years until I left Palm Beach for good, I spent as much time at Jane's house as I could. But that very first day stuck with me most of all. After we had put our lunches together to sit in her TV room, I remember looking down at the sandwich on my lap and wishing with all my heart that someday I could live that way myself.

Chapter 23
Cotillion

Cotillion was an expected rite of social passage in Palm Beach that took place every year at The Breakers Hotel. It was a series of luncheon dances for the pre-teen ladies and gentlemen of our town in anticipation of the debutante ball we would all be attending when we turned 16. It was assumed that we had already been taught the basics of proper comportment at home, but the classes offered instruction on the finer points of etiquette and ballroom dancing which were skills required of the well-born — and my diligent parents had signed me up.

Of course, it was required that all young members of society dress accordingly, with stockings, white gloves, and Sunday best dresses for girls, jackets, and ties for boys. Upon arrival, we would enter through the stone portico on the right side of the hotel to the reception line. The lessons began there. We would be expected to introduce ourselves properly to the event hosts and hostesses. In greeting, the girls were required to take each host or hostess's hand, execute a proper curtsey, and a confident "How do you do." Boys were to speak up and offer a firm handshake.

Inside, the tables were set with pink tablecloths and small pastel floral arrangements. The required luncheon plates and multiple silver forks, knives, and spoons were all there for the meal. When we entered the room, there was a flurry of activity as we found our places. Feigning nonchalance, we searched the place cards with a calligraphic "Miss" or "Master" followed by our names, each card accompanied by a sense of doom as we realized we would likely be seated with strangers. Soon we learned it would be even worse than that. When we located our designated seats, we were placed next to a member of the opposite sex on either side. The expectation was to learn how to comport ourselves as the "misses" and "masters" our place cards told us we were.

A matron sporting a bouffant hairdo and a conspicuous corsage served as hostess and mistress of ceremonies. She introduced herself and presided with careful and studied etiquette, along with an iron-fisted knack for quelling the effects of burgeoning testosterone. Inevitably a few of the boys chose misbehavior over perfect compliance. At the merest hint of such insurrection, all it took was a dark look and a firm "tut-tut" to drive a troublesome young man back into his seat amid the silent expectation of the room, all heads turned in his direction.

"Ladies and gentlemen, when you are seated, you may put the napkin in your lap," she instructed. "Keep in mind that the outside fork is for salad only. The glass to the right is yours, as is the butter plate to your left. I trust you know that anyone may pick up a tea sandwich with their fingers, but French fries must always be dispatched with a knife and fork."

The meal progressed through the expected courses.

"Soup must always be consumed by skimming the spoon on the surface of the soup in a motion away from oneself. And please — no slurping noises!"

There were a few snickers.

She continued, "Your roll is to be broken into bite-sized portions with the fingers, one piece at a time, then buttered and popped into the mouth, *one piece at a time*. Do remember, bread is to be eaten only after the meat is served. And when cutting anything on one's plate, the fork must be placed in the left hand, tines downward, until the cutting is completed. Then it is customary to place one's knife on the rim of the plate and move the fork into your right hand to carry the morsel to your mouth. Don't forget: Olive pits and any other unwanted items are to be transferred discreetly into one's hand and gently placed on the rim of your plate. When you have finished eating, place both of your utensils together across your plate so your server knows you are finished. Used napkins are to be folded neatly and placed to the side."

The room was thick with a kind of malaise that only comes with the commingling of hormonal pre-teens of both sexes thrown together for an embarrassing purpose. I imagine there wasn't a soul there who wouldn't have made haste for the door, stripping off the shackles of their fancy clothing in favor of being just about anywhere else.

As we ate, there was little conversation. All the while, my only thought was, "How much longer?! How much longer?!" I kept my eyes on my plate as much as possible, straightening the hem of my dress under the table and generally doing whatever I might do that would go unnoticed to pass the time. Looking up, I noticed some of the boys sneering when our hostess's attention was turned elsewhere. It seemed to me the boys had even less interest in the lessons than I had, and their free-wheeling rudeness made me cringe. When the meal came to an end at last, we were asked to fold our napkins and assemble in the ballroom.

There, the boys and girls were segregated on opposite sides of a vast space, and the boys were told to cross the floor and graciously choose a partner. Girls were to accept this kind offer, no matter their personal feelings. It was a setup for unease in the extreme for most girls, and it could not have been any different for the boys. Inevitably, the best-looking boys chose the prettiest girls at once, causing a kind of frenzied traffic jam wherever those girls stood. Then, as those girls were taken, things progressed through the remaining choices down to the wallflowers and the less attractive boys until all were matched up.

As I was quite short and immature-looking, I knew I was not a prime choice. Embarrassed, I waited. I remember my horror as girl after girl was selected until finally, there were only a few boys left to make their choices. I spotted an unnaturally tall and gangly individual with an unpleasant face looking my way. He began to cross the large room in my direction, an Abraham Lincoln of a boy, his height far beyond his years and body weight. I averted my eyes, hoping with all my might that he wasn't coming for me. Ultimately, he made his way to my spot, and I was obliged to dance with the boy whose belt buckle was in closer proximity to my face than his head. I was mortified and felt sorry for him at the same time. He hadn't much choice himself but to choose me, and I had no alternative but to accept this excruciating form of humiliation.

Once we all had partners, the dance instruction began. Our social education wasn't complete without a rudimentary understanding of the cha-cha, rhumba, foxtrot, and waltz. Seemingly out of nowhere, the matron produced a suitable partner for herself, and we all stood at pre-dance attention, one hand holding our partner's aloft, the other either on our partner's shoulder or around their waist, heads turned and waiting for instruction. When dancing together, boys and girls were expected to keep a prescribed distance from each other's bodies, which at the time was a welcome relief, as it was awkward enough to be touching at all.

"One, two, three. One two three. Gentlemen, step to the right." We went through the motions looking like our partners were the source of some sort of unpleasantness, which was mitigated by the gulf of air between us. The enforced bodily distance was just fine with me. The only bright spot in the whole sorry transaction was imagining how someday, I might dance with someone more attractive to me and would know what to do by then. I have no doubt my poor partner felt the same way.

Eventually and mercifully, the occasion would be at an end, and the "young misses" and "masters" were released to the waiting cars outside. We dispersed, ushered back to nearby homes, our parents assured of our successful climb into the lofty social circles of Palm Beach's upper crust. These scenarios repeated themselves with varying but similar outcomes throughout the Cotillion season until its blessed end.

I can only suppose my parents, having come from more modest beginnings, thought this was some sort of opportunity for us because later on, my sisters were sent as well. By the time my mother received the fancy engraved invitation accepting me as a candidate for the debutante ball, she was over the moon. She said that they had only just begun to accept girls who were of Jewish descent. By then, I was almost 16 and I was certain it was a "club" I didn't want to join. I remember my mother's anger and disappointment when I refused.

Chapter 24
Junior High School

By 1967, I was 13 years old. My parents transferred me to Palm Beach Day School, not far up the street from my former school. I hadn't thrived in the other school, and no doubt, the move to this one was an attempt to make a positive change for me. It didn't work. I was miserable. I was a full year younger than most of my classmates — undersized and physically immature for my age — factors that combined with disastrous results.

Early on, at a school event, I recall my shame for having to stand in line amid the fourth and fifth-graders when the teachers arranged the entire school body in sequence according to height. Worse than that, I was half-Jewish and half-Italian-Catholic, which, in a place like Palm Beach, relegated me in the eyes of my predominantly blue-blooded peers to the status of something akin to a beast of the field. How they even knew my ethnicity was mysterious. I can only assume that their parents relayed this fact, telegraphing a level of distaste for "them," which played itself out on the playground.

It felt like torture. Each morning in the seventh grade, Marie, a girl who had the locker next to mine, bent down to my ear and, sneering, whispered, "Dirty Jew!" Every time she did it, I froze, lacking any experience with such behavior or the protective armor to insulate myself. Instead, I took my punishment silently, with no outward reaction. Inside, I was horrified but was helpless to think of a comeback, much less to deliver one. And so the misery continued every day for more than a year, well into the fall of eighth grade. We'd gotten the same lockers we had the previous year, and Marie showed no signs of stopping. Finally, the day came when she pushed me beyond my limit, and I broke. I didn't even know I had a limit until then. That morning, as usual, Marie bent down to me and smiling slyly, delivered the familiar phrase,

"Dirty Jew!"

Suddenly, an utterly unexpected flood of pain and fury overwhelmed me. Without thinking, I closed my fingers into a tiny fist and punched her as hard as I was able. In a split second, she had crumpled to the floor, the wind knocked out of her. I stood there frozen and terrified by what it was I had just done. I had no plan to do it. I certainly hadn't any idea I *could* do it. She was much bigger than I was, and I was afraid of her. I wasn't sure what would happen next; I waited in fear, not knowing what else to do. My only thought was that surely my actions would now make her even more hateful. But instead, she caught her breath, straightened up, and quietly pulled her books from her locker. She never spoke to me again. The following day at our lockers, not a word was spoken, but I knew what she was thinking, and that knowledge was enough to leave me still dreading our daily encounters.

Although my locker mate had been silenced, the misery of that school was not confined to her. As is so often the story for kids in middle school, the indignities were legion. Early in the seventh grade, I had also acquired the nickname of "Cheetah," a reference to Tarzan's famous chimpanzee friend. The name stuck, both because of my diminutive size and the fact that my mother would not allow me to shave my legs. The girls in my class would giggle knowingly to each other as they observed the dark hair on them, a trait from my Italian heritage. It was a characteristic that stood out in the sea of blue-blooded, fair-haired children, and I was mortified.

The nickname Cheetah was so painful to me that when I would find an occasional and unfortunate banana in my lunchbox, I would quietly sidle over to the nearest garbage can to slip it in as quickly and discreetly as I could. I was desperate to avoid having one seen by my tormentors. I didn't dare eat a banana in school ever — as much as I liked them — and I never spoke a word of it at home, ironically ensuring that a banana would continue to turn up in my lunchbox. I was simply too ashamed to say anything. Sadly, the name stuck so well that when my poor sisters enrolled there, they suffered the same indignities.

If it had only been these few experiences, my middle school misery would have been hard enough to bear, but it was magnified each day when it was time for phys ed, which was compulsory. Initially, on the day my parents took me to tour the school, there was a terrible field hockey accident. As we approached the playing field with our tour guide, an ambulance stood at the curb waiting to receive a girl with a bloody head injury.

"Get out of the way!" they yelled while she moaned and vomited as they passed us. It left an indelible impression on me. No one in our house had ever had much interest in sports, not even my father, and the activity seemed alien and pointless to me as it was. But after that day, field hockey in particular, and by association, all field sports, seemed dangerous, and I had no interest in them. Still, it was required, and I had to take part, no matter how reluctant I was.

It was a classic story: It never failed that I was the last one chosen for any team. The appointed captains would select their players, person by person, until they were divided into two groups, leaving only me. "OK... I'll take Helen," were the words pronounced with regret when finally, they had no choice. They had reason to be reluctant. I was good at ballet, but I was hopeless at sports. Because I was physically small, the opposing team would position one exceptionally sturdy girl across from me on the field. The player's nickname was Tarzan, a nickname she seemed to enjoy much more than I did mine. I can remember her barreling toward me from the opposing side. It was like facing down a freight train. I could think of nothing else but to sit down on the field and cover my head. The coach yelled from the sidelines, but I stayed where I was, terrified by the hurtling mass of muscle and bone coming my way. I knew that being more willing to get hurt wouldn't help my cause anyway — nothing would change my status with my classmates. And going back to the locker room afterward was no better.

A Florida law was passed back then requiring all students to shower after sports activities. In true "Carrie" style, like the Stephen King movie, these were opportunities for an ultimate humiliation. Many of the girls were already well-developed, and on some afternoons, a prank was afoot to reveal my poor flat chest for all to see. Wordlessly among them, an agreement would be made, and one girl would yank back the flimsy shower stall curtain, leaving me exposed and naked to the world. The girls watched in hushed and gleeful complicity, giggling under their hands while I flinched and grabbed my small school-issued towel in an attempt to cover myself up. It had already happened several times, perpetrated by one or another of the heartless girls until I got wise. It was bad enough that I had to change into my gym clothes beforehand. At least at those times, my childish "training bra" and underwear gave me some small protection, but I simply couldn't bear the thought of being caught totally naked again. Instead, I would go into the shower stall, close the curtain behind me and change out of my gym clothes as quickly as I could. I would wait with my feet up on the bench while I ran the water, quietly pretending to shower. After a time, I would shut the water off and exit the stall, straightening my clothes as I went. It wasn't a perfect strategy, but it was better than having none at all, and I made it my habit after sports every day to preserve whatever shred of dignity I had left.

At night, after my sisters went to sleep, I spent long hours pouring my heart out to Greg. I'd had a classmate try to put a contraband cigarette out on my arm at a birthday party. More than once, someone spat in my face for no apparent reason. I lived in daily fear of the inevitable school humiliations. In English class, Mr. Burns would ask me to read aloud. He called on me often, and I was the only one he ridiculed. When I stammered, which was often, Mr. Burns would shame me in front of the others, saying how stupid I was that I couldn't read the passages properly. He did this so regularly that at some point, Greg must have mentioned it to my mother. To her credit, Mom promptly went into the school to have it out with the headmaster. Much to my astonishment and relief, the teacher stopped calling on me in class, but the other assaults on my sense of self-esteem continued virtually unabated.

I was sure that there was something wrong with me. Other people had real problems, not me. I had everything anyone could want. My parents often told me how lucky I was. I knew I must be weak, and I was so ashamed. Without Greg, I could not have survived.

"You'll be OK, Helen. There is absolutely *nothing* wrong with you! You are smart and beautiful, and you are a kind and good person! They aren't worthy of you. Someday, those horrible kids will be gone, and you will have a wonderful life. They'll get theirs!"

How Greg arose early every morning after the countless nights' sleep I took from her, I will never know. Her steadfast reassurances that I wasn't a repulsive person helped somewhat. She blamed the kids with absolute authority, and I tried to listen. Still, the torture was unrelenting, and eventually, even I knew the only relief coming would be the day I could leave the school and those people for good.

I can't say for sure how much my mother and father knew of my trials at the school. I know that Greg reported at least some of it to them, but my parents seemed to be made of tougher stuff. It seemed our suffering was inconsequential to them compared to their own experiences growing up. The fact was, my parents saw me as an overly sensitive child. They told me that's what I was in so many ways. I had no right or reason to question it. They knew better than I did.

Chapter 25
The Escape

At this point, the difficulties at school only added to my general sense of free-floating anxiety. Headaches and panic attacks were frequent, often knocking me back and sending me home where things weren't much better. I had already missed half of sixth grade, and things didn't improve in seventh or eighth grade either. I didn't understand what my problem was, and everyone else was worried too. I'm sure Greg and my parents were disappointed when the same troubles followed me to my new school. The move had failed to improve things, and by the first half of eighth grade, I began to dread continuing into high school with that same group of kids. I just didn't fit in. My parents decided to consider the options.

The obvious choice was to leave me where I was at Palm Beach Day School. It went to the twelfth grade, and in some ways, it would be the simplest decision, but they knew I wasn't thriving there. Graham-Eckes, the other private school on the island, was the second choice, but it was an unknown. It seemed likely that enrollment at Graham-Eckes would throw me into the same snobby and mean-spirited mix. Lastly, there was Twin Lakes High, the local public school in West Palm Beach. Lately, a number of racial skirmishes had been reported there; in one case, a kid's throat had been slit, and no one felt this was a viable option.

One evening in the fall, there was a dinner table discussion about it. For the local families, nothing was quite as attractive as a legacy spot in a prestigious northern school where they had a connection. Generally speaking, those schools were for the well-to-do, and no one in our family ever had the money for such an extravagance. But now, this was a possibility for me, and my father knew of a few good ones. At Kent School, he even knew the headmaster, who was an old friend. As the pros and cons of various schools were considered, Greg suggested Dana Hall School in Wellesley, Massachusetts, a place she knew well. Years ago, she had lived in a neighboring town and hoped to send her own girls there when they were my age. Unfortunately, a sudden change in her financial situation had made it impossible, but Greg spoke of Dana Hall in glowing terms, and my father agreed to take a look.

In the end, Dana passed muster with my father, and my parents arranged for a whirlwind tour of three of the schools on the list. Traveling north with my parents, we visited each campus with some excitement. By the time we'd finished our tours of the first two schools, I was beginning to feel unsure about leaving home. But when we got to Dana Hall, I felt an immediate connection. The campus was beautiful, and I was totally impressed. Everyone we met there was warm and friendly, not just the admissions staff, but the students themselves. I could imagine how nice it would be to go to a school like that.

I knew the friendship at Kent was a draw for my father, and I hoped he wouldn't be disappointed, but that connection was his, not mine. My preference was Dana. When we returned home, my father sent in applications to all three schools. He felt it was important to have choices. Now the applications were out the door, and all we could do was wait and see if I would be accepted.

On the morning the envelope arrived from Dana Hall School, Greg was there. Years later, she told me how my father sat at the breakfast table with it unopened in his hand.

"I feel nauseous just looking at this," he said, locking eyes with hers. "What if it is a rejection?"

Greg was optimistic. "Go on. Open it. She's gotten in," she said to him.

Carefully, with his table knife, he slit the envelope open and read the letter. Greg had been right. He smiled at the news and congratulated Greg on her clairvoyance, but soon enough, a dark cloud crossed his face, and with a defeated tone, he commented, "I'm just not sure she is ready to go so far away from home. She's young, and she's been having so much trouble."

He spoke with Greg about what he knew of my fragile nature. After all, at the time, I was having panic attacks and headaches, and I was taking barbiturates at night to sleep. He shared with her his doubts for my success. After all, he reasoned, there had been multiple doctors and various medications with no success. How would I fare all alone so far away from all of them?

"Here is my problem, Helen," he said to me later that day. "I'm afraid you can't hack it away from home." I understood he had his reasons. We both knew what they were. "You've never been away from home before — not even to a sleep-away camp. I worry now if I send you, you'll want to quit and come home right away."

I hesitated. What could I say? I wanted a chance to try it,

but he was right. Going so far away was a scary prospect for me. How could I possibly know how things would go?

Then thoughtfully, he added, "I will make a deal with you. If you decide to do this, you will have to agree that you won't come home before Christmas. I want you to prove to me that you have given it a good try. If you can't agree to this, you can just continue in school where you are, or try Graham-Eckes. Either would be fine with me. To be clear, once you go, you must stick it out until you come home for Christmas break."

Naturally, the idea of going so far away from home was frightening for me. I knew that leaving Greg's protective sphere would be hard. I had only just turned 14. Still, it was Greg who had originally recommended the school, and I had gone there to see it myself. The school grounds were appealing, and everyone there seemed so nice. In the end, the connection to Greg and my own brief experience there was good enough. The calculus was simple. I was so unhappy in Palm Beach that I figured nothing could be much worse. I didn't hesitate for long.

"I'll do it," I said.

"Good for you!" he said, smiling broadly. And that was that. I'd made a commitment. Now there was no turning back.

That September, my parents flew with me to Massachusetts for orientation and to spend a few hours before returning home. The day passed for the three of us in a flurry of new faces and new things to be learned about the school and my new life there. There were mealtimes to know along with information about classes and study halls. There were also dorm rules to be learned, presented by a merry-go-round of people who greeted us and then added to my stack of schedules and guidebooks, all to help with my transition. The day went by at a dizzying pace when, suddenly, my housemother poked her head inside the room to announce that it was time for all parents to leave. I'd been so busy up until then that I'd had barely any time to ponder what was just about to happen.

I was only 14 and a half years old when I watched my mother and father walk away from me down the hallway and out the front door of my new home in Wellesley. I felt a hard and painful lump in my throat as I watched them leave, along with an unfamiliar and powerful feeling of loss. The feeling was transitory.

I turned around and went back into my room where the excitement for my new adventure returned. Now I could unpack my bags and get to know my roommate. For so long, I'd been reliant on phenobarbital to get to sleep. Nervously, I checked through my things to locate the large bottle and set it on my dresser well before bedtime. Judging by its contents, I reassured myself that I had enough to carry me through until Christmas vacation.

But then something happened. I could not have anticipated anything like it. That night, I settled in at my new school with my new and unfamiliar roommate, a thousand miles away from home. It was a curious thing, but suddenly, I felt sleepy. I thought I might not need the two tablespoons of medicine. My roommate turned off her lamp, and I followed.

And for the first time in years, I fell asleep on my own.

I couldn't fathom why, but I didn't need the phenobarbital anymore. Still, I kept the bottle with me for a few more years as a security blanket. I wasn't sure I wouldn't need it again, but I never did, ever. That night was a turning point that I couldn't have dreamed of, not in my wildest imaginings.

Once away at Dana Hall, I never had another panic attack. The change was stark and utterly surprising to me. I never again wept for no reason, and my migraines and stomach aches went away completely. The truth was, I was set free from the stress which had been my invisible and daily burden. I had not recognized the far-reaching effects it'd had on me. Now it all came to a sudden halt, and a fuller understanding began with a slow dawning. Could it be that all those troubles, both emotional and physical, had been the result of living at home? How was that possible?

While I lived with my parents, I had always known that Greg was my miracle. Now Dana Hall would be my second. All the stress and its fallout were gone, now replaced by a period of self-discovery and peaceful enjoyment. It was a healing time for me in countless ways. I began to learn that it was OK to be just the way I was. I saw myself for the first time as a person who wasn't ugly, needy, and oversensitive. The world opened up to me, and I was eager for it. I would always remember these first years away from home as some of the happiest of my life.

While I was away at Dana, my father wrote me letters. Aside from that first conversation about whether I would go or stay, they were the first interactions I'd had with him, separate from my mother and the family group. Suddenly, he was taking the time to ask me personally about what it was like at school. He seemed curious about me, and what I thought of the world I had just joined. It was the '60s, and there was so much going on. He asked my opinion concerning things I might have noticed in what he called the "wild-eyed newspapers." His letters opened a window into a new version of my father. Suddenly, he wanted to get to know me. The focused interest he showed felt new and unusual, and it was wonderful.

By the Christmas holidays, the whole world had changed. At dinner on my first night home, I chatted with everyone, telling them all about my Dana Hall adventures. I had already made some good friends and I even liked my new teachers. There was a lot to tell — about my dorm and my new roommate and the girls who lived with me. I told them about going with new friends into Boston and Cambridge on the train and how we spent time exploring Wellesley too. I had even seen snow, something I hadn't experienced since Mamaroneck. By the time I saw it again, it seemed entirely new to me. My life had changed and was filled with novelty. I was clearly enjoying every minute in my new situation. As I spoke, my father kept chuckling to himself, seemingly tickled by some private thought he was having.

When we were finally alone that evening, I asked Greg whether she had noticed how strangely he behaved during dinner.

"Yes, of course! You left a little girl, and now you have come home a young lady. He is delighted to see such a transformation."

It didn't make sense to me. I was still only 14, and I certainly didn't feel like any kind of lady.

"I only went away last September! What's so different?" I asked her, glad to be the source of a positive response but finding it hard to understand. Now it was Greg who was chuckling.

"Oh my dear, you have changed more than you know. I see

it. You've never come to the dinner table and chatted so openly. Everyone in this house has witnessed how happy you are, and it is wonderful, so wonderful to see. And your father? He could hardly contain himself! It's obvious this change has made him very, very happy."

Carolyn and Debbie seemed to notice something different too, as both of them lingered in my room while I unpacked that night. This was unusual for them, and suddenly it was me who noticed a change. I was a curiosity to them now, having been away for longer than I had ever been before. I had gone missing and lived to tell the tale. They seemed to be competing for my attention, telling me stories about life at home and at school to catch me up on the news.

"Debbie has a new cat," Carolyn offered, as I carried my things from the suitcase to an open drawer.

"Really? When did that happen?" I asked, looking at Debbie for answers.

"She's just an alley cat," Carolyn added, quick to respond, even as I looked to Debbie.

"You don't know anything, Carolyn! She's not an alley cat!" Debbie countered, then turning back to me, she said, "She's a Maine Coon cat, and somebody abandoned her, I think."

Then she added, "I named her Toto, like the dog in 'The Wizard of Oz.'"

"Nobody can touch her. Only Debbie. She only comes to Debbie," Carolyn piped in, quick to add as much inside information as she could.

Debbie's face glowed with a sense of pride. "Yeah. Nobody's

as patient as I am. She only trusts me," she added.

"Where is she? I want to see her," I said, scanning the room and the open doorway for any sign of Toto.

"Oh, she's outside somewhere right now. You'll get to see her tomorrow," Debbie answered. "She doesn't sleep here."

That evening, after the girls had gone to bed, Greg came back into my room to chat before bed. I would have preferred to sleep in her room, but suddenly it seemed babyish, and I just couldn't ask. Greg sat down beside me on my bed and placed her warm hand over my own.

"Oh, my, you're growing up so fast... and you really do like it there?" she asked, with an intonation of barely concealed pride and satisfaction. She knew how I felt.

"Yes. I *love* it there," I answered.

"Aaaahhhh," she sighed. "Hearing that does my heart good."

"Thank you, Greg. I am so lucky you knew about Dana," I told her.

"*Welcome home, Sweetheart.* We have all missed you," she answered, kissing me goodnight as she always had. It was good to be home and near her again.

As I lay in my old bed, the full force of my new situation came to me as it had on my first day at Dana Hall. I realized once more that I would never live at home again. Not really. I would visit everyone on vacations. There would be Thanksgiving, Christmas, Easter, even whole summers, but I was no longer the permanent resident I had been, and my life had changed forever. The hold they all had on me before had quietly diminished during the few months I had been away. I lay in my

bed and cast my eyes toward the bathroom. Even the secret door
no longer evoked the feelings it had once, not so long ago.

I had another life now, one filled with new people, activities, and challenges, and this was where my future began,
wherever it might take me. The truth of that thought washed
over me along with a curious sense of nostalgia and a distinct
pang of regret for my old life, even as I knew that moving away
was the best thing that could have happened. Before now, Greg
was my protection, and since I'd gone, I missed her and that
sense of safety. I knew I always would, but now I looked forward
to the coming choices that would shape my adult life. I knew this
was necessary for me, as well as for my happiness. To return
home was no longer an option. Greg was right. I was growing up.

Chapter 26
The Shift

Now that I was only home for vacations, my disconnection from most of the kids in Palm Beach felt complete. Despite all the time I had lived there, I had virtually no real friendships among my old schoolmates. How could I? Not only had I fallen short by their standards, but I had suffered mightily because of them. While in Palm Beach, I'd felt insignificant and insecure — even defective — for not fitting in, having little insight into the reasons why.

I suspect it was the values of the parents, and by extension, their kids that made things so hard for me. None of my new friends cared about money or connections to high society. They didn't care that my father was a Jew or my mother Italian Catholic, in fact, in my new situation, my background didn't seem to matter at all. Ironically, many of my new classmates had also come from wealthy families, but Dana Hall was a liberal northeastern school and the values of kindness and respect for others were fostered there. Now my own sense of self had shifted, and I possessed a new self-confidence. I felt sorry that my sisters were not having the same wonderful experience along with me, but there was nothing I could do about that. I was where I needed to be at long last.

During my first year away, Dad's health began to fail in earnest, and he decided to retire. He divested himself of his

interests in Funk & Wagnalls and sold the Kings Point house; he
didn't need to be in New York anymore. I was sorry to see the
house go, as I had such fond memories of our time there. Now
the family was in Florida full time and I needed a new strategy in
order to enjoy the time away from my northern friends.

By some natural stroke of luck, there was a group of boys
who started showing up regularly at the house. They may not
have been close friends, but I was grateful for their company. I
know they were thankful too, for a place to while away the hours.
None of the kids who came over were a part of the "in crowd" of
Palm Beach. They were Jewish, except for Wallace, whose more
patrician background was utterly unimportant to him. There
were a few girls I spent time with too, ones who weren't snobbish
like most of the ones I knew in Palm Beach. Thanks to those
vacation times, we rediscovered each other and began to get together when we were all free and searching for something to do.

While I visited one-on-one with the girls, the boys arrived
en masse to play billiards and hang out in the pool house, a two-
story building my parents had recently built off to one side of
the swimming pool. It was meant to be an entertainment space
for my parents, but more often we used it as our own meeting
place. My mother let me entertain and carry over snacks from
the main house when we gathered. The staff already kept the
bar area fully stocked with juices and sodas for anyone who was
thirsty.

When entering from the pool, we would cross a broad living room to the back corner where a cast-iron spiral staircase led
down to the bottom floor. The downstairs had the old New

York pool table, and an upright piano. The couches and chairs were arranged together with an intimate and clubby feel. At the back of the main room was another door with access to the sloping yard. If the boys couldn't find a ride, they would bike over on the lake trail and enter through one of the two back gates, coming up the yard to that door. The makeup of the group changed over those four years, depending on who was available. On any given day, the core group consisted of Marty, the son of my father's lawyer and business partner, along with Reed, Marty's friend, and everyone's friend, Wallace. Others joined in too, depending on who else was around with nothing to do.

We were the school vacation group. Some were enrolled at the local public high school in West Palm, while others were at Graham-Eckes. In my first year away, my mother monitored our get-togethers by checking in now and then, as Greg was often busy with my sisters. It was the beginning of a lovely few years of intermittent friendship, which doubtless was a boon to all of us. It was a time when we were too old to play with our younger siblings but not old enough yet to drive a car. Marty lived down the street and often walked up the hill with one of his friends. Wallace didn't have parents who would transport him, but he didn't live too far away either, so he would take his bike and show up whenever he could. There were other occasional visitors to the core group, like David and Paul, boys who came with Marty at first, but then they came over on their own.

No doubt, the pool and pool house with its billiards table were the main draw, but that was fine with me. It was so nice to finally have a group of friends coming over when I was home.

The fact that it was a group of boys only made it more fun. Lacking brothers of my own, Marty and his crowd were a novelty. When I lived in Palm Beach full time, I hadn't enjoyed any sort of regular company, much less the company of boys, so it was fantastic for my sisters and me when they visited. We would swim and horse around in the pool for an hour or two, then dry off and go into the pool house to chat, play pool, and use the stereo. Often, when we first entered the pool house, Wallace would seat himself at the piano and play for a while. All along, there would be plenty of friendly banter and teenage gossip, and soon the many billiards matches would begin. We blasted the Doors, the Stones and others endlessly on the stereo until it was time for everyone to go home.

Carolyn was too young to have much interest, but Debbie liked to sidle into the pool house when we were there, and stand by the pool table to watch the games.

"Hey, I bet you a dollar I can beat you," she'd say, in a nonchalant and innocent tone.

Even though Debbie was a few years younger, she was a budding pool shark and as competitive as ever. Looking at her, the boys thought she would deliver an easy dollar into their pockets.

"OK. You're on!" one of them would say, smirking at Debbie's boldness.

Debbie would quietly and efficiently knock all the balls into the pockets she called before the boys had time to absorb what had just happened. The first one would part with his dollar, only to have the next boy follow out of a sense of ego, sure it had been a fluke. Of course, they could beat her!

Some days, Debbie would return to the main house with two or three dollars, gleeful that she had bested them, and looking forward to her next payday. The boys were amazed that such a little girl could be so good at the game. Debbie never failed to show up if there was a new kid in the mix to wager that she could beat him too. Of course, everyone else would egg that boy on.

Pretty soon the boys were wise to her and refused to play for money anymore. Somewhat disappointed, Debbie would play anyway, just for bragging rights and the thrill of being the girl nobody could beat — and they usually couldn't. Despite her age and size, Debbie had a distinct advantage. She practiced tirelessly at our own pool table.

As time went on, Dad was getting more fragile, and Mom was more occupied with him than ever. Although I always enjoyed my time with Greg, as a budding teenager, the relatively rowdy band of boys fit the bill on vacations. It was a happy time for me, but in my general absence, nothing else had changed for my sisters and some things were about to get much worse. Carolyn confessed that when I came home to visit, things were actually better for her and Debbie.

"Mom is nicer to us in front of you," she said. I wasn't sure what to make of it at the time. She didn't strike me as much different. But things had changed considerably for me, and Carolyn and Debbie were getting older. It seemed odd that my mother had begun to put on a good face for me too. Before now, she had only done this for the benefit of her friends. Still, I had to take Carolyn's word for it, and it made me sorry to think that this was the case. I knew how changeable Mom could be, depending on who was watching.

We three girls began speculating among ourselves about how long Greg would be allowed to stay on with us. At the time, she was already in her late 70s and was visibly slowing down. We weren't sure how much longer she could stay on. Without her, we knew that things would get harder for all of us. She was a vital buffer in our household, and we dreaded the day she might leave. What we did know was that since Dad was home full time, Mom was not likely to let her go just yet, and we were right, but we could see that things were changing.

Now with Funk & Wagnalls and the Kings Point house gone, Dad seemed to lose focus and was slipping physically. There were subtle signs. His hands were shaking a little more while he ate his breakfast. He didn't complain, but we knew he felt less well. At least for the time being, he had stopped playing tennis and jai alai and we noticed there was less of a spring in his step. Still, he was a fighter, and he always seemed to make a comeback when he faltered. We never imagined anything else, even as the writing was on the wall.

Chapter 27
Trouble

On November 27, 1969, I was a sophomore at Dana Hall and home for the short Thanksgiving vacation. At the time, we were all sitting in the Florida room waiting for Grandma Speciale to arrive for dinner. From where we sat, we could see the formal dining room. The long table was a vision of perfection, carefully arranged earlier in the day for the holiday meal.

Before each chair was a setting with our good sterling flatware, cut crystal goblets of varying sizes, and my mother's newest and favorite acquisition, whimsical plates from Hungary, all hand-painted with little fruits and insects. One of our best cutwork tablecloths was spread out beneath them with matching napkins neatly folded at each place. My mother's favorites, yellow roses, were mixed with white Japanese mums and baby's breath in the long low vases that allowed a clear view from any seat at the table. The taller candelabra beside them effectively divided the table into three equal sections.

Grandma Speciale would be walking up the street from the house the grandmothers had shared for so many years. Grandma Morse had died last February, and this time, she would be arriving alone. Aunt Ida, my mother's sister, and her husband, Uncle Joe, had only recently moved to Florida from Yonkers. Dressed in their Sunday best, they were sitting together and enjoying cocktails when Grandma arrived.

"Mama! Mama!" Aunt Ida called out to her as she entered the room, hurriedly rising to kiss Grandma on the cheek. "How are you? You look so pretty today. Is that a new dress?

It wasn't. My grandmother answered Ida's usual fawning with one of her famously unenthusiastic shrugs. With a weary sigh, she plopped heavily into an armchair, her face still sweaty from her walk up the hill. Rummaging in her pocket for her crumpled wad of Kleenex, she mopped her brow, her face brightening as she noticed us. Stretching her arms in our direction for a kiss, we were happy to oblige. My parents wished her a Happy Thanksgiving and offered her a glass of wine. She settled in. Now sipping her drink, she was content to relax and listen.

Ignoring her mother's lukewarm reception, Ida continued where she'd left off, prattling on to my mother about the merits of one kind of fabric versus another for the curtains she had ordered for her new home. All the while, my mother scurried about, lending Ida half an ear while putting the finishing touches on the side table where she would place her traditional dish of lasagna; it was the one thing she always cooked herself on Thanksgiving. The turkey and the lion's share of the meal was still the cook's responsibility. We could see Roseanne already busy pouring ice water and sparkling wine into the various glasses at the dining table.

Finally, my mother set the hot casserole dishes of lasagna out on the side table. At the same time, Roseanne, in her dress uniform, hurried to light candles in each candelabra and flipped the switch for the chandelier. Coming to the edge of the Florida room to face us all and bowing slightly from the waist, she announced respectfully, "Mr. and Mrs. Morse, dinner is served."

Nodding again to all of us, she turned back into the kitchen to begin service. By then, the house was fragrant with the smells of the beautiful dinner to follow, and everyone was hungry. We arranged ourselves at the table, with our father seating himself at his usual spot at the head. Mom sat to his right side and me to his left. Ida placed herself, as she always did with Joe, on the other side of my mother, while Debbie and Carolyn sat near Grandma and Greg.

As soon as we were seated, Roseanne reappeared to place the individual salads, baskets of rolls, and gravy boat on the table and returned to the kitchen. She then brought out the massive silver tray with its mounds of sliced turkey, aromatic stuffing, and mashed potatoes. Stopping at each diner, Roseanne held the tray for us as we served ourselves. Next, she came out with the smaller tray with sweet potatoes and green beans almondine, while a gravy boat was passed from person to person. Those who also wanted lasagna went to the side table to scoop some of my mother's creation onto a smaller plate to bring back to the table.

Dinner proceeded as usual. Aunt Ida held court entirely for our mother's benefit, prattling away in her heavy Yonkers accent and between bites, regaling us kids with stories of their childhood. She liked to revisit many of their hardships and never failed to include the story of my mother's arrival into the family. Grandma brought home her new baby girl, acknowledging that she would be Ida's responsibility. It was Ida's favorite story for Mom. To us kids, it seemed she felt the need to jockey for position as the most important of Mom's sisters, cultivating the favor she already had. We knew the whole enterprise was unnecessary. Mom was already sold on that narrative and agreed with every detail. We kids had only recently begun to notice this little bit of theater, but it became almost comically predictable once we had.

"Mama was workin' so much back then, and when she brought you home and she tol' me, this baby is for you! Isn' that right, Mama?" she said, turning her focus briefly to her mother.

"Mmm-hmm," Grandma shrugged and continued with her meal, never looking up from her plate.

"I changed your diapers and dressed you and took you wit' me everywhere. Isn' that right, Mama?

Grandma shrugged again. She was busy eating.

"Oh, yeah. You weren't just my baby sister. You were my very own baby gurrrl," Ida purred adoringly, all the while watching Mom's face for signs of approval.

On this particular Thanksgiving, my father seemed a little subdued. He wasn't commanding the conversation as he ordinarily did. He appeared preoccupied, and there was a vague look of displeasure on his face. We kids had to question our own actions, wondering if we had done something to cause his mildly sour expression, and we were half-waiting for a sudden disclosure of what it was. The moments passed without any clues, so we turned our attention back to our plates. We always tried to serve ourselves a reasonable amount from Roseanne's tray, remembering the rebukes that would come if, in our enthusiasm, we took more than we could eat. On holidays, it was a challenge to keep from overserving ourselves, with so many of our favorite foods appearing all at once. Meanwhile, Aunt Ida continued to address my mother.

"You know, Claudia, Barry Rosetti died last month. You remember him? From Yonkers? Deli man? He and Joe used to play cards together... Right, Joe? Funny guy. What a shock! Carmen, his wife, was devastated. One minute he was there, and then boom! He was gone... Right Joe?"

Uncle Joe answered with his usual smarmy smile to all of us, leaning on his delivery of the critical word in response.

"Mmm-hmm. Gawwwn. Just like that."

With this, my father muttered under his breath, "I am the only figure of death at this table."

My mother, whose antennae were tuned in to my father's every waking moment, turned her head toward him with a questioning look. I heard it, too, and cast an eye toward my mother. Ida hadn't noticed and was continuing her story when my father rose from his seat and proceeded to excuse himself.

"I'm sorry, everyone, but I am feeling a little tired. I think I might go lie down for a bit."

Containing her alarm, my mother said, "I'll have your plate brought back to the kitchen for later. Can I get you anything just now?"

"No," he said wearily, and then hesitating, he said, "Maybe a ginger ale... Please go on without me. I'll see you all in a bit."

Then turning, he exited, heading for the master bedroom. My mother rang for Roseanne and asked for a ginger ale, and the soda appeared almost immediately. Still seated, my mother said, "Go bring this to your father," passing the glass across the table to me.

When I walked in, he was lying on his back on top of the covers, still fully clothed except for his shoes. His eyes were shut, but upon hearing me, he opened them briefly.

"Thank you, Helen," he said wearily and closed them again.

I stopped quietly at the landing to look back at him for a moment. Was he only tired, or could this be something worse? Was it possible that this was the beginning of another heart attack? I didn't know what they looked like, not really, even though he'd already had so many during my short life. I hadn't witnessed one from the onset. From what I could observe, he looked well enough. I wanted to speak to him, but I dared not disturb his rest with anything more, so I dutifully returned to the table.

When I got back, my mother asked me with some urgency, "How did he look? Is he resting?"

I answered as best I could and resumed my place at the table.

"I want you to go check in on him again in a little while. I'll let you know when."

"OK," I said, glad to be of some help.

The meal continued then, somewhat awkwardly, our constant awareness of the empty chair now a necessary part of the conversation.

"Is he all right?" Ida asked.

"We'll see," was my mother's answer. Ida shot her a meaningful look.

"I didn't notice anything before he got up from the table. I mean, maybe he was a little quiet, but nuttin' else. Right, Joe?" Ida offered.

"Mmm-hmm," Joe answered, smiling again, completely oblivious. "He's probably just *tiiired*," he said, and shrugged his shoulders.

I could see that my mother wasn't so sure. About 15 or 20 minutes passed when she asked me to take another peek at him.

"Don't wake him if he's sleeping," she warned. "Just have a look."

And so I went. I entered the room stealthily, tip-toeing down the hallway to the top of the two-step rise above the main bedroom floor, where I could take a look at my father unnoticed. He was still clothed and on top of the covers, but this time, he was shivering very slightly, with a peculiar expression on his face I had never seen before. How can I describe it? There was a slight smile on his face while he shook. It looked like defiance. It was as if he was in some sort of an internal battle that he was determined to win. The whole meaning of the situation was beginning to hit home for me when I reported back to my mother.

"His eyes were closed, but he was shaking," I said, "and *smiling.*"

With this, my mother hurriedly rose to call Dr. Levitan, a pediatrician who lived just down the road and had made regular visits to the house for us kids. He was the only doctor we knew who lived on the island, and he would be able to look at him and make some immediate assessment.

The rest is a blur. I can't remember if we ever went back to finish anything that remained on our plates. The beautiful table and all its splendor suddenly seemed hollow to me, a bland and empty exercise. None of it improved the situation. None of it mattered. It is likely the pumpkin pie, and my mother's favorite, a pumpkin cake she always got from a local bakery, would sit untouched that night. Our appetites were gone. I can't remember when it was that Grandma or Ida and Joe left. I don't even remember the arrival of Dr. Levitan or my father's subsequent removal to the hospital. The worry and its fallout superseded everything. It had indeed been a heart attack of some sort, and the doctor wanted him checked in for tests and observation. And so he went.

I can't say how I spent the rest of my vacation before returning to Dana Hall. It couldn't have been more than a couple of days before I was due back north to finish the semester. Of course, we always expected the crisis would pass, and he would come home. This time was no different. I don't recall thinking that there was any chance I would never see him again. He would pull through somehow, he always had. This heart attack didn't seem so bad; surely, the doctors could help him. And he was tough, the toughest person I knew. Going back to Dana wasn't hard. I knew I would be back home for Christmas, and all would be well.

The time passed quickly. I finished my papers, took my exams, and soon enough, I was packing my bags to fly home again. Dad was still in the hospital. As it turned out, the tests they gave him indicated the heart attack he'd had at Thanksgiving was concerning enough to keep him there a little longer, until Christmas, just as a precaution. I was on my way back home on Saturday the 19th, and the doctors saw no reason he would not be coming home the following Tuesday, just in time for Christmas eve. That was the plan anyway.

When I arrived home on Saturday, my mother had already managed to have the usual substantial holiday tree set up in the Florida room, a real treat in the tropics, where otherwise, such trees did not exist. The smell was intoxicating, and I can remember taking a deep and appreciative breath when I entered the room. As always, she had hung all the familiar German glass ornaments and a full complement of heavy leaden tinsel and candy canes. The gifts were already under the tree, except for the few which would be coming from Santa. We knew those would appear later on, just before we were to open all of the presents as we did every year, on Christmas Eve. Dad was never up in the mornings, and our parents likely felt it wasn't fair to make us wait until well past noon to open presents on Christmas day, so this was our family tradition.

Dad had indulged Mom around holiday celebrations from the very start. Mom wasn't much more religious than Daddy, but Easter and Christmas were important to her. We'd always had surprise deliveries from the Easter Bunny, and at Christmas, our mother liked to go all out. Jesus and Catholicism had no part in the proceedings. It was Santa and the Easter Bunny all the way.

Our father even went so far as to dress up in the red and white get-up every year, pretending to be the real thing. He was hardly a portly Santa Claus, prancing and "Ho Ho Ho" -ing all over the house, but my sisters would watch agog with excitement. For all we knew, this was the real Santa. The magic continued every year until the day he forgot to take off his slippers, and I recognized him. The fact that it turned out to be him wasn't a disappointment. For me, at least, it was proof that he cared, and that was enough to make the loss of Santa a pleasant surprise.

Now I was home, and I would finally see him in person again. Almost as soon as I'd settled in, I heard from my pool house crew. I also got an invitation for a date from another local boy on that Monday. I was flattered and excited about it, happy that my vacation would once again include visits from my old friends. And now, I even had a suitor.

My mother went to the hospital every day to see my father. On Sunday, she returned home to say he wanted me to visit him on Monday afternoon. He was asking for me! And there it was. The choice was slightly uncomfortable. Should I cancel with the boy and visit Daddy, or go on the date and see him when he got home? I asked my mother what I should do, and she said it didn't really matter. She hated hospitals and likely felt there was nothing pleasant in a visit there that wouldn't be much nicer at home.

"Go on your date," she said sympathetically, your father'll be home soon enough. It's only one more day anyway."

And so, I proceeded to go on that date, feeling slightly guilty, yes, but satisfied with the overall plan. It made sense. I would see my father tomorrow.

Chapter 28

Gone

It was Tuesday, December 23, 1969. We had all been through this before. My father was coming home from the hospital again. Mom had left a few hours earlier to go get him. Even though the doctors were releasing him, he would need more quiet and rest. When they walked in the door, Mom would usher him straight to bed. We would be allowed to visit him there. Maybe he would be able to get out of bed for a short time tomorrow to watch us open our presents.

He'd had 10 heart attacks in the 15 and a half years since I'd been born. The doctors had kept him in the hospital this time since Thanksgiving, just for good measure. We knew he would be spending almost all of his time in bed when he got home, at least for the weeks to come. The doctors would want him to stay there for a reasonable length of time. They always did, but we also knew he would only tolerate it for so long before we would find him up and doing things at his desk. Even this wouldn't last. Soon enough, and without his doctor's permission, he would be sneaking off to play tennis, coming home feeling invigorated, his shirts translucent with sweat from a challenging game in the tropical heat. He would walk in the door, throw his car keys down onto the telephone table and go directly into the pantry for his after-game bottle of Coca-Cola. Standing at the smaller refrigerator, a towel around his neck, he would pull out a frosty bottle, pop the cap off, and happily down half of the bottle before he came up for air.

"Ahhhhhhh. That's good!" he'd say, with his irresistible daddy grin. "What a workout. I must have lost five pounds!"

Once, with a showman's sense of drama, he set his Coke down and said, "Watch this," and on the spot peeled off his soaked polo shirt. Going to the sink, he wrung it hard over the tub. I was amazed to see the droplets fall from the tightened folds into the stainless tub beneath. I hadn't seen anyone sweat like that, and my wide-eyed reaction seemed to make him as happy as a little kid. For me, it was an impressive show of vigor. I'd never seen my father do much more than sit at his desk, putter in the garden, or drive his car into Manhattan.

As far as we knew, the happy days of tennis would be returning soon. At least, they always did. I remember dawdling around the house while I waited for Mom and Dad to arrive home. At some point, I found myself again admiring our splendid tree. The star at the top nearly touched the high ceiling where it stood, splashed by a flood of warm sunlight spilling through the vast floor-to-ceiling windows. Mom had done a beautiful job. It would be even prettier tonight when Dad would be home, and the little lights would be lit. All would be well. I smiled, knowing that when he saw it, he would approve, possibly appreciating too, that he had been able to come home just now, at our favorite family holiday, having dodged yet another bullet.

I had just recently begun to know him better through his letters to me at school. For the first time in my life, I was able to anticipate his interest. It was only since I'd left for Dana Hall that he was showing me his softer side more consistently, and the experience of this more loving aspect was all the more precious because it had come so late. Today, I knew he was looking forward to seeing me, and I felt the same way. Once he had settled in, we would no doubt chat about Dana Hall. I could imagine my joy seeing the pride in his eyes as I told him of my latest activities at the new school. His enthusiastic encouragement and advice on my minor struggles was an incredible balm for our relationship. I was thriving, and the old and difficult days were over between us. I was content.

And so I waited for them to come home. Time passed, and at some point, I must have gotten bored downstairs. I climbed the staircase to go and play records and noodle around in my room. I could hear Carolyn and Debbie in theirs as I passed it. Greg must have been in her own room, too, relaxing at the time. Settling in at my little stereo table, I kept the music low so that I could hear my parents when they came in. I had lost track of time when I finally heard the metallic scrape of a key turning the lock. I looked at my clock; they were extremely late. Silence. It was odd, because I hadn't heard the door shut behind them nor my mother calling up to us to announce their arrival. I rushed down the long hallway and out to the railing at the top of the stairs to listen. All was quiet. A bad feeling began to creep in. Something was wrong. I had a flash of fear for what was next but managed to squash the thought down long enough to leave my spot at the top of the stairs and make my descent.

From the front hallway, I rounded the corner within view of the living room. I was stunned that the room was littered with people. My first thought was, "How did they all get in so quietly and so fast?!" Standing in the doorway and quickly scanning the room, I saw that the Levys were there, Aunt Ida and Uncle Joe, my cousin Bobby and his wife, Grandma Speciale, and even Greg. There were also a few people I didn't recognize. No one was talking, and a strange silence filled the room. My mother was sitting alone in the center of our largest couch. Her mascara-smeared eyes turned toward me. Before she spoke, I knew.

I gasped audibly.

My mother held her arms out to me and said, her voice wavering, "Help me, Helen. He's gone! He's gone!"

I ran to where she sat and held her, my arms wrapped around her shoulders. She placed one hand on my forearm. I couldn't speak. I couldn't cry, either, the girl who cried too easily and too often. Now it was my mother who wept bitterly.

It was as if a small plane had passed overhead unseen that afternoon and dropped its payload somewhere over my father's hospital room in West Palm Beach. While I had been cluelessly fooling around in my room, he'd had three more heart attacks in rapid succession. Now the nuclear blast had traveled back to the house and left utter chaos and injury beyond repair. Nothing would ever be the same. My primary reference point was gone, and with it, my very sense of self. I felt vulnerable and ravaged, as though my skin had been peeled from me. I had only just begun to understand that he did love me after all, and he'd been snatched away, not just from me but from my sisters too. He was gone from all of us now, and it was over. My heart ached unbearably with regret and unrequited love.

Seeing the sorrow on her face, I felt sorry for my mother too. She had devoted herself exclusively to him. She barely knew us, and now, no doubt, she felt alone.

What happened after that is a blur. I was so immersed in the sea of my own roiling emotions that I barely observed my sisters' reactions. I know I felt an extra pang for Debbie, who began to cry pitifully when they told her the news. I felt only minor surprise when Carolyn, being only nine years old at the time, asked if she could be excused to go and play after a brief cry. Beyond these two details, I remember nothing else until dinner. I recall intentionally seating myself in my father's chair at the head of the table. No one told me to do it. I needed to feel closer to him; I also felt the need to signal to my mother that she was not entirely alone, that he was still partly there through me. She took no notice of this while Roseanne served us dinner in the long silence which was now our lot. No one was hungry.

That night, I lay in bed in Greg's room, listening in the darkness as Greg talked and wept alternately. It was a shock to see her so beside herself. Greg loved my father dearly, even more than I knew. She spoke at length about the times she'd had with him. I had observed they shared a sense of humor and companionable camaraderie for a long time, and I always assumed she cared about him. Her sorrow itself was not surprising to me, but the depth of it was. I just hadn't realized. In the moment of my most profound grief, it was comforting that Greg cared so much for this man who was now gone to both of us. I lay in bed that night, listening to her, asking questions, and adding details in agreement. I comforted her where I could. And when she seemed to have said all she had to say, during a moment of silence, I said to her,

"I can't cry, Greg. I want to cry, but I can't!"

"Don't worry about it, sweetheart. You will; believe me, you will," she said.

"What's wrong with me?" I asked, more urgently. "But why can't I cry now?"

"You will cry when it is time for you to cry. Now let's try to go to sleep. I love you, dear, so very much."

"I love you, too.'

"Good night."

"Night, Greg."

The following day, Christmas Eve, passed uneventfully. In our house, we opened gifts after Christmas Eve dinner. When we had finished our somber meal, my mother rose from the table and stated quietly but firmly that we should proceed. Dad would want us to open our presents, she said. Debbie and Carolyn were still young, and it was clear that the pretty boxes under the tree were beckoning. We were all grateful for any sort of distraction from the events of the last 24 hours.

Placing themselves beside the tree, my sisters began to open their gifts until none were left. While they sat surrounded by their newfound treasures, my mother retrieved a small flat box from under the tree and placed it into my hand. I protested at first, as I had no interest in opening any of my presents just then, but she insisted. Looking down at the tiny festive label, which read, "For Helen, From Santa." I took off the paper. Prying open the outer box revealed a flat cloth case which I recognized as a presentation case for jewelry. I opened the dove gray flap, and a chill went through me, swiftly followed by a flood of renewed and bitterest grief. Lying on the white satin interior was a replica of my favorite costume jewelry necklace, the one I had been wearing nonstop on my last visit home at Thanksgiving. It was a delicate necklace of gold chain with pearls, long enough to put on by simply passing it over my head. My father had noticed it only a few weeks earlier and had remarked to me, "You really like that necklace, don't you?"

That was all he had said about it. Now, on the satin before me was the very first gift I had ever received directly from him, a replica of the necklace but in real gold and pearls. I took a giant breath and now wept, awash in grief, clutching the case and its contents to my chest as if it were my father himself.

It was Christmas Day when we all dressed in the morning for the graveside service. The limousines pulled up, and we were off, winding our way through the streets of Palm Beach with a full police cortege, the governor of Florida out front, rolling across the northernmost drawbridge and northward again onto the mainland toward the cemetery itself. The governor had been to the house only a few times, having enlisted my father's backing at the last election. He was not an old friend, and it felt

wrong that he was there. We barely knew the man. I can remember feeling angry too, that he thought so much of himself
that he'd put his car in front of my father's hearse. Who did he
think he was anyway? His fake smile and cloying familiarity had
always bothered me.

The governor didn't belong at the funeral at all, much less
leading the whole group. But I had no choice. I remember looking out the window as we passed pretty homes and shops with
their festive decorations. The smiling Santas and happy reindeer
everywhere seemed ironic to the point of cruelty on a day so filled
with agony. For me, this holiday would never be the same. An
emotional charge would settle into every crevice of the Christ-
mases to come that I could never shake, no matter how I tried.

When we arrived at the cemetery, a large crowd was already
seated and my father's mahogany casket was waiting to be low-
ered into the ground. A podium with a microphone was set up,
and various speakers shared stories about my father and gave
their condolences to the family. No one would be sitting shiva
for him afterward. My father had been proud of being a Jew, but
he was an atheist. Still, among the speakers were a rabbi, a
Catholic priest, and even a Protestant minister. All three had
known him well and asked for a moment to speak. He would
not have objected to the prayers being said over him, but he
wouldn't have requested them either.

On this day at the cemetery, I was oblivious to it all. The
words at the gravesite were white noise. This moment was the
closest I would ever be to my father again, and all I could do was
concentrate on the chest he was in. My eyes never left it. I was

now in my own little world with one thought only: I wished
with all my might that I had X-ray vision to see him just one
more time. I wanted to rush up and throw open the top so I
could hold him. I wanted to be near him, really near him, and I
saw the blasted box as an impediment. Jews never had an open
casket, and this, I think, was the moment in which I understood
why some people did otherwise and had their loved ones on display at funerals. I wanted to see him. I wanted to be closer to
him. My heart was nearly exploding with the need.

Soon enough, the service was over, and people got up to
leave. Instead, I made my way to my father. I don't know how or
when I did it. No one seemed to notice, and I had no awareness
of any others when I stretched my arms across the expanse of
shiny varnish, warm now in the Florida sun. I lay my cheek
down and clung to my father with unspeakable longing and regret. I have a vague memory of a mournful stream of words spilling from my mouth, but I have no memory of what I said. The
pain was unbearable. I don't know how long I was there. For
that one last time, I was alone with my father, the man whose
love I had only just begun to know.

At some point, our kind family friend Mitchell, some
years older than I, came to where I was and gently tried to comfort me, saying it was time to go. I remember being blind with
sorrow and rage for being pulled away. I swore at him — I may
have even taken a swing to make him leave me alone. I didn't
want to abandon my father there in that lonely spot. Mitchell
seemed to understand my anguish and slowly managed to convince me that it was time. When I finally turned around, I saw

that everyone else was gone, except for the cars that waited for
us. Mitchell kissed me goodbye, and we left too.

Chapter 29
Firing Greg

The summer after Dad died, Carolyn and Debbie went with Mom and our neighbor, Mrs. Hewitt, on a three-week tour of Europe. It was a trip unlike any other, as Mom had never before included any of us in her travels. Being a teenager and out of state during the school year, I liked the idea of staying home in Palm Beach. I would have a little time to myself. Besides, it wasn't appealing to take a trip with my mother, especially with Mrs. Hewitt as her primary companion.

With only an elderly Greg to handle things, Mom had left Aunt Ida to assist in overseeing the household in her absence. This was a first, but we didn't think much about it at the time. We also didn't know about the hidden agenda for this plan.

Mom and the group were getting close to their expected return when I took a short trip of my own for a couple of nights. I don't recall where I went, probably to a friend's house. The following is Greg's account of what happened while I was away.

One morning, while everyone was gone and the house was quiet, Greg had just settled down to work on her needlepoint. She heard someone open the front door and called out from where she was sitting at the breakfast table.

"Ida, is that you? Out here in the Florida room!" Greg said casually, not suspecting anything.

Ida rounded the corner and stood in the broad doorway.

Without as much as a "Hello, how are you?" Ida said coldly, "I came to tell you your services are no longer needed."

Ida wasn't wasting time on niceties and held her ground where she stood, looking coldly at Greg, who remained seated, the tapestry needle still in her hand.

"What?" Greg wasn't sure she had heard it correctly.

"You can pack your bags and leave today."

"I beg your pardon? You're not my employer," Greg said, offended by the suggestion.

"I may not be your employer, but I am her sister, and she has authorized me to do what is best. Pack your bags, and we will ship the rest to you when you are settled.

Greg might have even guessed a day like this was coming. Since Dad died, she knew that Mom might have had some thoughts about the timing of her retirement. She knew it would happen someday, but not like this! It was beyond the pale. Greg knew that Ida had never liked her. She simply couldn't imagine my mother would ever tell Ida, of all people, to ask her to leave — and not like this, with everyone gone and with no notice. After all, Greg had been a part of our household for 16 years. Surely Ida wasn't serious. She felt blindsided.

Greg rose from her chair, "What about the children? Mayn't I stay long enough to say goodbye to them?"

Ida stood unmoved. "They don't wanna say goodbye to you," she said dryly.

Greg knew this was a lie. She knew we kids would be upset when we found out she had been fired. Greg also knew there was nothing she could do at the moment to talk her out of it. There was no use arguing. Instead, Greg climbed the stairs in tears and packed her things. She was 78 years old, and by then, she had been with us since I was a baby. When Greg was done packing, Ida called the taxi and the cabbie carried her bags past Ida's cold and watchful eyes to the car outside. There was no thank-you for her many years of service; none of us were there.

Within a few short hours of Ida's edict, Greg was on a plane bound for New York. She immediately went to her daughter Marjorie's in Forest Hills, where she could live with her and the rest of the family.

When my mother and sisters returned, Mom feigned ignorance and said that it was probably for the best. I was shocked and angry, but I had no choice but to accept the situation. She said what was done, was done, and we would be OK. We weren't so sure, even though I was 15, and Carolyn and Debbie were 10 and 12 by that time. We were no longer babies, and my mother probably felt she could handle things on her own.

We knew that Ida had been lobbying my mother to get rid of Greg for some time. Everyone else had heard her grousing, but she didn't do it in front of Greg. What none of us had expected was how effective Ida had been in convincing our mother that it was time for Greg to leave. For the many years to follow, we kids blamed Ida for Greg's ignominious send-off. How could it be Mom's fault? It was so unthinkable that we didn't consider it. Even Mom had more integrity than that.

As much as we might have liked to do it, we understood why we couldn't call Greg now and just ask her to come back. It was true that she was getting on in years and that she might be better off with her own family at that point. Still, we were upset. It wasn't Greg's retirement itself that bothered us, it was the cruel manner in which she was dismissed.

It took a good number of years before the truth of what had happened began to reveal itself. It came to each of us gradually, as we all, in our time, re-examined the events tucked away in our memory. It had been easy to blame Ida for events as they unfolded. We already knew her to be a conniver, someone who constantly said and did things to ingratiate herself and influence our mother. But as time passed, there was no denying it. Ida would never, *could never*, have made such a move without explicit permission from our mother. In hindsight, we could see our mother's frustration and jealousy toward her elderly and far too beloved employee as motive enough.

Ida had merely been the hatchet man and subsequent scapegoat, while the trip to Europe had been a perfect subterfuge to get it done as blamelessly as possible. Our mother likely knew what we would make of Ida's part in this, and at the same time, it would be painless for her personally. Did she feel even the tiniest bit of guilt for the heartache it caused Greg? Of course, she should have, but we will never know. It is clear that Ida was willing and able to take a bullet for Mom that day, and no doubt, Mom was grateful for it.

In the end, it was only Greg who never knew. It was simply too much to shoulder, and she couldn't bring herself to see it, believing instead, as we girls had in the beginning, that it was all Ida's doing. My mother would never, could never, have done such a thing. Greg had been such an important part of our lives for so long — and surely, there had been so much sincere affection between them that could not be shaken by anyone, not even a sister.

Over the years that followed, every time something came up to remind her of that day, the memory would bring Greg to tears. It happened often enough when I was with her on one of my many regular visits. We would be sitting together, laughing and fondly reminiscing, when something would jog her memory in that direction, and she would ask me what I had made of that day. How could Ida have been so mean-spirited? Surely Mom didn't know what Ida had planned! What could have precipitated such an action? She was mystified, and I had no intention of adding to her misery on the subject, so I played along, pretending to be mystified myself. The answers were all there for her to see, but it was just a bridge too far. It was unthinkable. And so it was, the sense of confusion would come and then recede again, never finding the obvious answers too painful to bear.

Back then, when I learned what had happened, there was some comfort in knowing how well-situated Greg would be in retirement, living with her family. She deserved a happy retirement. She may have been dismissed from our household in a cold and inexcusable manner, but I knew she would be received home with joyful love and appreciation. Greg had spent so many years away from her daughters except for that one week per year for as long as I had lived. Now she could have time with them.

Meanwhile, Ida continued her not too secret campaign to insinuate herself into the management of our home, but ultimately, her efforts failed. No doubt, she would have welcomed an invitation to become the new Greg and Guardian of the Household. Ida had mentioned an interest in this possibility more than once. Of course, she likely would have expected to be paid for it, too. We knew that she had been charging our mother for years for the small sewing jobs and favors she'd been doing here and there. At the time, we had reasoned that she might have needed the money, and no doubt she did. Mom had so much, and she paid her willingly. The exchange seemed benign, even if it seemed a little odd. We chalked it up as something she and Mom did as a mutual kindness, but it would have been galling for us to see her getting paid at Greg's expense.

The facts and tone of Greg's dismissal changed our view of Aunt Ida. Her ongoing solicitousness toward our mother became nearly unbearable to witness. Where before we only saw her adoration for Mom, now, a cruel and selfish aspect of her personality had been exposed. The blinders were off, and we never felt the same about her again. My sisters and I took to calling her "Ida the Spidah " behind her back. It would take a few more years for me to comprehend my mother's part in the ugly event.

Now the two key people in the house were gone. First, it was Dad, whose presence had a moderating effect on our mother, and now Greg, our rock and shield, had been let go. For us, these changes triggered a cascade of effects much bigger than any of us could have foreseen.

Chapter 30
The Fanatic Soul

Debbie's emotions were deep and all-consuming, and her opinions on just about any subject could be rigid to a fault. I knew how fanatical she could be.

She displayed an intensity, both in action and feeling that she brought to everything. Debbie could be excessively selfish and possessive at times. Often she was aggressively paranoid, a trait hardest for everyone to navigate. The overarching theme was that our parents had abandoned her in her earliest years. They hadn't loved her or provided her with the nurturing she had needed. The often harsh and cold treatment all three of us had suffered from our parents affected her state of mind, much more so than it did Carolyn or me. Debbie believed that people were basically insincere and fickle with predictably selfish motivations. For her, the world was uncaring and unreliable. She trusted few, not even me.

And now Dad and Greg were gone. With these losses, life got even bleaker for Debbie. Her view of the world was darkening. It seemed the chip Mom observed on her shoulder years earlier had grown to become a predominant part of her persona.

Originally, I thought of Debbie's moments of cruelty and generally bad form as something akin to my own malaise, but with an angry twist. Intuitively, I felt she might benefit from a change. Dana Hall School had done so much for me. I thought it might be wonderful for her too. I spoke to Debbie about it, and she seemed to like the idea. It didn't take much to convince Mom. She took Debbie for an admissions interview.

It didn't go well. By my mother's account, Debbie sat the entire time with her arms folded defensively across her chest. She was sullen and gave one-word answers to every question put to her by the cheery admissions officer. We all knew my sister could be shy and uncomfortable with strangers. We also knew she might appear withdrawn, but the admissions officer couldn't have known this, nor it was her job to care.

Debbie was not admitted. Until that moment, I hadn't imagined she wouldn't do well or that anything could possibly happen to make them say no. I was sorry to hear the news, not only for her sake, but for us as sisters. Where once I had been excited to think Dana Hall could be a positive change for her, now it had become just another disaster. I had hoped the shared experience would bring us closer together as sisters. Even if she would never admit it, I understood well what this latest failure meant to her, and I bitterly regretted ever having made the suggestion.

Back home, Mom enrolled Debbie at Graham-Eckes, the other private school in Palm Beach. At least it was a change of venue from the private school that had brought us so much suffering. But this rejection, like others on Debbie's growing list, merely served to reinforce the idea that the world was against her. It provided yet another reason for her to protect her vulnerabilities and remain ever-vigilant. To her, people were unkind and ungenerous, and she had to do battle on her own behalf.

To be honest, Debbie was most often the creator of her own

misery. As a teen, she began to demand that friends make her their one and only priority. It was easy to see that eventually, they would be forced to fib here and there about their activities if they wanted to have a life that included anyone else besides her. They had to juggle excuses, and it wasn't easy. They had their own lives and friends and family who also needed their attention, and of course, nobody could keep up with such high expectations.

The crimes were generally minor, but not in Debbie's mind. Tensions would arise if anyone said they were busy or unavailable when she called. From Debbie's perspective, she expected no more than any loyal friend would. If someone didn't drop everything to accommodate her, there was hell to pay, and they would never enjoy the status with her they once had. Any explanation for inattention was suspect, and as the list of infractions inevitably grew longer, things only got worse. It was an endless loop of ill effects. Under the yoke of Debbie's standards, friends were more likely to make excuses. Ironically, Deb hated fibbing even more. She might discover that they had told a white lie about their availability, resulting in total ex-communication. From that moment on, she never trusted them, and once out of favor they became objects of pointed suspicion and never-ending thoughts of revenge. Her anger was unrelenting.

"Wait until she wants something from me! Wait and see what she gets!'

I would try to reason with her.

"But think about it. Of course, she has other friends!" I'd say. "I bet she was afraid to tell you the truth because she felt guilty about saying no. She was afraid of hurting your feelings.

Maybe she even had it planned for a while and couldn't break the date!"

"It doesn't matter! That's not the point! There is no excuse for it. She *lied* to me! Headache? My *eye!*" she'd exclaim, "She went to a *movie* with *Sylvia!*"

She found the unavailability unbearable, but the lie was the frosting on the cake, giving legitimacy to her righteous indignation.

She resented what she saw as the theft and disruption of her time with her friends. Indeed, I knew not to linger when Debbie had people over. She was concerned that I might try to "steal" her friends and even accused me of it when all I'd ever done was say a pleasant "Hello" while passing through the room. All I can imagine is that her friend might have said something like, "She seems nice," and that's all it would have taken to set her off. I knew to keep moving.

Debbie's difficulties with friends and family were bad enough, but things were about to take an even darker turn. Now that Greg was gone, Mom had started taking Debbie and Carolyn to the movies. One time they went together to see "The Exorcist," a movie about demonic possession. I remember feeling a little horrified when I heard Mom had taken them. Carolyn was so young. I was still in college then, and I hadn't seen it myself because of all the press — and I was a horror film enthusiast! It's funny to think of it now. Horror films have come so far beyond those dated special effects, but back then, they were new, and the movie had a reputation for being the very definition of a real scare. Mom knew this and she didn't want to go by herself. It was

OK if her girls got scared too, just as long as she had company. The three of them trundled off to a local theater to see it. Sometime after, on one of my visits home, Debbie confessed that the movie had changed her life.

"Changed your life?! You're kidding, right?" I said, watching her face for a glimmer of the joke. Seeing none, I remember thinking, "Uh-oh."

"No," she said emphatically, with a severe expression.

"That stuff is real."

I could see she was in earnest, but I scoffed reflexively.

Insulted now, she responded, "It *is*, Helen. Just because you've had no experience with it doesn't mean it doesn't exist. You think it's a joke, but it's not! I *know* it exists."

"What exists? The devil? Actual satanic possession? Levitation and heads turning 360 degrees? Come on, Debbie! How can you say that? It was a scary movie — a *movie!*" I said, trying to get a foothold.

Tearful now, and her voice swelling with emotion, she said, "Sure, the movie's just a movie, but what it's showing you isn't! Haven't you heard or seen something that you couldn't explain? The paranormal is real, Helen!"

What I didn't know at that moment — what I couldn't have known — was that Debbie had been fostering such ideas for quite some time. Seeing "The Exorcist" didn't create this sense of conviction, it had merely given her ideas some legitimacy, and a reason to express her long-held beliefs. I didn't hear the following account until many years later, but it all makes sense in hindsight. It was Leila, Debbie's most trusted and lifelong friend, who told me a revealing story. She began by saying it was about the fancy marionette puppets we had.

I knew those puppets well. They were our most complicated toys because the strings tended to tangle badly. Pelham was a European toymaker, and the fancy wood and lacquer marionettes had come from the FAO Schwartz in Palm Beach, one by one, over the years. There were six of them: Peter Pan, Pinocchio, a witch with a broomstick, a poodle covered in white rabbit fur, and a Dutch boy and girl in traditional dress who wore little yellow wooden shoes. The characters didn't match any of the Disney versions we were familiar with. They were formal and slightly peculiar looking, with none of the usual cuteness of American toys. We played with them often, learning how to make them walk, dance, and interact with each other.

I honestly can't remember which ones were mine. Some of them must have been, but Debbie was so possessive of them that it seemed they all belonged to her. By the time I moved out and into the more grown-up room across the hall, they effectively *were* hers. I thought they were kind of weird-looking, but Debbie seemed to have a strange attachment to them, even into adulthood.

Leila began,

"*We were about seven or eight years old at the time. On that day, like many others, I was at your house to spend the afternoon. Greg was occupied elsewhere when Debbie leaned in to say something to me. Her voice sounded spooky.*"

"*I have something to tell you, but you have to swear you won't blab it to anyone else,*" *Debbie said.*

I paused.

"Swear it! Swear! I won't tell you unless you do!" she said ominously.

"I swear."

"You'd better not tell!" Debbie warned, eyeing me one more time as if she could tell whether or not my word was good." Eventually, she began again in a calm voice,

"So I was lying in bed going to sleep the other night when I noticed something." She paused and then went on. "I had a strange feeling that I was being watched. When I opened my eyes, there they all were – standing on their own at the end of my bed, looking at me!"

"Who was looking at you?"I asked her.

"The puppets!"Debbie said in a quavering voice, her eyes telegraphing the horror of the memory.

"But, Debbie, that's impossible!" I said, astonished. I was only a little girl myself, but I knew that this account could not be true.

"It was a dream. It must have been a dream!" I said almost plaintively, wishing Debbie was not telling me this story.

"No! It wasn't! It wasn't! I swear! You have to believe me! It was real! I was awake and I saw them!"

Leila told me she had argued a bit longer, confident it couldn't have happened, but Debbie persisted, and eventually, she quit arguing with her. She knew that Debbie wouldn't calm down until she relented and told Debbie she believed her. Leila was perplexed, but she knew she could never share Debbie's story with anyone. If she did, Debbie would never forgive her, and Leila's own strictly religious mother wouldn't let her play with Debbie ever again. For all these years, Leila never told anyone about it.

She understood Debbie had some wacky ideas, but overall, she seemed fine. This event was a one-off, and she never asked Debbie about it again. What Leila could not have foreseen was the development of Debbie's beliefs from that point into adulthood. They would only grow stronger as she matured.

Many years later, when Leila told me about the incident, it took on more significance. Is it possible Debbie made the story up out of whole cloth? Yes, I suppose it is. Debbie could have used the story as a means to draw Leila closer. Debbie needed to feel people were bound to her both by word and action. Promises and confidences were essential. The puppets and any other secrets they shared were important to their friendship.

Had Deb told me that story instead of Leila, I would have told her it was only a dream too. After all, this was the logical explanation. I also know Debbie's insistence that the story was true would have bothered me. I might even have thought there was something wrong with the both of us. There we were, imagining things and being frightened by our overly fertile imaginations around the same age. I'd already had so many nightmares and "experiences" with the secret door. If I was going to be honest, I didn't have a leg to stand on. She probably would have seen my stories as further proof that the supernatural was real. If not for her unshakeable belief that the puppets were standing at the end of her bed, I would have guessed that Debbie had the same girlish interest in ghost stories as anyone, including myself.

We were simply hurtling through our childhoods, each of us with our quirks and neuroses, no single one of them a clear indication of future successes or failures. It's too bad no grown-ups were there to counter Debbie's story, and Deb never told anyone about it aside from Leila.

Years later, when Leila shared the puppet story with me, the memory of my conversations with Debbie took on a hopeless aspect. With the puppets, she had accepted early on that the paranormal was frighteningly real. By the time Debbie told me about "The Exorcist," her belief in the paranormal was already deep-seated. I realized there was little I could have done then to dissuade her.

I was a non-believer. I felt it was simply a trick of the mind, something that occasionally happens, but nothing to support an entire belief system. I had experienced similarly inexplicable events, the moving hook on the secret door among them, but I knew my own neurotic imagination had created those.

For me, that first conversation about "The Exorcist" was a red flag, however insignificant it might have looked to anyone else. At the time, I hadn't heard the puppet story yet, but even so, I remember having a sinking feeling that Debbie was heading into dangerous territory. The exact nature of the danger wasn't clear to me, but I saw how her paranoia was driving people away. At the same time, she seemed to be adopting beliefs that made her terrified to be alone, and it had me worried.

Chapter 31
The Aftershock

Time was passing slowly in the molasses of our collective sorrow. I had made an early escape and continued to do well enough, but Mom, Debbie, and Carolyn each struggled to find a path forward. The death of our father was, in almost every way, the end of the life we knew. Nothing was the same, both the good and bad. With our father and Greg now gone, stability of any kind vanished completely.

While our father lived, Mom had been behaving herself, burying any questionable impulses beneath the altar of our father's good opinion — playing the idealized wife — ever-loyal, supportive, and subservient. Now that he was gone, the already-infrequent visits from his relatives dwindled even more. Mom had never bonded with them, and that lack of attachment now showed itself in full.

Louise was the only one left from my father's side who saw us occasionally, but she had been married and living in New York with two young children for some time. Since she'd had the kids, she simply couldn't visit as often. The others on Dad's side stopped coming altogether. While his family had almost completely receded, Mom's side came to the fore. When they visited, her preference and favorable judgments were sought after. Many of them were still dependent on the monetary support and ongoing small favors my father had provided over the years. She complained about it often, but we could see that she enjoyed this rise to power. Now she was in control of the family fortune, and she saw herself as nothing less than a benevolent empress on high. Mom held court among them, expecting to be treated with the deference she felt she now deserved, and she began to look down on all of them, something we had never seen before. We kids observed this change with surprise and dismay, and we missed our former family life.

It was obvious, too, that Mom didn't want anyone within the family to be close, except maybe, to her. Her insecurities and paranoia fed into divide-and-conquer strategies, and no one was immune. She routinely badmouthed each person to us and likely to everyone else, leaving all of us confused and unsure of ourselves.

Ida was a money-grubber and a conniver. Her daughter Joan was an ingrate and way too fast with the boys. Theresa and her husband Charlie were idiots. Josie was a certified nutcase, and her husband Joe was an impotent zero. She even referred to her own mother, Grandma Speciale, as an ignoramus from the old country. Almost no one received less harsh judgments.

Although Mom called everyone names, she expected all of us to be diffident and loyal to her. For Mom, fealty was everything, but it was a one-way proposition. She demanded it simply because it was her due, no exceptions. Mom continued to give small amounts of money to family members, but only if they asked for it properly with a generous serving of humble pie. She needed control and simply couldn't relax unless she had a chokehold on everyone, no matter what it took.

Remarkably, the years immediately following our father's death were quiet otherwise. The shock of Dad's death and Greg's departure were still fresh for all of us. There were no more changes to the household except that the boat was sold and its captain went with it. Things improved imperceptibly. Mom became the tiniest bit kinder to us. She seemed to realize that we were all she had now, but that didn't change her basic nature. She wasn't any more maternal. There were no hugs or declarations of affection, although she was taking us out to the movies and for dinners occasionally. We liked the feeling of being more important to her. Sometimes, when I was home, she took me with her to the dog track. It was her hobby now that she was all alone. I was old enough to be admitted, and she seemed to want my company. It was nice for both of us.

I don't know of any other mothers and daughters who bonded at the dog track, but we did — at least as much as we could. When we went there, she was more animated and carefree. When she won, which was often, she seemed genuinely happy. Mom was good at picking winners and seemed to enjoy teaching me the racing form. She even offered to place bets for me now and then. This was the first time I spent real time with my mother, and it was the most one-on-one fun we would ever have.

By then, I was coming home for the three months of summer and for the multiple vacation weeks at Easter, Thanksgiving, and Christmas. That meant I was away a lot, but I wasn't too worried about everyone because things seemed to be going smoothly. Debbie noticed it too. I can recall talking with her about the new Mom. We speculated that maybe our home life had changed for the better. Although she was busy tearing her way through the rest of the family, badmouthing, setting up rivalries, and demanding that everyone kiss her ring, she changed toward us. Of course, we had to toe the line. We were used to that, but, oddly, she seemed to appreciate us girls more. The thing was, we were also aware that it didn't feel normal, and we wondered if it would last.

Mom even began to confide in us a bit. She made a few comments that she felt old and unattractive. We knew that losing Dad had been hard on her, and we tried in our way to rally around her. We knew she missed having a man around. All her friends were married, which was awkward, and she was almost 50. Of course, we never dared to express our opinions concerning her status as a single woman. We felt she wouldn't welcome them anyway. Things were going along well enough, and we didn't want to rock that boat. But we assumed she would be happier if she found someone.

We were aware that she had begun going out at night once in a while, and we wished her well. We were getting accustomed to life as it was, but all the goodwill we had built did not serve to solidify the tenuous sense of comfort between us all. In hindsight, it was fleeting. Life as we knew it was about to change again. And this time, it would be much worse.

She met Travis in a bar on Singer Island. Her friends were alarmed and had warned her privately. "A bar?" they asked.

"Who can you meet in a bar?! You're 51 years old! What are you going to do with a 34-year-old Southerner with no education and no career?"

She was furious with her friends.

"It's easy for them to have their opinions, " she said indignantly. "They all have someone. They don't care about me! I'm the one who is all alone now, and I'm not gonna stay that way. To hell with them!"

Travis was tanning by the pool with a six-pack of beer by his side when Mom introduced him to my sisters, ages 12 and 15. When they approached, he was bare-chested and in red short shorts, his lean, tanned body stretched the length of a chaise on our patio. His brown hair was parted to one side, and a longer forelock flopped over one eye with youthful nonchalance. Gripping a beer in one hand, he held the other up to shield his eyes from the sun.

"Travis, these are my girls, Debbie and Carolyn."

He raised his head slightly from its rest as she introduced them.

"Hey," he said, his southern drawl immediately apparent.

Then dropping his head back down again, he closed his eyes. No chit-chat, no questions, not even a hint of feigned interest in the girlfriend's children to curry favor with their mother. I was away at Dana Hall then and heard about it from my sisters.

Mom and Travis were married within four months of that day, with enough time afterward for my mother's facelift before my graduation in June. When they arrived for my big day in Wellesley, he was a total stranger to me, and I hardly recognized her. It was in the early days of plastic surgery, and hers was so tight it hurt to look at her.

That summer, things began to happen. Travis stopped going to bars and traded his pickup truck for a hunter green Rolls Royce. Still, he drank all the time. I can remember sitting unseen out by the pool one evening and watching him in the Florida room go to the once-locked liquor cabinet to pull out a full fifth of whiskey. He unscrewed the cap and tipped the bottle to his lips, gulping continuously, only setting the bottle down after he had managed to drink over half of its contents. Then, with languid deliberation, he popped the top of a bottle of ginger ale and took one sip for a chaser before setting the smaller bottle down and stalking off.

Things quickly went out of control. I was there during several of his drunken rages when all of us, Mom included, would have to lock ourselves upstairs in my room while he tore the house apart downstairs, bellowing and smashing things. We could hear the sounds of breaking glass and the rumblings of furniture being overturned while my mother dialed for the police from my phone.

By the following September, I went off to Sarah Lawrence. I was excited to be starting my college career but worried about what might be happening back on the home front. I continued my old Dana Hall habit of calling home once a week. I was suspicious, but no one said anything. Mom usually picked up the phone and spoke with me for a minute or two before putting Carolyn and Debbie on for a brief hello. When I asked how everything was going, their answer was always, "Fine, just fine."

During Christmas and Easter, Travis stayed pretty much on his best behavior, and I began to think he was changing his ways. I was wrong.

By the following summer, any illusions I might have had were completely gone. Obviously, he wasn't going to stop drinking. I wondered how the three of them could stand all the scary theatrics and chaos he created. Mom was the only one among them that had a choice, and I couldn't understand why she tolerated it.

By the following fall, I was even more worried about them all. I had to return to college, but I knew that nothing was right — and no one would tell me anything. I already knew Travis was dangerous; I had seen the behaviors myself. A couple of months in, I called home as usual. This time, though, I got lucky, and Carolyn picked up the phone.

"Are you alone in the house right now?" I remember asking.

"Yes."

"How is everything?"

"Fine," she said simply, but I knew better.

I pressed harder, reminding her that I already knew that things couldn't possibly be fine. Here was her chance to tell me the truth.

"Please, Carolyn. Be honest with me," I said, pleading.

At last, she relented, and with every word, my spirits sank further. It was a horrible story, but I knew she was telling the truth. She proceeded to tell me how recently there were times after school she would find our mother bruised and bloody. Mom always made excuses: She tripped and fell. She bumped into something. Barely a teenager at this point, Carolyn knew it wasn't true.

It got worse.

Travis had been sneaking upstairs when Mom was out, pushing Carolyn against a wall and fondling her. The man was a monster.

It was my second year at Sarah Lawrence College and the end of the first semester, with a pileup of work and papers I still had to write. I had no choice. I dropped everything immediately and booked a flight to Florida to confront my mother and her new husband. As soon as I got to my hotel room, I called my mother.

"Hi," I said, "I'm in West Palm Beach at the Marriott. I have to talk to you."

"Oh God, you're pregnant!" she said in a panic, thinking the worst had happened. Why else would I show up?

"No, Mom, but we need to talk. *Alone.*"

Within an hour, she was at the hotel. We sat in my room as I confronted her. She was angry at Carolyn for telling me, but what seemed to bother her most was that I had found out about it at all. At the time, it wasn't clear whether she already knew what Travis had done to my sister. I don't recall asking her if she knew. Maybe I didn't want to know. I'm not even sure.

The idea that my mother might have known was so horrible I'm sure I found it impossible to consider it. I was relieved, at least, that she seemed incensed. She agreed with an angry resolve to go with me to the house and confront Travis, so we went.

The conversation took place in the den with Travis and my mother. He blamed Carolyn, as he sat back in his chair, smug and self-satisfied.

"She was teasin' me. She was wearing skimpy little thangs and flirtin' sexy like," he said in his thick drawl.

My mother was silent. She looked over at me.

My mind was racing. It was an outlandish lie, and we knew it. It was impossible to consider even for a moment that innocent, flat-chested Carolyn had seduced helpless Travis. Good God! She looked like a fourth-grader! She still played with dolls! The concept of Carolyn seeking the sexual attention of any man was ludicrous.

And anyway, why was I even listening to his side of the story? He admitted he did it! My heart was pounding. I was furious, and my mother remained silent. Why wasn't she speaking up? Why wasn't she defending Carolyn?! I was bewildered.

She waited. Finally, I broke the silence.

"THIS IS NOT OK! This is *horrible*. Mom! SAY SOME-THING!" I demanded.

"See what you have done, Travis? Helen has come all the way from college in New York because of you! Things are gonna change around here! They are going to change! I can tell you that!" Mom said.

It was a lame response. My heart sank. Why didn't Mom stand up for her youngest daughter? Why didn't she kick Travis out on the spot?

Afterward, I asked mom what she was going to do. She answered that she was sure he had learned his lesson.

"WHAAAAAT?" I thought, my mind reeling.

"It won't happen again," she said.

"And what about the reports I got of the bruises and cuts Carolyn saw on you?"

She shot Travis a look and then turned back to me.

In an angry tone, she said, "Now you can mind your own business. That's my affair. I'm fine, and he knows I won't tolerate it anymore."

"But," I said.

She interrupted. "He wouldn't dare!" she said as if any predictions she might offer for his behavior now would hold any water.

"That's the end of it, Helen. Don't aggravate me," she said now with a threatening look. "I'm a grown woman, and I don't need my teenage daughter looking over my shoulder."

I was angry too, but I knew I could only push her so far. I was only 19. I had no say, and I didn't know of any authority I could contact. As far as I knew, help was non-existent.

Before I left again, I took my sisters aside. Debbie now confirmed everything Carolyn was saying.

"He has a gun, you know. He showed it to us laughing like he might do something with it, the creep."

Debbie seemed unafraid, but I found her comments less than reassuring.

"Just stay away from him! And if you see the gun again, don't wait! Call the police."

I went on. "You've got to lock your door whenever you're

in your room. And if he lays even a finger on you or Mom again, don't stay silent, for God's sake! I want you to call me right away!"

Carolyn and Debbie agreed, and I returned to college full of trepidation, unsure I had done much good at all. Things couldn't be much worse, and I knew all I had really managed to do was to object loudly. I had to hope against all hope that Mom would do the right thing and leave Travis, but I could see that it was unlikely. I told myself at least my sisters knew I was watching. They knew I would come back. As it was, I returned to school in a tangle of fury and heartbreak.

The sorry truth was my sisters would have to cope somehow, making strategies to stay out of Travis' way. My mother was on her own. If it had been my choice, I would have kicked him out on the spot. Failing that, I wish I'd had the guts to take my sisters and move them out with me immediately. But back then, I had no idea of where to go or how I might support them, much less myself. My life so far had left me unprepared, without the confidence to take things into my own hands. Instead, it was my sisters who would have to do it, and eventually they did. It didn't take long.

Chapter 32
Runaway Brides

Tragically, Travis was allowed to remain in the house for a few more years. For the time being, the same horrible abuses Carolyn had described to me earlier continued. Everyone at home was in survival mode, and my mother had done little to protect herself or my sisters.

Debbie began to spend more and more time away from the house. Now she was 16, and she wanted to hang out with her friends. She also wanted to stay away from the difficulties at home and began going to nearby beach clubs any time she wasn't in school.

She set her sights on one particular lifeguard working at The Breakers. She would place herself carefully, sitting where he could not help but notice her, but far enough away that she didn't look desperate. Debbie liked strategy, and she had her target. Riley was a handsome young man, close to a decade her senior. He was tall, with a blond mustache, wavy blond hair to his shoulders, and a youthfully lean but muscular build. His bright blue eyes, dashing appearance, and blasé demeanor were a kind of catnip for Debbie. She wanted to be at the beach club anyway, but Riley made it irresistible.

While all this was going on, our mother asked no questions. She had other things on her mind and didn't seem to care. She was probably glad to have Debbie out of her hair.

After essentially two years of flirting by the pool, Debbie married Riley. He had no money and no detectable ambition, but Debbie was 18 now and had some limited access to her inheritance. Mom was in control, but she and Riley would manage. More than anything, it was an escape for her, and probably for him, too. Mom threw them an over-the-top wedding at The Breakers Hotel.

In the end, we all wished the newlyweds well, but privately most of us shook our heads. We were surprised when Mom helped with the funding for a small house in West Palm Beach. She wasn't really any more enthused than we were. Riley was an enigma. He seemed unknowable. Just as Debbie's possessiveness prevented us from befriending her cat Toto, she had kept Riley all to herself. On the rare occasions when we did see him, he was largely silent, all the while wearing a mysterious Cheshire cat smile, his blue eyes and straight white teeth nearly glowing against his tropical tan.

He pointedly kept his thoughts to himself and made no effort toward real conversation of any kind. He simply sat silently beside Debbie like an ornament, his lean arm slung casually across the couch cushion behind her shoulders. In lieu of small talk, he favored a knowing look and a choice word now and then. From what we could see, there were no real exchanges of affection or closeness of any kind between them. They were a good-looking couple, and that was all. It looked like an impending train wreck. We worried, but we knew when Debbie made up her mind, no one held any sway over her — least of all me.

The best I could do was to pray that she had made the right

choice for herself, but she hadn't. A couple of years passed, and Debbie's marriage to Riley failed. For a multitude of reasons, they were not a good match and parted ways.

Even before Debbie left for The Breakers on her big day, Carolyn was also thinking about how to make her escape. At age 15, months ahead of the wedding, Carolyn had begun to run away from home. She would simply grab the car keys and take off for whatever destination she could find. At least once, on her way out, she had the nerve to take all the money from Mom's purse. She went all the way to Massachusetts once, but she drove to Louisville, Kentucky, most of the time because she had friends there. Another time, she went on a trip to New Jersey with a boyfriend and came home pregnant. My mother sent her with a family friend to get the abortion, but nothing seemed to slow Carolyn down. Misbehavior and running away became a habit. To Carolyn, it was simple. She wanted out, and she was only getting bolder.

Whatever punishment Carolyn got later, it didn't matter to her. Apparently, it was worth the break from Mom and Travis. She would do it again and again. Mom would notice that both Carolyn and the car were gone, and she would call the police. An APB would go out, and the police would find her, if not on the road, then at her destination. When she was spotted, they would surround her car, and all 4 feet, 10 inches of her would emerge from the driver's seat, announcing to the officers her intentions.

"If you take me home now, I'm just going to do it again."

And so she did, until one day, Mom called me in utter frustration.

"God, Helen. I don't know what I'm going to do! I can't handle her anymore." She was in tears. "Maybe a reform school can handle her. I don't know."

"I always thought she would be my walking stick when I got older! How wrong I was! She's impossible — I am at my wits' end!"

This idea of a walking stick surprised and fascinated me. Why would my mother assume she could lean on us when she had so surely neglected us all along? To my surprise, I felt some pity for Mom. It was a tipping point for me. The blinders lifted, and I saw that she was totally clueless. Forget her daughters' problems; she couldn't handle her own. And I understood why Carolyn was determined to get away from such an impossible home life.

Suddenly, the answer was obvious. Why hadn't I thought of it before?! I could take Carolyn! Two years earlier, I had transferred from Sarah Lawrence to Kirkland College, but I had graduated recently. Now I was working at the Eastman House Museum in Rochester, New York. My life was stable, and it would all work out. She could come to me! I could find a larger apartment, and she could live with me and finish high school in Rochester. I felt it would be some improvement, and she would be with someone who loved her. I wanted to help. And that's what I did. At least I tried.

We moved into a roomier place near the museum and I enrolled her in the local high school. Every morning, I'd hand her the lunch I'd prepared along with her backpack and wave goodbye. Then I'd go back inside to get ready for my day. She seemed to be doing fine, and I thought I was doing a great job.

Sometime in the fall, I got a notice from the high school inviting me to Parents Day. I decided to go. It would be nice to meet her teachers, and I wanted to show my support. I didn't mention the plan to Carolyn because I wanted to surprise her. I figured she hadn't told me about it because it felt a little odd to ask her sister to come to an event that was for parents only.

That morning, I got up, fixed my hair, dressed in my nicest conservative skirt and blouse, and headed off to the school down Monroe Avenue, not far from home. I was only inside the building a minute or two before a stranger approached me and asked if I was Carolyn Morse's sister. The principal wanted to see me — but why? When I entered his office, he motioned for me to sit in one of the two chairs before his desk. His face was stony, and I began to worry. What's gone wrong? My mind was searching for an answer. Once we were settled, he wasted no time.

"I'm sorry, Ms. Morse, but we have only seen your sister Carolyn a handful of days in the last few months. I'm afraid we cannot sustain her enrollment here at Monroe High School."

What? I wondered how this was even possible. She was misbehaving again.

I asked for details. Then I begged. I wept. I pleaded, but he was unmoved.

"Please, please, give her another chance! She has been through so much. She has only just gotten here, and I know I can convince her to do better!"

We talked for a while, but the principal wouldn't budge.

"I'm sorry, but that's it."

Devastated, with anger rising in my throat, I went home and waited for her. I had tried so hard. I had moved to this larger apartment for her sake. Mom never made her lunch or stood to wave her off to school, but I did. I had bought her a bedroom set and all of the winter clothes and school supplies she needed. Mom hadn't helped at all; I paid for everything on my own. I had hoped Mom would offer, but she never did, and I was too embarrassed to ask. By then I had a modest income myself from a trust that had been set up for me after Dad died. Carolyn was still young and hadn't gotten hers yet, so I used mine. I didn't mind. The thing that bothered me more than anything was that I'd had such hopes for us as sisters. Now it seemed all for naught.

Around four o'clock, Carolyn came through the door and set down her backpack and empty lunchbox. I was already seated on the couch, where I had been waiting for some time.

"How was school today?" I asked, barely able to contain myself.

"Fine," she replied casually, having no idea what I already knew.

I was beside myself and revealed where I'd been that day and the reasons why. I told Carolyn what the principal had said. I was hurt and angry and demanded an explanation. I was shocked a second time when she told me she already had a plan — and it didn't include school, or even me.

"I don't care," she said. Her face was impassive, while I wept anew.

"I have a job at the Xerox store. I'm moving into an apartment with friends from work."

She delivered the news with a sense of resolve which was new to me. Carolyn had always been so compliant and easy-going, at least when she'd been younger. Now she was running away from me too. She was defiant and made it clear that there was nothing I could do about it. I tried to reason with her, but she would have none of it — she had made up her mind.

I hadn't known it, but she had been working at the copy store since September and saved enough to achieve her goal with no help from me. I was heartbroken. I had failed. Despite my objections, it wasn't long before she moved into the other apartment to embark on a life of her own.

It was there, in Rochester, where she met her first husband, Daniel. He proposed early, but they didn't get married right away. Instead, they went back and forth between Florida and Rochester like gypsies for a couple of years until they finally wed in Rochester. The event was modest and much more personal than the one Mom threw for Debbie. Carolyn had no interest in a fancy wedding that would involve dealing with our mother's controlling personality. Although the wedding itself took place in New York, they returned to Florida one more time before they decided once and for all that they didn't want to live in either state. It was a spur-of-the-moment kind of move, like the rest of them, and perfectly in keeping with Carolyn's impulsive nature and love of adventure. She told me how they had taken out a map of the United States. Carolyn closed her eyes, and blindly set her finger down. It landed on Murphy, North Carolina, and with the selection made, they moved there to settle down.

After our time together in Rochester, I seldom saw Carolyn in person again. Now, she had left us all behind. Years were passing, but the distance between us only grew. She did manage a visit to me with her firstborn in Massachusetts once. I also saw her once or twice at Mom's in Florida. There was no acrimony between us, but our lives had taken very different paths and Carolyn receded into the background again, just as she had in childhood. The phone became our primary mode of contact. I had difficulties of my own by then, and sadly, the demands and vicissitudes of our separate lives and the geographical distance only served to preserve the gulf between us.

Back in North Carolina, Murphy turned out to be a small and sleepy rural town, with no entertainment at the time, except the Henn, a small movie theater with a chicken silhouette on its marquee. Most of the town's social activities took place in its many churches.

Once they settled into their new home, Carolyn and Daniel started having babies. Along the way, they also began to buy up a number of dilapidated buildings in downtown Murphy. Real estate was already cheap, and they acquired them at fire-sale prices. Although we got word about the births of each of their three children, none of us knew what else they were doing at the time. All we heard was that the kids were healthy, Daniel was doing carpentry, and the marriage was going well.

In addition to the buildings in downtown Murphy, the pair took Carolyn's inheritance and bought a piece of land. There, they spared no expense in building a roller skating rink. There were helicopter lights, black lights, and mirror balls hanging from the ceiling, and at the sides, there were lights that flashed on and off with the music. The floor had hand-painted fluorescent graphics under translucent epoxy which glowed under the black lights when they were on. The facility was the state of the art as skating rinks go, and Murphy had never seen anything like it. While Dan managed the business, Carolyn ran the snack bar, making sandwiches and serving drinks. The new business was a resounding success.

After a good number of years, when we had finally decided that Carolyn was doing well, she announced that her marriage to Daniel was over. There was financial wrangling between them, but mercifully the divorce concluded quickly. She had done significant damage to her nest egg in the process, but at the time it seemed inevitable with buildings downtown that were hard to sell and all the money spent erecting the fancy skating rink.

Less than a year after her divorce, Carolyn told us that she had met someone named Toby and married him. I wasn't anywhere near North Carolina, none of us were, and the news came as a big surprise. No one had met him. All we knew was that Carolyn was in love and that this new guy named Toby had spent time in prison. It didn't look good.

She had been living a separate life from the rest of us for a long time, and I felt sorry I'd never been to see her where she lived. She hadn't been to our family hub at Mom's for a while either. When I had the chance, I drove up from Florida to spend some time with her. It would be my only visit to the state since she'd chosen Murphy for her hometown.

It was OK when she didn't invite me to stay with her at the

house. The distance between us had grown sufficiently large that I felt I had no right to feel hurt. She told me that with three kids, her life was too chaotic for overnight visitors. All right, I thought, maybe it was better to stay in a motel anyway; I would have more privacy. When I arrived in town, I called her.

It was then she said she had only one hour to spare. I wouldn't even see Toby. He wasn't going to be there. I wouldn't see the kids either. I had just driven 11 hours up from Florida specifically to spend time with them all, but OK. I didn't allow myself the luxury of feeling insulted. It stung, of course, but there was nothing I could do but roll with it. Things were what they were. I drove over, willing to settle for whatever time I might get with my sister. When I pulled up, a battered race car — one of Toby's — stood on blocks in the tall weeds out front. The house looked almost as tired as the car. The scene looked like something out of the movie "Deliverance." My heart sank.

I knocked on the door. Carolyn answered, and invited me in for a tour. In the first room, the family pool table, our father's pride and joy, stood grievously damaged. The force it must have taken to splinter its quarter-sawn oak undercarriage was a testament to the level of abuse the table had suffered. In the living room, our father's antique ivory collection stood on shelves along with heavy country-style decor and general household mess. The elegant pieces seemed out of place in the chaos of this house. Upstairs, one room was filled wall to wall with NASCAR memorabilia. Carolyn showed me the kids' rooms too, but didn't offer to show me her bedroom. That door was closed, with various padlocks and deadbolts in a curious cluster.

She hurried me away from it, saying they just didn't want the kids snooping around in there.

I had to wonder why, but at the time I didn't feel comfortable asking. It was unsettling. Toby's past, the general state of the house, the locks on the bedroom door — all were red flags. They were signs of something, but what? Things just didn't feel right, and suddenly I was worried about Carolyn again.

What came next could have been predicted, but back then, it was just puzzling and sad. Of course, many difficulties were yet to come for all of us.

Chapter 33
A Conversation with Mom

I was in my late 30s when my mother was diagnosed with a brain aneurysm. She was having more than her usual number of headaches, and her doctors in Florida had ordered a CT scan to figure out why. The answer was definitive. She had a balloon-shaped mass at the center of her brain.

Mom's long-gone brother died as a toddler from the same problem. There had been no reason until now to think she or her sisters might have had the same condition. None of them experienced headaches in clusters, and none had been seriously ill. Her doctors couldn't tell how long the mass had been there, but her headaches were worrisome. They told her she needed surgery. They were sure if she did nothing, it would kill her.

Reluctant to go under the knife, Mom delayed and delayed, saying that she felt fine. Sure, the headaches weren't fun, but she could tolerate them. After all, she reasoned, maybe she'd always had it. The doctors had admitted as much. A year or two passed, and Mom did nothing.

At some point, the headaches got much worse. The doctors were alarmed and scheduled her for emergency surgery. Days beforehand, Mom sent me a box containing some of my father's effects. It probably wasn't coincidental. The doctors told her the surgery was risky, and there was a chance she might not survive it. I'm sure she was thinking of this when she mailed the box.

She wanted me to have those things, just in case.

At the time, I was divorced and living in Watertown, Massachusetts, with my young son. I remember opening the package when it arrived. Nestled between sheets of tissue, I found my father's baby gown. There were also a pair of gray spats and a black beaver hat, both things he must have worn before I knew him. Along with these were various photographs, papers, and a large pile of letters. In the days preceding her surgery, I began to read the contents of each envelope. Every one of them was addressed to Dad with a similar closing. The purpose of the letters ranged from business to personal, but they all had one thing in common; they showed his life since 1954 had been a series of debilitating heart attacks and lengthy recoveries. The messages stood out to me as a sad chronicle of his ever-worsening health, but it was touching to see the expressions of affection and encouragement they contained.

As I read on, I suddenly understood the precarious situation my parents had endured. They were two people who always seemed hard, harsh, and utterly impervious. Now, as I was approaching middle age myself, I was finally able to understand the situation for what it was. My mother must have been beside herself with worry much of the time. They had married in 1953, and only a year later, the long and agonizing series of heart attacks had begun. By 1969, her husband, our father, was gone.

I hadn't finished reading the letters when my mother and I finally spoke. I'm sure the reason for the call was understood between us, even though not a word of it was spoken. We both knew there was a small chance this would be our last conversation, even though the doctors were optimistic. I wasn't able to be in Florida just then, and I wanted to touch base.

I called on the eve of her surgery to wish her good luck. I told her I would be thinking of her and thanked her for sending the box. We spoke for a while about the odd mix of items, settling finally on his collection of letters.

"You know, the thing that struck me the most was how often people spoke of Daddy's failing health," I said, sharing with her my deeper understanding of the difficulties she'd endured with my father.

"Yes. Everyone was worried about him. They all loved your father," she responded wistfully. "It kept me busy. There wasn't much time for anything else."

And then I did it. I blurted out the words before I could stop them. I hadn't even known they were coming.

"Yeah. You were never there for me."

There was a silence. "*Hoo*, boy," I thought. I knew I had crossed the line this time, and I held my breath.

"I know," she responded matter-of-factly.

Her words hit me hard. I didn't say anything, but the thoughts came flooding in.

Whaaaaat?! She knows? She *knows*?! All these years, and she knew it all along?! I searched everything I understood of my mother for the explanation. My mind was racing. The fact was, I could have imagined just about any response but this one.

The moment "You weren't there for me" had passed my lips, I imagined all kinds of potential responses: disgust, anger, ridicule or indifference, any of them, and in any combination —

and I braced for it. When instead she confessed she knew, I was utterly unprepared.

"What do you mean?" I asked as casually and calmly as I could, aware that I was in dangerous waters.

"Well, I had a lot to deal with, you know. He was always sick."

"I understand," I said, the tendrils of a newfound sense of empathy rising as my defenses fell.

"It wasn't easy for you," I said, surrendering to the sensation. "I don't think I got it until I read all of those letters."

The bulk of them had one common thread. They ended with the same message year after year., "Don't leave us yet, Joe." "We're worried." "Sending prayers that your recovery goes well." "Hope you are out of the woods soon."

"I never thought of what it must have been like for you, always thinking he might die at any moment."

"Yes. It was hard," she answered. And then she paused and said the unthinkable.

"I am sorry, Helen," she said. "I'm sorry for whatever it was I did to screw you up. I don't know why I am this way, but I am."

The whole world shifted imperceptibly at that moment, and with those few words between us, a sense of peacefulness settled into my heart. It didn't change what had happened but it served as balm and bandage for the sensitive little girl who had always blamed herself for her own neediness. It didn't matter that she couldn't understand everything. It didn't matter if she never repeated it again. She said she knew and that she was sorry.

It would have been fantastic if the conversation had stopped there, but it didn't. Now comfortable about expressing my concern for my mother and about the next day's procedure, I asked stupidly, "So, how are you feeling about the surgery?"

My mistake.

She responded angrily.

"What do you think?! I'm nervous! Wouldn't you be nervous? Goddammit, Helen, what a ridiculous question! They're going to open my skull up and play around with my brains! That's how I'm feeling! I can't talk to you anymore. I'm gonna go now."

I had wanted her to know that if she was worried, she could talk to me. I only wished to open up a dialogue. Lulled into feelings of closeness and well-being after that last big revelation, I had made the mistake of letting my guard down. Now, instead, the spell was broken.

"I'm sorry, Mom. I thought you might want to talk about it. I wasn't trying to upset you. Really."

"All right. I'm gonna go now."

"I love you, Mom. I'll be thinking of you tomorrow."

"Yeah, yeah. I have to go."

After replacing the phone receiver in its cradle on the kitchen wall, I sat back down at the table to think about what had just transpired. I should have known better. When was I going to learn that things would never change between us, even now? She was different from me — so different — and nothing, not even her brief confession, could change that.

I scolded myself for my dogged need for connection. I would never change, and neither would she. I felt that I had failed miserably at providing some pre-surgery solace, the one thing I'd intended that day.

Still, the earlier part of the conversation had been remarkable, and I was comforted in a way that felt new and different. Ironic. I'd given up expecting much long ago. Suddenly there was this moment of genuine introspection and honesty that changed everything for me, even as she was busy proving she hadn't changed one iota.

I felt giddy, crestfallen, and grateful, all at the same time. I was somehow lighter in the knowledge that she had understood something of our lives together. After years of longing for a sense of closeness, suddenly I had gotten it, if only briefly. But that was enough. It was a feeling of great abundance. I only wish she had given the same gift to my younger sisters.

Chapter 34
Love Lost

After her divorce from Riley, Debbie married again a few years later. James had a reassuring warmth, and we all liked him. Most of all, we felt relieved. For many of us in the family, marriage hadn't been a successful enterprise. Debbie needed someone steady and caring, and he seemed perfect. They weren't planning to have children, but they seemed happy with that arrangement, and none of us questioned it. We were glad that Debbie's life seemed to be turning around. As far as we could see, her new marriage was going well.

Before her surgery, things had improved for Mom too. It had been a few years after the fiasco with Travis that Mom met and married Arlen. He was younger, even younger than Travis, but he was a decent man who adored Mom. We were all grateful for that. What followed was a series of blessedly uneventful years, and it seemed that everyone was doing well.

It was then that Debbie began a correspondence with a former high school teacher from Graham-Eckes. It seemed harmless enough at first. This was a close friendship, nothing more, and her former teacher lived in a distant state. As time went on, there were occasional in-person visits, but the relationship between the two women was platonic until the day it happened.

As Debbie described it to me later, James was out running

errands while she and her friend relaxed, casually chatting and splashing around in the pool. During all the letter-writing, a natural bond had formed between them. Aside from Leila, Debbie didn't have many close friends, but she had especially liked this teacher when she was in high school. Now Debbie was happy to have such a fun and vibrant woman in her life. She saw her as a soulmate and new best friend.

And then it happened. While the two were talking in Debbie's pool, her friend crossed over to her, and in an emotional moment of closeness, kissed Debbie full on the mouth. It was a lingering kiss, and in Debbie's mind, it changed everything. Debbie was surprised by the kiss, but it was the pleasure she felt that shocked her more. It set her mind in motion. Nothing else happened on that visit, but after her friend left, Debbie suffered terribly. She struggled with the idea of her failed loyalty to her husband and questioned if she were gay. She wasn't sure she could live openly as a lesbian. She and I discussed these questions often, and she took her time, cautiously thinking them over for nearly a year.

I can remember the regret I felt for James's sake, mixed with a sudden suspicion that Debbie's actual sexual preference might account for some of her ongoing struggles. I was glad she was being careful and warned her that it might be a mistake. My comments were tempered with the thought that I shouldn't stand in the way of her nature. If she were gay, she would be much happier with this friend, and I told her that, too. It was a torturous decision for her, and I did what I could to listen and be supportive. I knew not to push her one way or another. Any counsel I might give could spell disaster for her and for me as her advisor.

Eventually, her attraction and love for the former teacher won out.

Before she even spoke to her friend, Debbie separated from James. She felt it was only fair to break up with him before she committed to someone else. She felt she owed James that much. And so she left her relatively solid marriage for what was essentially an unknown, choosing to vacate the first before she was sure of the second.

Debbie waited months after her split with James to finally speak with her former teacher. For her, it was a difficult and long-considered decision. Eventually, when she was ready, Debbie declared her feelings. The woman's response was swift and definitive.

"Oh, Debbie, Oh, no... Haha! You've got the wrong idea. I'm not gay. I'll never be gay!"

Debbie was devastated. Her suffering was unbearable. She had discarded the one person who had been loyal and steady in favor of someone whose impulsiveness would now be her downfall. It was after this incident that Debbie's terrible spiral began in earnest.

There was nothing to be done. James would not take her back. He had met someone new, and suddenly she found herself alone with nobody but herself to blame. Her depression and suffering were unrelenting, but then things got even worse.

Mom died. Ironically, it wasn't the long delayed removal of the aneurysm that killed her. The doctors had succeeded at that, but the delicate procedure had left her with permanent brain damage. They had warned Mom that this was one of the potential results. Now she was imagining she'd had lovely lunches with Cary Grant and Doris Day. Mom even called me once, thinking she had been convicted of murder. She begged me to come and get her out of prison, tearfully swearing she was innocent of the crime. She was out of her mind.

To his credit, Arlen continued to cater to Mom, keeping her at home and fussing over her as he always had. He felt sure that eventually, her old self would reappear, but it never did. Now her power over us was gone. Mom no longer recognized any of us.

Before the operation, we girls had joked with each other that maybe the brain surgery would render us a kinder and gentler mother. Suddenly it had come to pass. Once they administered the proper drugs to control her volatility, she seemed docile and happy enough, except for one thing.

Mom was still going after Debbie. When she visited, Mom would eye her suspiciously and make unpleasant comments. Mom knew even then she didn't like this stranger, and it would reduce Debbie to angry tears. All I could do was remind her that Mom wasn't herself, and that she didn't know what she was doing. But secretly, my heart ached for her.

When the end came, it was sudden. The appearance of
Mom's cancer was an accidental discovery. She had only begun
to complain about a pain in her side when they took another
scan, and at that point, no treatment was possible. She died
within weeks of her diagnosis, never knowing she was ill.

While she lived, Mom's emotional hold on Debbie had been
complete. When she died, at least in the very beginning, Debbie
seemed to be relieved. She had blamed Mom for so much. This
was no surprise. Their relationship had been contentious from
the start. Both were suspicious by nature and their personalities
had often clashed. Now, the looming wave of loss and unfinished
business crashed over Debbie's head and took a toll on her psyche.

It wasn't long before James and his new girlfriend made
plans to marry. Debbie was all alone in the house, and she
started noticing signs that our mother's ghost was visiting her.
The situation became a long and complicated odyssey with no
partner to protect her from her own state of mind. Instead, Debbie immersed herself in the study of all things paranormal, hir-
ing psychics and shamans for their advice. She "educated"
herself on the subject in every way she could, reading books and
attending lectures. Her mood was black.

By now, it felt like she had been depressed forever and she
was talking about suicide more frequently. It wasn't entirely

new. Debbie had made threats as early as her teen years. Lately, she had come to see suicide as an escape and relief from her depression and the paranormal events she was experiencing. Debbie discussed both things incessantly, and it irritated her that we couldn't agree on either subject.

All I could do was be patient and let her talk it out. I tried to be a voice of reason and a neutral sounding board for her. It was a long and agonizing time for me, and I did all I could to lend emotional support. As I saw it, the quality of her life, even her life itself, was in the balance. On the subject of suicide, she was insistent.

"I just don't know how long I can do this anymore. You'll be fine. I know you will. You'll have your life, and I'll be at peace."

"Don't talk that way, Debbie. Please. Let's talk about how to make things better instead."

"Get ready, Helen; I'm gonna do it. I just don't know when."

I would protest, telling her it wouldn't be so easy for me and that she had no concept of her value to me or anyone else. I would miss her terribly, and others would, too. I reminded her that there might be some other solution coming.

"What if they are just about to come out with a new drug for depression? It's happening all the time. Maybe the next one will change everything for you."

The idea wasn't unreasonable.

As for the haunting, I couldn't dissuade her. I didn't believe in the paranormal, and Debbie's new and passionate interest became a growing concern. The scary experiences she reported were less compelling as proof of spirit activity than evidence of

some sort of breakdown in her perception of reality. It precipitated many arguments between us, despite my efforts to avoid
them. I learned I had to take a different approach.

"What if Mom isn't trying to hurt you? What if she simply
wants to make contact because she's sorry for how she behaved
before?

"You just don't know, Helen," she would say, a flicker of
something softer crossing her face, then adding,

"I just can't take it anymore.".

In her opinion, suicide was the only answer. Endlessly, I
denied that this was a rational decision. I wept. I argued. I reasoned. I begged. Year after year, I did these things. I knew they
might not help, but I had to try.

"You think these experiences are all fake," she'd say angrily.
"Mom was here! I was talking on the phone last night, and there
was crackling on the line!"

"Debbie, I'm sure there is some sort of normal explanation
for that. Phone connections aren't always perfect. It happens to
me all the time, and I don't automatically think it is some sort
of haunting,"

"No, that's not it," she'd say, "At the same time the static
happened, the lights started to flicker!"

She felt this was proof.

"I don't know, Deb, but it sounds like there might have
been some electrical storm happening nearby. Florida is the light-
ing capital of the world. You know that. It was probably a passing
storm — maybe in Lake Park or Jupiter — somewhere nearby."

These comments would only make her angrier.

It was around this time that Debbie hired a psychic. Simon would help her figure out what was going on. She began seeing him often, inviting him to the house to conduct his investigation. Debbie wanted an expert to confirm or debunk her experiences, and he was more than happy to oblige.

Debbie described how scared she was. Now she was hearing strange sounds at night. She swore that small objects were being moved from one spot to another around the house. She felt sure she wasn't alone.

"I checked with Simon, and he says there is no doubt it was Mom. No doubt! He has been connecting with her. "

"But Debbie," I'd say.

"He's the real deal, Helen. Simon knows his stuff. You just don't know. You think you know, but you don't. So what else is new? You always think you know more than me!" she'd say bitterly, then adding: "Just because you think you do, doesn't mean you do! You're such a know-it-all!"

I told her I didn't know everything. I said I was only trying to find alternate explanations for things.

"Mom's haunting me, not you! She loved you! She's always had it in for me and she still does! If I had the guts, I'd just kill myself! She's dead now, but she's still following me around! I can't take it anymore."

By now, she was weeping inconsolably.

She was convinced Simon was helping her fight this battle. In him, she had finally found a champion. He was giving her the fierce loyalty that she'd always wanted. It seemed to me that Simon was filling her already fragile head with more problems and that Debbie was becoming more and more reliant on him.

Simon was a gay man, and I knew that the relationship was platonic, but I was worried about her dependence on him even without a romantic connection. He was there often, at her beck and call, and had managed to convince her he could control the lights and even move furniture around her house remotely. What's worse, it turned out Debbie was seeing Simon three and four times a week in addition to countless phone calls. Until then, I hadn't known the frequency, and I was shocked.

The spirit world had long fascinated her. Now it was playing on her mind and would be her undoing.

I had given Debbie moral support for many years, but I couldn't convince her that she wasn't being haunted. After the litany of losses, personal failures, and unfinished business, she was in trouble.

The hurt she carried from childhood was always lurking just beneath the surface of every conversation between us. I did all I could to shore her up, but it wasn't helping. Debbie seemed to like picking fights with me and did it as often as she could. My only choice was to avoid the battle as much as I could. I didn't take her barbs personally.

Suddenly, it all made sense. Before now, I had thought of Debbie's peculiarities as simple flaws in her personality. She used to be a puzzle to me, but now the pieces had fallen into place and I came to understand that she was suffering from mental illness. I knew she needed me more than ever. The thoughts running through her mind had warped her sense of things.

I knew a big part of her was angry with me, and in her view, she had reason. I felt sorry that there was no one else to take up the role of champion on her behalf, not for my sake, but for hers. In many ways, for Debbie, my kindness toward her was a bitter pill.

I had been the golden child, a hard fact that would never change. I comforted myself that at least her dislike for me was equal to her love for me. I knew my role. I was the strong one, the lucky one, and it was for me to be tolerant. I set my mind to shoulder the blame when she demanded it and do what I could to help her navigate the wrong-headed direction I knew she was taking. I needed to save her from herself. At least I had to try.

Chapter 35
Dark Times

Debbie saved her paranormal arguments for me. She knew the other family members would dismiss them out of hand. This meant that there was effectively little general support for her. Debbie had cut Carolyn out of her life for some minor infraction years ago and she had alienated everyone else, one way or another. They avoided her when they could, shaking their heads and talking behind her back. She was exhausting, and they wanted no part of the drama. This also meant that aside from her therapist, I was the only one to fully understand how ill she was.

Still, she shared her general depression and thoughts of suicide with those who would listen. Most of the family had already tired of the complaints about her miserable life. She had plenty of money. What was the problem? Everyone assumed her behavior was willful unpleasantness and self-pity. They had lost patience with her, and I couldn't blame them. She wasn't easy, and besides, ours was not a family that pulled together for anyone. At some point, our half-sister Louise said in disgust,

"Just do it then! *Do it!* Or don't do it. I don't care, but I don't want to hear about it anymore."

Afterward, Debbie called me in tears. When I heard what Louise had said, I was horrified. Later, I argued with Lou, but she defended her position, satisfied that she told the truth. Louise had come to see Debbie as emotionally manipulative.

She wasn't entirely wrong to feel that way. Debbie brought everyone down, and to some extent, it did seem like manipulation, but Louise was wrong about one thing. This behavior wasn't fun for Debbie. No, Debbie was honestly desperate, and I worried there was a good chance she would go through with it.

I felt sorry for Debbie's pain and knew how serious any threat of suicide could be. I understood her, and right or wrong, I felt responsible. The thought of her suicide filled me with dread, and I resolved to do whatever I could to delay things, hoping a solution or treatment might arrive in time. Debbie needed all the love she could get, and the family simply didn't understand her or care anymore.

Meanwhile, Debbie had already gone through more therapists than I could count and had fired all of them. When she didn't like what they had to say, she showed them the door. Now she had one who agreed with every paranoid thought she put forth, but at least she was talking to someone other than me. It was clear this man knew — rightly — that if he contradicted her, she would fire him. She'd done it many times before. Now her longest-lasting counselor, a man who was fully licensed, went along with her in utterly unprofessional ways. He even took a trip to Ohio with Debbie at one point just to be available in the hotel room next to hers. All I could think was that *any* therapist was better than no therapist at all. It was an impossible situation.

I had begged Debbie for years to check herself into McLean, a premier hospital in my state for psychiatric treatment. They offered all sorts of cutting-edge technologies and programs, and she certainly had the financial assets to do it. I called McLean Hospital to gather information for her on what they offered. At one point, I was living close enough to McLean to see its campus from my back window. I told her I'd hang out with her there. I could even bring the morning coffee. She needed a psychological assessment. She even admitted to me that she needed help but argued that they couldn't provide it; no one could. On this point, she was unshakeable. I spent years trying to steer her in that direction but to no avail. She simply wouldn't go.

Debbie had been taking different drugs on and off to treat her ongoing depression, with little relief, and no doubt, she had questioned her own sanity. But Simon didn't think she was crazy. He confirmed her every suspicion. For her, this was a relief. She was simultaneously impressed and charmed, but he was also actively frightening her. By Debbie's account, he was demonstrating his powers in ways that were scary. When he wasn't attributing signs of paranormal activity to our mother, he was claiming credit for them himself. He had her convinced he could do scary things that she would witness remotely. And she told me she did.

Debbie's relationship with Simon had become utterly alarming. I already knew her innate personality mixed with a fascination with the occult was a dangerous combination. Simon seemed able to take Debbie's demands for attention in stride, but he was on her payroll. Her willingness to pay seemed ill-advised and maybe even dangerous. It was clear he was doing more harm than good. Simon was busy confirming and validating every one of Debbie's paranoid beliefs while at the same time adding to them.

I warned Debbie that placing such faith in a psychic was not a good idea. I said it seemed she was becoming too dependent on someone whose motives didn't look good to me. I also told her I felt Simon had a malevolent side, preying on her willingness to believe.

Debbie was furious. She told me off and hung up the phone. This time I didn't call her back. Feeling weary to the bone, I let her go. I couldn't change her mind, and the constant arguing and desperate attempts to help her had worn me out.

When Debbie finally did call again, about a year had passed since we'd spoken. It was the longest separation we'd ever had.

On the other end of the line, Debbie sounded more broken than ever. She said she hadn't been in touch because things ended badly with Simon, and she was embarrassed. The truth was, saying it "ended badly" was an understatement of epic proportions. It was then she told me the story.

After she and I had stopped talking, Debbie had packed her things and moved to Arizona with Simon. He already owned a house there, and she bought one nearby. She confessed she hadn't let me know what she was doing because she rightly predicted I would object. The following months were a nightmare between them for many reasons, all leading to the last argument, which took place in his living room. After some yelling on both sides, Simon retreated to his bedroom. Debbie waited in the living room, thinking maybe she should let him cool off.

When Simon didn't return, she knocked on the door a few times. Getting no answer, she went in. What she found there was more horrible than anything she could have imagined. Debbie found Simon hanging from the rafters. She managed to cut him down and called 911. Panicked and terrified, she tried CPR until the ambulance arrived, but it was too late.

The police questioned Debbie extensively, trying to determine if she'd been involved. They told her not to leave town, a place that was thousands of miles away from anyone she knew. She'd only met a few of his family members, but now they were suspicious. The police interrogated Debbie for several days, and she was called back for a number of lengthy interviews before it was over. Debbie described to me her distress while the investigators did all they could to get her to confess she had strung him up herself. It was a kind of torture. She had lost this man who meant so much to her, and now she was being accused of killing him. Simon was a large man, and eventually, the police realized she would never have had the strength herself to hoist him up in order to hang him. In the end, his death was ruled a suicide.

Still haunted by my mother and now traumatized and broken by her experience with Simon, she returned to Florida. It was at this point she got back in touch. She told me that she was still being haunted by Mom, but now Simon was haunting her too. There was no question in my mind that she believed this. I could hear the fear in her voice. While she spoke, I held my head in my hands.

Desperately worried, I convinced her to come and stay with me in Belmont, Massachusetts, where I lived at the time. Debbie had never accepted my invitations before, but this time she agreed. When she stepped off the plane, I could see how she had suffered. The stress and mental anguish had contorted her features into a mask-like expression reminiscent of a victim in a horror film. She looked terrified and strangely demonic at the same time. I could hardly believe this was my sister. Her eyebrows were skewed with a diagonal arch that was unfamiliar to me and gave her face a bizarre and frantic appearance. None of the softness of her features remained. When her staring eyes locked onto mine, I confess I felt spooked. That night, she insisted on sleeping in my room, and so we climbed into my big bed together. Before I turned off my bedside light, Debbie turned to me and said in utter earnestness,

"I wish I could just die here tonight in your arms."

My heart broke for both of us. I knew I couldn't talk Debbie into getting help voluntarily, and I was afraid of what could happen next if I did nothing. The following morning, saying I had an errand, I went instead to the Belmont Police Station and asked for their assistance. The situation was officially out of hand. Debbie needed help, and I felt I could no longer do it alone. She needed to be committed.

That evening, when the first police cars arrived, lights flashing, Debbie turned to me, half smiling, and asked in a theatrical tone,

"Helen, what did you do?"

As the fire truck arrived along with an ambulance and then

more police, she was now laughing out loud.

"Officer, there has been some huge mistake," she said in her best "all is well" voice. She was so good at it.

"I am fine. *Really.*"

The officers were having none of it. They took her and placed her in the ambulance, and I followed behind in my car.

They kept her behind locked doors while I went back and forth to her psych unit in Melrose, bringing supplies and sitting with her outside at a picnic table. She ranted bitterly about how foolish I was to do this to her. As it turned out, she was right. All they did was take her belt from her and make sure she had no razor to shave her legs for the three days. They made her do crafts and asked her repeatedly if she would still kill herself if she were released. She reported how she'd laughed at the doctor, telling him to his face that once he released her, she could kill herself if she wanted to, and there wasn't a thing he could do about it.

After only three days they released her, and I went to pick her up. By her account, they had given her no therapy and no plan for the future. No help at all. I remember how sheepish I felt when she got back into the car. I'd had no idea that this was how it would go. Afterward, I felt naive to think they were going to work on finding effective treatment of some kind. But now I knew. There would be no help forthcoming for Debbie. She forgave me for doing what I had, but she never let me forget it.

Debbie went home to Florida a few days later and I promised her I would never try that again. I was running out of ideas. I didn't know what to do.

Debbie was already seeing a psychiatrist who had put her on ever-changing medications, but clearly none were helping. Worse yet, she was addicted to Xanax and was getting extra pills without her doctor's knowledge. I asked to speak to the doctor, but he refused, even with Debbie's permission. And so I did the only thing I could. I talked to Debbie on the phone as often as she wished. I spent hours upon hours trying to prop her up. There were times I thought I was making progress, only to find I'd made none at all. Finally, she allowed me to help her find a different therapist — this time a good one. But by then, it was already too late. The whirlpool had her in its grip, and she was circling toward the drain.

Chapter 36
Circling the Drain

"Bitch!" was the last thing she said.

It was the parting word on a long and rambling phone message she left me. Debbie had so much to say that she needed to leave a second one to finish her thoughts.

Prior to this message, I hadn't heard from Debbie in a few months. My repeated calls had gone unanswered except for this one long and hate-filled invective. It was evident that Debbie's paranoia had gotten much worse.

The whole mess had started with a CD compilation of old Super 8 movies of the extended family. Some years earlier, Mom had a local business make CD duplicates for each of us. Even though the movies lacked sound, they were the closest thing we had to a lifelike record of the family, and we treasured them. Dad was the primary cameraman, but it also contained some footage of him which made the CDs even more precious. Unfortunately, Debbie lost hers, so I promised to send her a copy.

The problem was that I had moved again, and I just couldn't find it. I assured Debbie that I was looking everywhere. All I could do was state and restate that she would have one as soon as I could locate it, but this didn't appease her. To make things worse, she refused to ask Carolyn about it because they weren't speaking. Eventually, I asked Carolyn about it myself, but she wasn't sure where hers was either. So I kept searching. It was a disaster. Debbie convinced herself that I was enjoying every minute of what she considered intentional torment. As the weeks passed, her impatience and paranoia grew exponentially, along with my frustration. I couldn't convince her that I was being honest and would locate it eventually. Just before she slipped into this most recent period of silence, a good number of our phone conversations concerned the CD and Debbie's accusations of my controlling, selfish nature.

"You're the one who has it," she said in the message. "You just don't want to look for it. I bet you know exactly where it is. How could you? *Really, how could you!*" she said bitterly, now weeping.

"It's just a small favor. It would mean so much to me- and obviously, *my* feelings are not that important to you. I'm an inconvenience, and you're *enjoying* this. I *know* you are. Admit it!"

Now she digressed to every time I'd slighted her. She expressed her anger at what she saw as my deliberate disbelief in the paranormal and reasserted her certainty that Mom and Simon were haunting her.

Debbie had found a new psychic, Marla, who confirmed these "facts," including the idea that I was purposely withholding the CD. A majority of Debbie's recent phone messages covered this issue. Marla, her new best friend, told Debbie that her suspicions were correct. The psychic was the expert, and Debbie now had *proof*.

She rambled on, telling me how she had developed her own psychic powers. She could sense the presence of souls who had passed over and knew why her chairs were being moved out of place. Her phone reception was still spotty and poor, all evidence of the souls who refused to go away. She'd paid another expert on the subject of hauntings to come to the house twice to bless it and burn sage in every room. She felt threatened by the ghosts and she was furious with me.

I knew she was losing her grip on reality, but there was nothing I could do. She hadn't answered my calls for months. I thought about flying down to Florida again, but there was a good chance she wouldn't let me in. I had been putting out Debbie's fires for years. I spoke to her on the phone for three and four hours at a time. Over time, her delusions had grown in scope and intensity. When I would call her, the quavering "hello" on the other end of the line signaled that the phone call would be a long one. Near the end, the phone conversations increased in length and number until suddenly they stopped altogether.

It was only a year or two earlier that Debbie had called me in desperation, confessing she'd invited a homeless woman, a stranger, to come and live with her. She thought another person in the house would diminish her loneliness. I was stunned. I had thought that even Debbie had more sense than this. They'd been together in Debbie's new house only a few weeks before Anna May became surly, unkind, and even threatening.

Distraught, Debbie begged me to help her get rid of the woman. I told her I would try. I flew to Florida with the idea that I would get to know Anna better and figure out a strategy to get her to leave voluntarily. Legal action would have taken a while, and with Debbie's fragile state, I knew she wasn't up to the task. After the hasty trip, I arrived at her door. Debbie let

me in, and we settled into the chairs at the tiled wrought iron
table in her courtyard. The woman was still in her room, and at
first, Debbie and I sat in silence. The screened-in pool area in
front of us had a view of her back yard which extended to a
stand of trees in the distance.

Between the pool enclosure and the trees were a multitude
of animal pens. Debbie had recently built this house and tried
to fill her empty life with animals. As it was, she already had several dogs and kept a couple of Appaloosa horses off the property, but this didn't satisfy her. She decided to become an exotic
animal breeder, too. At the time, I remember advising her that
such an enterprise might be too much, but she persisted. She
quickly set up shop, commissioning the construction of a good
number of enclosures and filling them with smaller exotic animals. Now it was clear to me that the animals had not improved
things for Debbie. The homeless woman was proof.

As we seated ourselves, the familiar cacophony of lemurs
and monkeys screeching and howling filled the silence between
us. I remember how Debbie looked in her ubiquitous jeans and
tee-shirt, leaning forward on her elbows. She kept her baseball
cap tilted downward to shield herself from direct eye contact as
the smoke curled upward from the Marlboro between her
fingers into the warm Florida air. The large ashtray in front of
her was overflowing with butts, and a gentle breeze scattered a
few telltale ashes across the table's surface in a careless pattern.
The half-finished glass of Diet Pepsi at her side stood with ice
melted, leaving a transparent layer of water over the darker
liquid below.

This was her favorite spot. She sat in this same place whenever we talked over the phone for all the days, afternoons, and evenings endlessly rehashing her misery. We had tried to unravel the complicated difficulties between us, along with her troubles with life in general. Occasionally, the lemurs would send up a communal vocalization that was so loud we had to wait for them to finish to resume our conversation. If it wasn't the animals, it was a train passing on the track nearby that held us silent and waiting to resume.

And here I was again. Excusing myself, I went inside to get a drink and returned to Debbie, now prepared for the task.

"So," I said, breaking the silence between us.

I could see under the tipped bill of her cap that Debbie's mouth had already begun to screw itself into an expression of grief. Tears began to roll down her cheeks, and we sat together quietly, listening to the sounds coming from the pens, each of us knowing that this latest problem was only the tip of an inconceivably large iceberg.

"Try not to worry. I'm here now, and I can help you fix this."

"But *how?*" Debbie asked, her voice in a tearful whisper. "She told me I can't evict her. The law says she has the right to stay here."

Her emotions were swelling in earnest now, but her eyes stayed cast away from mine. "I'm so stupid! What was I thinking?!"

"It's OK, Debbie. I will figure out a way. She will leave. I promise."

Anna May was a woman in middle age with a tired face and a demeanor that spoke of the hard life she had been living.

In the following days, I encouraged her to pour her heart out to me about her issues with Debbie. I empathized. I took her for rides and errands in my rental car so that we could talk privately. Anna May shared bits of her life story with me and confessed she had family members in Georgia that she hadn't seen in years. I sympathized with her and managed to get her thinking about the advantages of reconnecting with them. She didn't have the cash for a bus ticket, I knew that. At some point, over lunch at a restaurant nearby, I broached a plan. Wouldn't she prefer to return to Georgia and get reacquainted with her own family? I offered her a bus ticket and a motel room for the night. She agreed, and by the end of the meal, she was set to go home to Atlanta the following day.

When we got back to the house, Anna May went to her room and packed her things. Debbie was sullen and wouldn't say goodbye. But I delivered her unwanted guest to the motel, apologizing on the way for Debbie's cold farewell. I wished Anna May luck and told her I hoped better days were coming.

When I returned to the house again, the deed was done. At that point, Debbie demanded to know if I had spent any money in getting the woman to leave. I lied and told her no. Debbie could be ungenerous with her money, and this woman had crossed her. I knew admitting the truth would have galled her endlessly. She was always on the verge of rage as it was, her paranoia infecting every possible situation.

These days, by the time Debbie had stopped talking with me about the CD, I imagined it was only a matter of patience. This was nothing new. I could wear her down. I would simply keep calling, and eventually, she would answer the phone. I had no idea how bad it had gotten. Then I got a phone call from Florida. It wasn't from Debbie.

"Hello," said a stranger's voice. "Is this Debbie's sister Helen?"

"Yes, who's this?"

"My name is Sue. I'm a friend of Debbie's. She and I do business. I'm an exotics breeder."

I didn't say a word, waiting for what was coming next.

"I'm sorry to bother you, but I'm calling to let you know that this morning I had Debbie Baker-Acted. And I had them take away her gun."

I knew about the Baker Act, Florida's legal term for a psychiatric commitment. This would be the third time. Some years earlier, it had been her therapist who'd done it, the one who had been so unprofessional. Once she got out, she continued to see the same psychologist, successfully holding that act of commitment over his head as a sort of leverage. The second time she was committed, it had been me — and now this.

Debbie had been committed again, but this time, the circumstances were even more serious. Sue proceeded to tell me how she witnessed Debbie storming after an employee who made a minor mistake in feeding one of the exotic animals. The employee was a kind and gentle young man who was not prepared for the onslaught. Sue reported watching as Debbie beat him to the ground in a vicious fit of anger. All the poor guy could do was to cower beneath her on the lawn while she talked to angels no one else could see, striking him repeatedly about his head and body, and peppering her words with cruel and very personal in-sults. It had been a torrent of violence and uncontrolled rage mixed with utter psychosis, and I believed every word of it.

Sue tried to intervene, but Debbie was too far gone to listen to reason, and she continued her attack while Sue had managed to call 911. The police came and invoked the Baker Act. Fortunately, the young man was not injured and Debbie was carried off to a waiting ambulance and whisked away.

Since she'd returned home from Belmont, Debbie had talked almost gleefully about the fact that she had a gun. She laughed at my worry and said that she would use it on herself at some point, and there was nothing I could do about it. I knew she was right. In Florida, as it is in many parts of this country, virtually anyone can buy a gun. Aside from arguing, I had to put it out of my mind. Now, I felt a real sense of relief to know that it was gone from her house, and for even a moment now, Debbie was safe.

Sue ended our conversation, giving me the name of the hospital where Debbie was locked up. Thankfully, the young man did not press charges. He was concerned about her too, and I was grateful, but I was heartbroken for him, for her, and for the whole mess. At that point, it had been about three months since she'd yelled, "Bitch!" onto my phone message.

Soon enough, I was able to contact the people in charge at the hospital. A court hearing was to take place, and I was asked to become Debbie's legal guardian. They needed to medicate her against her will, and they needed a guardian to give permis-sion. I agreed. Of course, I was willing on both counts.

Debbie was in the hospital for a while. During that time, they called me numerous times as the doctors tried to stabilize her. Eventually, they succeeded with a cocktail of drugs that seemed to make a big difference. I spoke with her myself over the phone a few times, and she seemed much improved. After a few weeks, the psychiatrist called to tell me that the judge was about to release her and asked if I had any objection to such a plan. I told the doctor that I felt it would be a mistake, that I knew she needed much more care. I asked if the judge might reconsider. He did, but the preservation of Debbie's safety was not to last. Two weeks after that, I was told that they could not, by law, keep her any longer.

"I'm sorry, Ms. Morse, but we have done all we can. Legally, she has the right to go home. She seems stable enough. Rest assured we will be sending a home health aide to visit her every day for the time being to make sure that she continues on her medications."

"If you send her home now, she will eventually stop taking her medications, and she will spiral right back to where she was. She needs serious help! Is there nothing more you can do?

I was desperate.

"There are no other real options. I'm sorry. Your sister has legal rights that protect her." The doctor paused, then repeated, "I'm sorry."

And so it was done. Debbie went home. It was no surprise to me when she wouldn't answer the phone when I called her there. It rang until it diverted to her message recorder, and silence regained its hold between us. In the meantime, the home health aide had come for a week or two, and then, with Debbie's insistent and Oscar-winning assurances, the aide signed off on her case. I had no way of knowing this. I'd also had no idea there was a second gun. The only thing I did know was that whatever was happening, it wasn't good. Still, I had to hope I was wrong. I had no other option. I kept calling, but she wouldn't pick up the phone.

OK, I thought, maybe she doesn't want to speak to me, but perhaps she will make her way somehow. She had seemed so much better in the hospital. The truth is, when all you can do is hope, that is what you do. And so I did.

I wondered how she was and hoped for the best, knowing that the best was not likely to be what was coming next.

It wasn't.

Chapter 37
My Last Day with Debbie

It was July 2, 2013, in Belmont, Massachusetts, and it was dinnertime. My husband and I had just sat down with our friend Tom, who was joining us. The landline phone rang, and I rose to take it in another room.

An unfamiliar voice introduced himself as a detective from the sheriff's office in Palm Beach County. He asked to speak with someone named Helen Morse. That was me, I said. He asked if I had a sister named Deborah Morse. "Yes, I told him," and my mind began to spin. Had she attacked somebody else in her employ? Had her recent bizarre and belligerent behavior been a factor in some recent altercation? He went on to say that he was sorry to inform me that my sister Debbie was gone. They had found her body today. I paused.

"Oh," I said.

A co-worker had called the department to ask for a wellness check, and they had found her.

Then he said something about an investigation happening. How did he get my name, I wondered.

"OK."

The coroner had her body. They had taken her and would not be releasing her back to us for some time. It appeared she had put a pistol into her mouth and pulled the trigger.

"Oh."

There were personal effects that they had gathered, including the pistol. He said I could keep the gun, or the department would dispose of it for me. What did he say? I felt like a deer in the headlights.

"No," I said. "You can dispose of it."

He told me that they would hold her other things for pickup by the family. They would keep her body.

"OK."

I was numb. I remember thinking about what impression he must have of me, given my lack of reaction. Was it normal for someone getting this kind of news? I was dry-eyed, unemotional. All I managed to ask was,

"What do I do now?"

I needed him to tell me what to do. Surely, he'd been through this before. He answered that he couldn't say. That decision was up to me. I told him I was coming.

I hung up the phone and returned to the dinner table to explain what I had just been told and excuse myself to pack. Tom offered to leave, but I asked him instead to stay and keep my husband company.

It wasn't long until the plane's wheels hit the tarmac in West Palm Beach, and I took a rental car to the lawyer's office where Debbie's ex-husband James was meeting me. There were legalities to discuss, and they needed to do it in person. When I entered the office, James and a lawyer I'd never met were already there. They rose to greet me. Once the introductions were made, we proceeded with the task at hand. The lawyer informed me that Debbie had left her entire fortune to others. She had left none of her assets to anyone in the family except James, as executor of her estate.

The plan was familiar. She'd told me of it, at least in part, many times before. At those times, I'd tried with all my might to talk her down off the ledge. I reasoned with her. I tried to refuse her the pleasure of discussing it, but every time, she insisted. I remembered again the sense of exhaustion and despair I felt at those times. I had done all I could, but she would not listen to reason. If she could scrape together the courage, she would kill herself. And now she had.

The lawyer continued. It was the details of her will that were yet unknown to me. A small portion of the money would be held in trust to throw off income for life to her best friend. There were also a few one-time gifts to others. After that, the balance would go to a university animal studies program and a couple of animal shelters.

"OK."

I told the lawyer that I had no intention of challenging Debbie's wishes. He responded that it was good because there was nothing I could do about it anyway.

"OK. Thank you."

Debbie had left me all the items from our childhood home. She left nothing to Carolyn, not a single thing. This was not a surprise. Debbie could be cruel. During one of those terrible conversations, she told me that this was what she would do, and she was adamant on that point. I knew Debbie would have disapproved, but I decided that I would now divide those things fairly between Carolyn and me. In this, she would have no choice.

There was a brief discussion about the condition of the house. There was a mess and it had to be cleaned up. As executor, James expressed dismay that the required crew would cost the trust around $3,000. Body fluid removal was considered hazardous and therefore expensive. He had already looked into it.

"No. I will go," I said.

James offered to come with me. After all, she was his ex-wife, but it was easy to see that he didn't relish the idea. He added that he wasn't sure it was a good idea for me to go it alone either.

"No," I said. "I'll be fine. I want to do it."

There was no question. I needed to be alone with her. There would be blood, they warned, and Lord knows what else. I didn't care. It would be my last moment alone with Debbie in the world as she left it. I needed to be alone with what was left of her.

My next errand was to drive to the sheriff's office. They handed me two paper bags through a plate glass window. They contained the items retrieved when they had found her. On the outside of each was an official-looking strip of yellow tape emblazoned with the word "Evidence." Debbie's name and a few other details were hand written below the tape. I carried them back to my rental car where I could open them in private.

Inside the larger paper bag was a worn brown leather shoulder bag with western style details on its flap. I wasn't familiar with this purse, but it looked like something Debbie would have owned. I opened the flap and looked inside. There, I found a wallet with a few ID cards, a small translucent violet comb, a pink frosted lipstick and a few crumpled receipts. In the smaller bag was her necklace, a wide woven chain of gold, not quite a choker. I kissed it, and put it back.

Sitting there in the police station parking lot, I felt like I was encased in cotton gauze, moving through the world unable to feel my own skin. My mind was racing, but I found it impossible to focus. Just as it was when I'd lost my father, I was strangely unable to cry. I put the car in gear, and made my way to the grocery store.

I was sure there would be a bucket at Debbie's, so I didn't bother to search for one. Instead, I bought rubber gloves, sponges, and a bottle of bleach along with some paper towels and a Vitamin Water, and I drove to her house.

Armed with the entry code, I managed to open the electric gate and pulled into the driveway. I passed the Mamaroneck lions, and drove into the broad courtyard, parking the car next to one of hers. I was prepared to open the front door with the key James had given me. Instead, I found it unlocked.

I pushed on the door to the inner courtyard and walked into her world. Sounds of yips, barks, and whining filled the patio. All four dogs were still there, sorely in need of attention. One snarled at me, teeth bared, backing away and ready to charge, unsure of my intent. It had been a long while since they'd enjoyed the company of an attentive, loving mistress. It was apparent they no longer thought of any person as a potential friend, much less one who was only vaguely familiar. Even Peanut, the smallest one, backed away and circled just out of reach. All of them cried out in anxiety at me, their intruder and possible rescuer.

They had been ranging alone in the enormous space for
days. Dog feces and dried puddles of pee were everywhere.
There was no food or water in their dishes. I filled their dishes
with water from a spigot and then found the dog food. Debbie
kept provisions for all the animals in a small house to the left of
the pool. The cages and enclosures for the other animals scattered across the large backyard were empty — all of them. The
many lemurs, three or four monkeys, and two kinkajous were
gone. So were the pony, the anteater, and the tortoise, no doubt
sent away to various other animal breeders in preparation for
this day. Debbie had planned. A couple of empty cages stood inside the screened patio as well. They all gave silent testimony to
Debbie's efforts to fill her life with the love she couldn't seem to
find elsewhere.

The dogs kept barking, expressing their communal resentment for my presence. Why had Debbie abandoned them? How
could she do this to them? How could she do this to me? I
looked at the wrought iron table where we both had sat together
so many times. Behind it loomed the enormous sliding glass
doors. I stepped up to them and stood for a moment with my
hand on the pull. I could see the marks where the dogs had
been hurling their bodies in an attempt to reach their injured
mistress. Dog vomit and paw prints mixed with nose prints and
smears spread across the glass, horrifying proof of a scene that
had taken place only hours earlier. I could see the pool of blood
on the floor on the other side of the door. It had inched across
part of the small throw rug that Debbie had placed at the entrance to prevent the dirt and Florida sand from entering her

pristine inner sanctum. Now the rug was soaked with a crimson ellipse extending beyond its fringe into a puddle beyond. Nearby, a thin smear of blood remained as well from some part of her body's fall to earth.

I imagined her there beforehand; upright, looking resolutely out the door, balancing on two bravely shaky legs, heart pounding, breathing, alive. And then she was gone. Debbie's last trip. Did she suffer? The coroner said no. I wanted to see her, but the coroner said she would not recommend it. I tried to understand. I wanted to see her looking peaceful. The coroner told me I should not see her at all. She smelled terrible, she told me. I didn't care. I wanted to see Debbie. I asked the coroner if she might cover Debbie's face and just let me see her hands, even one hand. They were beautiful like my mother's. I would recognize them. The coroner said no. She was emphatic. Reluctantly, I agreed. She assured me it was for the best.

And so, in the end, all Debbie allowed me was this pool of blood. Now I was here, and she was not, except for a puddle of human essence on the floor. No one told me to do this. It was my choice. My crazy choice. My last act of love. My heart hung heavy in its cage. I left the spot and walked through the massive house like a tourist on an expedition of sorrow.

It felt like a hotel that hadn't yet opened. No artwork hung on the broad walls. There was one teaspoon in the double deep sink. A table stood with 12 chairs. There were empty shelves everywhere. I passed into Debbie's bedroom. The glass wall and slider facing the enclosed patio were covered entirely in foil sheets taped together with no opening for sunlight to breach the aluminum fortress. I'd offered to come down and help her buy curtains to help her make the place homey. We could even order them online, and someone would come measure and install them. The answer had always been no.

She had done this instead. It looked like a bedroom inside a poorly defended bunker. There was a sweet stuffed animal, a lemur, on the bed stand. Her bra was thrown to one side. Her bed with the massive headboard was rumpled and empty just as she'd left it. The rumpled sheets and blanket were left thrown open as if she had just gotten up. It was a sacred place, and I dared not disturb it. In the bathroom, all was in order. The towels were hung, neatly folded on their bars as if she'd never used them.

I needed my camera. I had been a photographer all my life. I had brought it as one brings an old friend for support. I took pictures. I needed to take pictures. I did it blindly, paying no attention to exposure or shutter speed. I had forgotten to set them; it didn't matter at the time. I took pictures like a thief in a palace. I needed to immerse myself in it. I needed to memorialize the damage and knew I would never have the opportunity again. I thought if I could keep something of this moment in time, I might be able to mend myself with it later.

Through the photographs, I wanted to make sense of it and maybe create something out of this tragedy. I might transform it into a thing that had some worth. She hadn't done this for nothing. *It couldn't be for nothing.* I wouldn't allow it. I *couldn't* allow it. I was her big sister. I had wanted to protect her. I would prevent this last moment from disappearing into nothingness as she had disappeared from me. Somehow, with the photographs, I could find something meaningful in what was so unspeakably horrific. I returned to the kitchen and filled a bucket I'd found in the garage with bleach and water. Then I took a few pictures of the spot where she fell.

I knelt and lifted the throw rug. The blood poured dripping from its fringe as I awkwardly tried to fold the now strangely heavy rug and get it into the uncooperative garbage bag. I tied a knot at its opening and set it in the far corner. A sweet metallic smell lingered in the air and sickened me with every breath. It was an odor like nothing I had ever experienced before. The blood was dark and thick but was already drying at the edges, peeling away in plaques from the tile beneath it. With each stroke of the sponge, the blood seemed to increase in volume until the water in the bucket could no longer be used to dilute it. I repeatedly poured what was left of Debbie down the sink and refilled the bucket. It felt all wrong.

I longed to dip a piece of cloth into the crimson ocean at my feet. I wanted to take some small part of Debbie to keep with me forever. All I had was the T-shirt on my back. I talked myself down, telling myself that this impulse was sick — as sick as she had been. Instead, I cleaned it all away. I did it as my last gift to her, scrubbing her floor down to the fresh and uncaring tile.

When I was done, I sat on the couch, facing the spot where she fell. Behind me, Debbie's sheepskin jacket was neatly folded where she'd left it, on one of the large leather cushions. Before me, the sun was getting low and throwing its light sideways through the glass. It reminded me I needed to clean the dog vomit and mess still there on the sliding door. It was then, by chance, I looked higher up on the glass.

If I hadn't been standing in that precise spot that day, I might have missed it. Suddenly I saw the greasy marks of a Christian cross on the glass. Each panel had one. They looked like they had been drawn there by a finger dipped in oil. I stood and looked around me and saw there were crosses smeared onto every door and window in the room. Traveling through the house, I found them everywhere. Before this, they'd been invisible. Now they commanded my complete attention.

Debbie told me she'd invited a shaman to bless the house. These crosses were the fruit of one of her many attempts to rid it of the evil spirits. She was frightened and in a hopeless state of solitude, literally out of her mind with fear. There had been nothing I could ever say or do to give her any comfort, no matter how hard I tried. The crosses spoke to me of her aloneness. They told the story of a beloved sister condemned to her own mind's unbridled menace and the only path to the relief she was able to find.

I had gone to her house that day in an act of penance for all I knew had driven her into that dark place. I went to allow her that one final vengeful blow, knowing that it was something she might have wanted. And I could take it. Somewhere along the line, I had become the stronger one. I wanted to hold her and comfort her once more in my sorrow and regret, but I would never have that chance. All that was left to me was one last moment of tender intimacy, to see the same things she had seen just before she was gone: the cigarette butts in her ashtray, the lone spoon in the sink, her bed pillow as she'd left it. I wanted to bridge the impossible and eternal chasm somehow. I wanted to make things right, but I couldn't. I never could.

I sat back down on the couch next to her jacket, facing the tile floor, now gleaming in the light of the setting sun. My thoughts returned to the adorable and brave little girl with blond ringlets who had been my childhood companion. I rested my hand on the soft fleece of her lapel, and I wept.

Chapter 38
The Wrecking Ball and The Bracelet

Back in the 1990s, our mother had sold the old Ripley house for an even larger one on the island's southern end. It wasn't long after she moved into the new house that she had the long-delayed brain surgery. I was in Florida a while after that disastrous event when we got word that the buyer of our old house was planning to tear it down to make way for a new one.

Rushing to catch one last look before it was razed, Debbie and I went there a day before demolition began in earnest. When we arrived, the crane with its wrecking ball stood looming darkly over the house. The front door was open, and we walked in to obtain permission from the head of the wrecking crew to have one last look around. Our first stop was the dining room, where Ripley's old French woodblock wallpaper and its scenes of India was still on its walls. It was too bad there would be no way to rescue these from the coming destruction.

The scenery of our childhood was about to be obliterated, and I wanted a memento. It was there in the dining room I took a photograph of Debbie in front of one of the fantastical panels. Her neutral expression and furtive sideways glance were fitting, standing there with a Tweety Bird logo stitched into her polo shirt in an unintentional but no less ironic statement. I asked her to stand against one of the panels with an elephant we'd loved so much. She said she didn't care where she stood for this memento of mine, but she did it anyway. She would never admit to any personal feeling for the place, but despite herself, there it was. I saw it when I took the shot, and it is still there in the photograph today, like a bit of life preserved in amber.

As Debbie looks to one side, her face clearly shows a sense of stifled tension, tied to the circumstances of our visit and the memories connected to the very wallpaper behind her. Half her face is in shadow. The other eye is illuminated. In it, I can see a slight flavor of the paranoia that I came to know so well. Her neutral expression and the Tweety Bird on her shirt couldn't protect her from what was coming next. The walls behind her had been silent witness to so much.

As we continued through the old house, most of the interesting architectural elements of the building had been stripped away, but we heard the secret room was still intact. Excitedly, I asked the crew foreman if he would mind if I took one of the closet hooks as a keepsake. As soon as he agreed, Debbie and I flew up the stairs to the closet for one last look.

I turned the familiar hook, and with a click, the secret door opened into the small room beyond. Now the room was completely empty. Mom's fur coats and the rack that held them were gone. The wall safe stood open and empty. Debbie and I stood there for a moment or two before we felt satisfied we had seen enough. I eased the hook away from its place on the secret door with just a few turns and put it in my pocket. It was an important part of history for me, and I saw it as a strange but fitting consolation prize for my childhood misery. I still have it today.

For Debbie, no cast iron hook taken from a door or any other souvenir could ease her suffering. It still had a firm grip on her. As she told me that day, this was justice at last. "Good riddance to this house! Good riddance to it all!" I didn't know it then, but the photograph I took in our old dining room was to be the last portrait I would ever make of her.

Not long after Mom died, Debbie and I forged a pact. Debbie knew I was horrified by the thought of her killing herself. I'd argued and pleaded against the idea for so many years, but on this point, she persisted. She seemed to feel a powerful urgency to prove to me that her theories and experiences with the paranormal were valid and real. She hatched a crazy plan, one that would satisfy this need. As reluctant as I was to entertain the idea of Debbie's demise, she wouldn't let the subject drop.

"OK, OK," I'd said. "First of all, I have to repeat — I want you alive. You know how I feel about it. I hate this conversation."

"No, no! I already know that," she said impatiently. "Just say it! Just say you will agree! I'm not dead now, but if and when I am dead, do you agree to have me come back and haunt you?" she asked with real intensity.

We went back and forth about it, but finally, I relented.

"OK, already! *If* you die before me, and *if* there is a spirit world, yes, you can haunt me. In fact, I hope you will. I give my permission right here and now! The truth is, Debbie, if you were gone, I would be happy to feel your presence near me."

And I meant it.

She seemed satisfied, but she warned, "You think you want this, but you won't! Don't be so sure of yourself. You'll see. You'll be as terrified as I've been!" she said to me in earnest.

I assured her that if she were gone, I would find her other-worldly visits comforting. From then on, every time the subject of the spirit world came up, which was in nearly every conversation we had, Debbie would remind me of my agreement. She seemed to relish the idea that she would get to show me once and for all.

When the horrific news came that Debbie committed suicide, the memory of our agreement floated back to me in full. Would I see signs of her presence now? Would I sense something? Now that she was gone, and I was there in her house, I confess a few grains of that conversation flavored my visit.

Over the days that followed, James and I searched the house looking for the things Debbie had specifically willed to me. The more personal items like clothing and jewelry were not spelled out in the will, but James was kind enough to let me have any keepsakes I wanted. He was already remarried and had no interest in any of them. I would ship half to Carolyn later on, but we had to go through all of it now. I didn't live nearby, and I had to get home to Massachusetts by the end of the week.

For me, there was only one of Debbie's possessions I really cared about. It was a piece of jewelry we had seen in a shop together several years before.

At the time, she and I both had admired it greatly. The yellow gold bracelet was from the art deco period, and had a series of small rectangular panels connected to each other with bits of double chain. Each panel was inset with onyx, and every panel and piece of chain was set with a tiny diamond. The effect was delicate and effervescent with sparkling stones. We both oohed and "oohed and aahed" over it, and a friendly argument ensued with lots of laughter.

"I waaant it!" I whined in my best baby voice.

I really did want it. The price was surprisingly affordable for such a pretty thing.

"No, you don't. I want it. And I'm going to buy it!" Debbie replied defiantly. Here she goes again, I thought. Always trying to dominate — but I could see she loved it too. This was going to be a battle between us, and yet it was an easy one, a fun one that didn't involve our family issues or anything else that really mattered. We argued now as loving sisters, a struggle without our usual heartache.

"Oh yeah? Well, I saw it first!" I said, enjoying the childish stance.

"So what? You have plenty of bracelets. And anyway, it fits me better!"

To my regret, she was right on both points. I was a bit of a jewelry hound, and her wrists had always been more slender than mine.

Eventually, I gave in, but not before we were both laughing
to tears, enjoying our selfish posturing. Ultimately, we agreed
that Debbie would be the one to wear it home but that I could
visit and borrow it now and then. We both knew this wasn't
going to happen, but saying so felt fair enough. She always loved
to win, and as much as I loved the bracelet, it was also good to
see her feeling victorious.

On the last day, when James and I had to comb through Debbie's
belongings, I kept an eye out for that bracelet. We carried out the
painstaking work from early in the morning until about seven or
eight that night, marking and separating things either for sale or
donation. At the end, just before I left for the hotel, we dumped
the contents of some desk drawers full of cards and letters into a
couple of old boot boxes. By then, James and I had sifted through
everything else in the house, and these were all that remained for
me to consider. It had been a long day, and I went back to the
hotel with the tattered containers under my arm.

After a quick dinner in the restaurant downstairs, I returned
to my room to examine the contents, unsure of what I would
find. Hours went by as I read each card and letter, separating
them into two piles. One stack to keep, the other, to toss. Late
into the evening, I lifted the last card from the bottom of the second box, and there it was. Lying in a small tangle, the bracelet

waited for me where it had been haphazardly tossed. I felt a chill cross the back of my neck.

The bracelet was the very last of Debbie's things to appear. Now I wept, heaving, holding nothing back, her message of goodbye held tightly in my hand. Eventually, a bit of calm returned, and through my tears, I unfolded the bracelet and laid it across my wrist.

I could almost hear her laughing as I failed again and again to close the clasp. The bracelet no longer fit. Perhaps she wanted me to know she was OK, but she certainly hadn't lost her sense of humor. I couldn't help but smile. Carefully, I placed Debbie's bracelet beside me on the bedside table and turned off the light. I laid my head down, exhausted, my mind flooded with thoughts of my dear, impossible sister and her unspeakable farewell.

After the appearance of the bracelet, Debbie's existence never asserted itself again. I know if it had been possible, her spirit would have visited me often, moving chairs and flickering the lights — perhaps even coming to me in visions or dreams. She'd fought hard to convince me that she would, and I confess to being a little disappointed that it didn't happen. I would have welcomed her presence. I admit I look for signs of her still. That said, the truth is, I need no external reminder of my sister. My mind goes to Debbie on its own, and the memory of her haunts me all the same. It always will. I imagine Debbie might feel satisfied with at least this much. These days, I have her ashes with me. She left no instructions for them to be scattered. I imagine that when Debbie made her final plans, there was no happy place she could think of for such a ceremony, but I was glad to bring her home.

Unwilling to bear a more constant reminder, I placed her marble urn high on a cabinet shelf in my studio and closed the door. I know Debbie would probably give me grief, complaining, of course, that I hadn't put her out on display. She had a macabre sense of humor, and I know she would have enjoyed the idea of being inside a container on my mantelpiece or in some other central spot. If she has anything to say about it, I hope she will let me know. Short of that, when the day comes, she will be buried with me, truly loved, as she always was, whether she ever believed it or not.

Epilogue

Greg went on to enjoy many years at home with her daughters. Even though I no longer had her all to myself, it was a great pleasure to see her leading a happy existence with them. By then, I was in my 20s, and despite the age difference, Marjorie and Eleanor began to call me their little sister. After all, we had the same mom. I visited as often as possible, and Greg and I spoke on the phone every week. We never lost touch.

As Greg grew older and needed more help, Marjorie and Eleanor didn't put her in a nursing home. They would never have considered it. Instead, they kept her with them and tended to her until she passed away at home on December 5, 1985, at 93. I think of her often, even now, and miss her warm and happy presence in my life. It is still a terrible loss, but I am ever grateful for the years I had with her.

Thirty years or so after her death, I had an opportunity to create an award at Dana Hall School in her honor. I named it the Katherine T. Gregory Award. It celebrates character and kindness, the very things which made Greg who she was. It is given out every year on Class Day to the student whose thoughts and actions speak to this ideal. She is the girl who has done the most good, either within the school or in service for those in the surrounding community and beyond. These fine young women are highly appreciated and admired by classmates and faculty alike, and it has been my great joy and privilege to be able to go back to Dana Hall to present it to the latest recipient.

Around the same time that Greg died, Grandma Speciale passed away at home unexpectedly. I was grateful that she had been spared the pain and indignities of a difficult death. She was an important bright spot in my life, and I remember her fondly. I admired her matter-of-fact acceptance of all things as they come. She was one of a kind, and she broadened my appreciation for the natural world in so many ways. Her love for birds is with me still, and I cannot see a shell on the beach or enter a garden that does not remind me of my time spent with her. Recently, I bought myself a rod and tackle, intending to take up fishing again, but I know it won't be the same without her.

In 1990, Mom had the brain surgery that brought an end to her active life. As the eldest daughter, I was grateful to Arlen for all the tender care he provided her, even though she no longer recognized or remembered him. By then she was calling him by our father's name, but he never corrected her. Just before Mom died, Arlen could no longer handle the care she needed by himself, and he had to place her in a nursing facility. She died thinking she was staying in a fancy hotel with terrible food. Arlen kindly buried her beside my father.

It was not long after that we got word of Carolyn and Toby's drug abuse. My mind flew back to the visit I made to them in North Carolina and the mystery of Carolyn's unavailability and the bedroom door with its many locks. The locked room had contained a large stash of crack cocaine, along with a gun kept on hand for protection. Now they were in trouble with the law.

Things did get better eventually, but not without one last tragedy. It was Carolyn's son, the middle child, who died of an overdose only hours after he had sworn to her that he was planning to quit drugs for good.

It was seven years from that terrible night before Carolyn and her husband were able to break free of drugs and turn their lives around. That was 26 years ago. They credit their church and faith in God for that change. The remaining children survived that dark time too, and so did the marriage. These days, Carolyn visits people who are incarcerated, speaking to them about her faith and its role in the path away from drug addiction. Toby still races cars when he can. Today, they are still together, and doing fine.

Looking back, I was nothing if not an earnest girl. I was a bit of a Pollyanna, having taken into my heart the lessons of honor and charity I'd been taught. My nature didn't always serve me well, but I tried hard, determined to do what I could. I never quite let go of the dream of happier days coming, not just for me, but for the people I loved. I clung to the comforting notion that there was goodness in everyone. The idea didn't always line up exactly with things as they were, but I wasn't entirely wrong either.

It's what made me try so hard and keep trying long past the time it was easy to do it. I had the willingness of a combat nurse to jump into the fray to soothe the wounded whenever I could. That was my nature. I always had hope, and if I could smooth the way, it was both my desire and my sense of responsibility to do it if. To be honest, I must also confess that I failed more often than I succeeded. Of course, there were disappointments, and frustrations, but what was hardest for me, more than any other thing, was the guilt I felt as the favored child.

I lost track of how many times I put out Debbie's fires or bandaged her wounds, doing everything I could in my limited power to help and protect her from a world that didn't understand and couldn't care. I gave her my best advice, but my expertise and my own reserves were limited too, and she was stubborn. I could only do so much.

Still, in many ways, I had become my sister's keeper. It wasn't a position I'd asked for, and it wasn't one that Debbie would ever endorse. In many ways, she resented me, and I accepted that. I had to. But she and I both knew there was no one else who could or would do it in my stead.

We all were who we were. From my perspective, no one is to blame for what that passed between us. Some of us were easy, and some were not. It might be hard to understand how anyone could love the ones whose outsized personalities and personal demons made it inevitable that they would do harm. They were the ones who could be cruel at times, but in all fairness, life had also been cruel to them. I had to understand and forgive what I could and cherish whatever goodness I would find in each. In the end, they were all members of my clan, my tribe — and I loved every one of them.

Eulogy

In the summer of 2013, somewhere between June 30th and July
1st, at the age of 57, my sister Debbie placed the barrel of a pistol in
her mouth and pulled the trigger. The police released her body to
the funeral home on July 8, 2013. As it happened, on that same
day, I held her memorial service. This is the eulogy I read for her.
She was inside the building at the time, but she had not yet been
cremated. As a visitor from Massachusetts, I returned home to await
her ashes.

*How do I describe her? She was an adorable child, all dimples and
delicate blond ringlets and skinny little legs that had knees patched with
band-aids – badges of honor for tom-boy activities.*

*Back then, our parents took delight in watching us say our prayers
together at bedtime. They particularly enjoyed it because our iconoclastic
Debbie – after thanking God for Mommy and Daddy, her Grandmas, her
sisters, and our dog, Pitapat – would conclude her prayer with, "And POP
goes the weasel!" – in place of "Amen." She liked to do things her way –
even then.*

*Debbie had a mischievous sense of humor and a devilish grin. In the
room we shared as children, she drew an imaginary line down the center.
All the toys were on her side. The bathroom was on mine. When she
needed to use the bathroom, I could choose a toy to play with. I was her
big sister, but she was the boss. It was always that way.*

And she was funny. I never knew anyone who could wear a lampshade and a makeshift monocle with as much jauntiness. And nobody – and I mean nobody – could think up better words in a rousing game of MadLibs. She was a fierce competitor, whether it was at a game of Monopoly or Old Maid, she gave it her all. Once, in seventh grade, she went out for the broad jump competition at school. She put so much effort into that jump that she had to spend three days in bed recuperating. And that jump, when measured, surpassed the distance of everyone, including boys some grades above her.

It was how she approached everything. She tried… hard.

And she died hard.

She couldn't see any other way out of the misery that plagued her one way or another, for much of her life. Many had hoped for more for her.

The truth is, Debbie never had a chance. The confluence of hard parents, bad luck and genetic accident combined with a series of bad choices that ultimately led to this unspeakable and tragic result.

People enjoyed her wicked sense of humor and that loving side she guarded so well. Those who really knew her were familiar with that side of her and the strange sense of accomplishment they felt when they could tease it forward. Sometimes she was hard on them, but I know with an absolute certainty that she was much harder on herself.

She was an original. There were people who stood by her when she let them – and others who tried but were sent away. Her expectations of others were immense. Her needs were complicated and even larger. She could be generous to a fault and then she could wage battle, taking no prisoners. She lived fiercely, but at some point that fierceness turned inward – and it left her with no safe haven – no place of solace – no chance for hope. Her illness took over and it took her.

I didn't want to say goodbye to you Deb. I didn't want to say goodbye to my adorable, bossy, big hearted, pain in the ass, tender, fragile, fierce and honor bound sister; the one with the big laugh and the strictest rules; the girl who wouldn't allow me into her pre-teen bedroom without the pass she'd written out for me; the girl who would begin a sisterly tussle with me, only to stop mid-air to comically ballroom dance with me before resuming battle...

She was the six year old who protected me – who, 20 pounds smaller, stood up to a neighbor boy and his threats to hurt her big sister – landing a solid punch to his solar plexus, and making sure he'd never threaten her again. And he didn't.

She was the teen who took delight in setting up her stereo at my bedroom door, blasting "Jeremiah was a Bullfrog," and waiting gleefully to watch me emerge bedraggled, angry, sleepy and confused – both of us dissolving into laughter and silliness.

She was the Tarzan to my Jane, forever in my memory swinging from that old banyan tree, pounding her chest and commanding all the beasts of the jungle – and her big sister too.

Goodbye to my childhood companion; my dear, darling hard headed little sister. You are in my heart and in my soul. You will never be far from my thoughts. I miss you today and I will miss you always.

The font used for the titles and chapter heads is IM Fell English.
The Fell Types are digitally reproduced by Igino Marini.
www.iginomarini.com

Made in the USA
Las Vegas, NV
25 March 2023